THE ECSTASY AND THE AGONY

Best Wishes,

Damien Tiernan

Damien Tiernan lives in County Waterford with his wife and two children. *The Ecstasy and the Agony* is his second book.

Also by Damien Tiernan

Souls of the Sea

THE ECSTASY

AND

THE AGONY

DAMIEN TIERNAN

HACHETTE
BOOKS
IRELAND

Copyright © 2010 Damien Tiernan

First published in 2010 by Hachette Books Ireland
A Hachette UK Company

Author cover photograph: Jim O'Sullivan

Some quotations have been taken from contemporary sources at the time.

A CIP catalogue record for this title is available from the British Library.

ISBN 978 14447 0683 3

Typeset in Bembo by Hachette Books Ireland
Cover design by Anú Design, Tara
Printed and bound in Great Britain by Mackays, Chatham ME5 8TD

Hachette Books Ireland policy is to use papers that are natural, renewable
and recyclable products and made from wood grown in sustainable forests.
The logging and manufacturing processes are expected to conform to the
environmental regulations of the country of origin.

Hachette Books Ireland
8 Castlecourt Centre
Castleknock
Dublin 15
Ireland

www.hachette.ie

A division of Hachette UK
338 Euston Road, London, NW1 3BH
England

This book is dedicated to my late father-in-law Paddy Mason.
And to all true Waterford fans.

Contents

1

THE ECSTASY

August 2008, and a cool Atlantic breeze hit the players' faces before they boarded the coach.

Suddenly, Paul Flynn recognised one of the golfers on the nearby fairway.

'That's Jack Nicholson, lads! Hey, Jack, how's it going?'

The famous actor looked up from the seventeenth, waved and took a deep breath before pushing his hands through his receding hair. He'd flown into Clare for a game of golf.

Some of the players wondered if they would get to meet him later, like the time John Mullane and Eoin Kelly met Wayne Rooney on a team holiday to New York. That had been the previous December when some of the players had gone to Madison Square Gardens to see the Knicks play the Boston Celtics. At half-time, Wayne and Colleen had appeared on the big screen, the announcer welcoming them as VIP guests. The Waterford lads had been sat way up, while the Rooneys were down close to the action on the court. Mullane and Kelly moved down closer, twenty rows away from Wayne, who was injured at the time and over for the weekend. The Celtics won eighty-eight to eighty-one and the Rooneys were ushered away through the VIP exit. Mullane and Kelly had followed and met them with the bouncers, who told them to leave.

'We're friends of Shayser from Waterford,' Mullane said to Rooney, who was wearing a grey hoodie and looking a bit perplexed. 'Tell him we said hello!' Mullane is good friends with Rooney's Manchester Utd team-mate John O'Shea. Later, Rooney told O'Shea that he met two mad lads from Waterford in New York.

The coach pulled away from the exclusive Doonbeg Hotel and Golf Resort, where rich Americans come to swing their titanium clubs, to take the hurlers for an early-morning workout at Quilty a few kilometres away.

The players were here on a training and team-bonding exercise and, this weekend, some will experience luxury like they have never experienced before – all in preparation to flake into the boys from Tipp in a week's time in the 2008 All-Ireland semi-final.

They plan to hurl like they've never hurled before.

Later that day back at the hotel, Dave Bennett, Paul Flynn, Tony Browne and a few others are sat overlooking the first tee on the Greg Norman-designed course. Green fees were €220 (Celtic Tiger prices!) and the boys looked longingly at the immaculate greens. They'd love a game now; Bennett plays off four, Flynners is even better, a one handicapper. They shake their heads as a Big Yank pulls his shot to the left. Maybe his bulging wallet in his back-right pocket unbalanced him. Hank is dripping wealth. The lads would love to be showing them how it's done, but there's some more training to be done for a match that will define many of their careers.

A match that they know – no matter what the result – people will talk about for years.

Just like they will talk about them, players who got their manager sacked only a few months earlier and who have trained like mad under a man many of them had despised. Players who have the Waterford public to answer to if things don't go right against Tipp.

It's been an emotional, exciting, turbulent journey for a panel of players who have brought their followers a decade of joy, mixed with heartache and many moments of breathtaking brilliance.

Theirs is the story of the angry teenager who has skill to burn but who never reaches his full potential.

But this match is the culmination of all those hard nights and hot days training to be the best. Since the back-door system was introduced in 1997, these players have undertaken, on average, ninety-one team sessions every January to August. They have come together 1,092 times to work, sweat and dream – and that's not including individual gym sessions.

Today, they find themselves in a familiar place but under very different circumstances. They remember the defeats in the semi-finals in 1998, 2002, 2004, 2006 and 2007 – five defeats. Five awful, nasty, dirty, tearful defeats. And each of their victors on those days didn't go on to win the All-Ireland, so they can't even say they were beaten by the best.

And now they have another semi-final. They can't lose another semi. They can't. 'Don't Stop Believing' has become the fans' anthem.

Will Davy Fitz, their recently installed, charismatic and sometimes controversial manager take them to a final? Or are they just so wound up that even if they had no manager, they'd still get there?

Earlier that Sunday morning, the coach stopped at Cusack Park in Ennis. Pat Fitzgerald, Davy's father, opened the gates, let them in and helped set up the cones for training. Michael Hearn, brought into the back-room team by Davy, had set up his specially adapted and imported baseball machines. Sliotars were being fired at 110 mph – up from 70 mph a few weeks previously – and balls could be dispersed every two seconds for time-based drills. Most of the players reacted quickly to the missiles and were able to hone their first-touch work. Outside of training for the goalies, management did not use the machines for high-catching practice, an aspect of the game some Waterford players were weak on. The great Liam Fennelly from Kilkenny always says the team that wins the aerial battle is the team that generally wins the All-Ireland, 'If you can soar for the high ball, you don't need much speed on your feet', as they say in Kilkenny. Wexford also worked with a baseball machine on their high catching when they won the All-Ireland in 1996 and Waterford management should have used the machines for more high-catching.

After a good session, the field was cleared and a selection of the 'Possibles' beat the under-21s from Galway in a challenge match (though without their influential Joe Canning).

The 'Probables' watched the game from the stand. Those on the field did well, in particular Dave Bennett, but he knew it wouldn't get him a starting position. His ankle was at him as he had strained his Achilles, probably a culmination of the savage effort they'd all put in since Davy had come to Waterford in June.

Back in Doonbeg, the players mingled and relaxed. Having beaten Wexford the previous weekend, they were here in Davy's backyard, getting ready for the test of their lives.

Davy told the players, 'Tipp think this is going to be won or lost on the hurling pitch but they won't know what's hit them.'

Davy Fitz is like a temperamental Icelandic volcano – he can be calm and collected when he wants to be, but the anger and desire to win bubbles over at most training sessions with fierce cursing mixed with cajoling in an effort to get the most out of his squad. And when he erupts, he can be scary. There should be 'Over 18s Only' certification on some of his half-time team talks. He divides opinion; he demands total commitment from players and has no time for smart arses. As he wrote in his autobiography, *Passion and Pride*: 'I have never had much time for smart young fellas, the lads that think they know it all. I prefer the unassuming types with a genuine love for life and the game of hurling.'

He is the only serving inter-county manager in hurling or football writing a weekly column in a national newspaper.

The hotel and complex at Doonbeg is luxury personified – the furnishings perfect, the beds in the four-bedroomed chalets King size and salubrious, and with thirty-eight-inch plasma screens with two dozen channels. Until a few years ago, Waterford teams hadn't really been doing the 'hotel circuit'. Some of the older players said they couldn't sleep in hotels and sometimes players had to bring their own pillows with them to help them sleep. But this was amazing. 'The theory behind staying in such a luxurious place was for the players to have a higher value on themselves,' says Michael Hearn.

The back-room staff knew each other very well, with some having been part of Waterford's epic journey for three decades. They had worked extremely hard with Davy over the past few weeks to make sure everything was done perfectly. Their attention to detail had verged on obsessive. That night, with the players in bed by 10 p.m., Davy and the selectors decided a few well-earned drinks could be had and taxis were arranged to bring them and some of the back-room staff to David O'Brien's pub in Miltown Malbay (David had been brought in by Davy to do the match statistics).

Everyone was up for training at 7 a.m.

The session at the nearby GAA pitch was all first-touch work and 'military' type of training that lasted just over an hour, after which everyone headed back to the hotel for breakfast. Some then went back to bed for more sleep, others had a chipping competition on the practice green with Davy. An hour or so later, they all met in a small room in the hotel for video analysis.

Peter Queally, one of the selectors, said they were going to look at the first half of the Munster semi-final in which Cork took Tipperary apart (Tipp went on to win the game with a superb second-half performance – though that wasn't going to be shown). But there was a problem with the video player and they had to watch part of a game between Clare and Limerick. When the Cork–Tipp section came on, the players watched closely and were asked for comments. A few said that to beat Tipp, they'd have to run at them.

Paul Flynn spoke up from the back of the room. He'd been studying the form of Tipp goalie, Brendan Cummins. 'I've noticed Brendan Cummins had thirteen puckouts, six went down one side, seven down the other.' Everybody turned to look at Paul to see what he was going to say next. 'The puckouts were low trajectory, so what we need to do is block his targets.'

Silence in the room.

'Go on,' said Davy.

'Very simple,' said Paul. 'You block the channels and you force Cummins to put the balls out high so a good centre-back will be able to catch them. And the way to do that is to bring out the midfielders or the corner-forwards and get in his way.'

They carried on discussing possible tactics. Forward Eoin McGrath would play a roving role in front of the full-forward line, hopefully creating confusion in the Tipp backline and creating space. And players were to be pinpointed with passes instead of sending up long, aimless high balls.

On Sunday afternoon, they got on the coach and headed back to Cusack Park for the last practice match before the big game. The 'Probables' played the 'Possibles' but the teams were mixed up a bit as the selectors had to try to sort out the full-back problem. The 'Probables' wore Waterford jerseys, with the 'Possibles' in the Portlaw jerseys, the closest of any Waterford club colour to a Tipp jersey.

Ken McGrath was put on the 'Possible' team facing the full-forward line that would start against Tipperary – John Mullane, Eoin Kelly and Eoin McGrath – but he wasn't happy there.

The experiment of trying Ken McGrath at full-back hadn't gone well for him. It'd been one of Davy's biggest gambles since he had come to Waterford, but even the sunshine on the warm August Bank Holiday weekend couldn't disguise the fact that it wasn't working. The old hurling maxim is true: 'You can make a centre-back out of a full-back but not the other way round.'

Ken McGrath is one of the greatest centre-backs in the history of hurling and had been a marvellous half-forward, but the strain of trying to make things work was evident. As they came off the pitch, there were nearly tears in Ken's eyes.

'My confidence is shot. I can't play there,' he told the selectors – Maurice Geary and Peter Queally. He may as well have had a big sign on his forehead blaring out: 'I'm pissed off!'

In the dressing room, Tony Browne and Paul Flynn listened to Ken. Would Tony be played at centre-half-back? Davy Fitz came in and called Flynners out, saying he wanted to talk to him.

Paul Flynn went to Davy and said, 'It's just as well it happened here and in this way. His confidence is shot and he can't play there.'

After the match, the coach then took them all to beautiful Dromoland Castle Hotel. Again, the lap of luxury.

Another team meeting was held, after which eight or nine of the lads chatted amongst themselves, a few of them having a slow cigarette, most of them knowing they wouldn't be starting against Tipp. The atmosphere in the room wasn't comfortable. 'A kind of feel-sorry-for-ourselves moment,' says Dave Bennett. 'If you're playing on the team, it's great, but if you know you are not going to be starting or even on the bench, it's very tough going.'

'It's incredibly hard when you know you are not starting,' says Tom Feeney, who gave fifteen years of his life to the cause. Apart from his family, hurling has been the most important thing in his life. 'It's head-wrecking stuff not being on the starting fifteen. It's like you have a sickness and you are going to die, like you nearly had cancer and you are just seeing out your time because hurling means so much to you. Being on the team, it's all about being on the team – I don't care what anyone says.'

Dinner was in a side room off the main dining room. No one was drinking. The lads had arranged a chocolate birthday cake for Davy, which was brought in after the meal by smiling staff. Everyone (well, nearly everyone) sang 'Happy Birthday'.

The players headed to bed early and, the next morning, went to an adventure centre at Killaloe for special team-building exercises – climbing poles, jumping, rafting, trusting your partner. It was all being recorded on camera and a compilation would be shown after training on Thursday to show how well they all got on together. They had great fun before everyone was brought back to Waterford to see their families.

Thursday and it was Walsh Park in Waterford city for the final training session before the All-Ireland semi-final.

The selectors knew that if there were problems in the full-back line, fear would permeate. So they decide to move McGrath to centre-back, as Tipp had a relatively young player, Seamus Callanan, at centre-half-forward and Ken was the man to mark him. But they wanted Tipperary to think they were going to start Ken at full-back.

The famous 'Diamond Formation', which was best exemplified in 2007 with Ken at centre-back, Michael 'Brick' Walsh or Jack Kennedy in midfield, and Eoin Kelly at centre-forward, was not going to be tried on Sunday – it had been previous manager Justin McCarthy's best system. Eoin Kelly functions best when he's making plays, not waiting in the corner for things to happen.

Davy had asked Dave Bennett to speak to the squad. Waterford players liked to go to the town end corner of Walsh Park for a private team chat after the final session before any big game. Even though he was not starting, Dave had no hesitation in putting the team first and in a team huddle on the pitch, Dave spoke from the heart, saying the fifteen who would run out with the jerseys on that Sunday had a great honour and that there were fifteen or sixteen other lads who would kill to be putting on the jersey this coming Sunday. He spoke about the history Waterford had with Tipp over the past twelve years. 'And when it comes to the knock-out championship, Tipp haven't been able to knock us out,' he pulsated.

The lads knew it. They were in an ideal situation. They liked being underdogs. Tipp hadn't been beaten all year, but the Premier County hadn't won in the championship in Croke Park since 2003 either.

Waterford players had been given a white-and-blue wristband, each inscribed with '+NBF' – be positive, next ball and family, the things that matter most. Some would wear the wristbands on Sunday.

They headed out to the Ramada Hotel for food and then went into a meeting room where a fifteen-minute DVD of their team-building exercises and training was shown, with backing songs from Eminem and others. Davy's voice could be heard urging players to do it 'for their families', to do whatever it took to win. There was also Ian McGeechan's famous speech to the Lions: that they were the chosen few that many had been considered but few were chosen. Shots of Brick Walsh lifting the Munster trophy in 2007 sent shivers down lads' necks. Some of the players nearly cried with the emotion of it all. They went home that night knowing they were going to beat Tipp.

The song that ended the DVD clips was 'To Win Just Once' by The Saw Doctors – and the lads knew that to win a semi-final just once would be magical, to break finally the jinx of losing semis – but would that be enough?

Saturday morning, the eve of the All-Ireland semi-final. The Waterford team got the 10 a.m. train to Dublin's Heuston Station. The previous year, they had travelled up by train on the morning of each of the three big matches, but Davy decided to change the routine. A garda escort was waiting for them and the team bus was taken straight to Croke Park for the Dublin–Tyrone football match. High up in the Hogan Stand, they zipped up their tracksuit tops to keep out the breeze. Because of the cold, a few of the players went down to the press box, to be joined by a few who had a fear of heights. Over the tannoy system, it was announced that Ronnie Drew had died.

Tyrone beat Dublin and the coach took the Waterford group to their favourite hotel for Croke Park weekends – the Marriott in Ashbourne, County Meath. They'd stayed there previously with Justin, before a league game with Dublin, but they had to put

Justin – and the semi-final jinx – behind them. Tomorrow, they had to win.

That evening, they had a meeting in the Blackwater Room in the hotel, to go through tactics – flip charts were used and roles reconfirmed. Then, they headed to their rooms and slept well because of the luxurious, thick Continental mattresses used by the hotel – and (something the players are unaware of) the special 'topper' duvet put between the mattress and the base of the bed.

After breakfast, before they boarded the bus, Davy got them all in a horseshoe circle and referenced Pádraig Pearse and the men of 1916. He looked each of them in the eye, speaking more loudly each time, as his eyes searched the windows of each man's soul as he repeated the question, 'I am prepared to die – are ye? Are ye all prepared to die? Are ye?'

Paul Flynn grabbed the groin of the man beside him and squeezed, daring him to shout out in pain and agony. 'Yes!' they all shouted in unison, the man being squeezed shouting the loudest!

As they took their seats on the coach to Croke Park, Flynn asked Michael Hearn, 'Is it England or Tipperary we're playing today?'

The players were told that Tipperary had already booked the Burlington Hotel for their post All-Ireland final reception. This was used to gee up the Waterford lads. Tipperary thought they were in the final before even playing in the semi!

Waterford were 5–2 with the bookies to win and Dave Bennett did something he'd never done before – he texted his old friend Donie Ormonde to put 'a nice few quid' on Waterford.

'Will u win?' Donie texted back.

'Put what u like on it,' texted Bennett.

One of the goalkeepers, Adrian Power, was the resident DJ for coach trips. As Croke Park came into view, he shouted, 'Wait till you hear this one!' and 'It's A Long Way To Tipperary' came on. The lads shouted and whooped and laughed. It was the ice-breaker. Davy thought it was the funniest thing; that it hit the moment spot on.

And Ken McGrath was happy, knowing he'd been moved out of the full-back position and would be playing in his favourite half-back spot. Davy had admitted the experiment hadn't worked and didn't think he'd persist with it for too long, as he had given it a fair try. And he'd assured people he wasn't one of those managers who thought he knew everything about everything.

Everybody on the coach felt that this was their day – the day of days to end the forty-five-year semi-final hoodoo.

Trainer Gerry Fitzpatrick felt it too, but he'd warned Davy that if they won, they shouldn't come off the field like they'd won the All-Ireland; he asked for any celebrations to be muted.

The tens of thousands of Waterford supporters didn't want to stop believing this could be their day. Around the world, Irish pubs were showing the match and Waterford fans on every continent were wishing they were in the Lower Cusack. In all, 53,635 people were in the stadium.

In the dressing room, thoughts were focusing and the adrenal glands were working overtime. The sound of studs on the non-slip floor competed with the thud of sliotars against walls in the warm-up area. Each player had his own way of fighting the demons in the final few minutes before the door was thrown open. Some went to the toilet at least three times; John Mullane hit his thighs with his hurley; others sat and breathed deeply; Ken and Tony geed up the younger lads; chests and backs were pounded.

'This is our day,' was the refrain.

In the final moments, Davy got the players sitting down for a visualisation technique where they close their eyes and try to see the game as it'll unfold.

Two minutes before Roger Casey opened the door, everybody got up to form a large circle, arms linked. Davy was in the middle, clenched fist, his words ricocheting from face to face. Each player was urged to say something, however brief, and they did, the intensity rising with each sentence. Captain Michael 'Brick' Walsh, the engine room of the team, made them believe even more in destiny. Shane O'Sullivan had never before been in such a circle, where unreal motivation became real, tangible, touchable.

Their time had come, all the talking had been done, the door opened and daylight beckoned. Thoughts affect feelings affect actions, and the intensity with which the Waterford players, in particular the forwards, tackled and hit their Tipperary opponents in the open fifteen minutes was mind-boggling. The highly fancied Tipp boys were being pulverised. In a man-of-the-match perform-ance, Eoin Kelly got Waterford going with a free in the opening minute, and a superb Ken McGrath clearance – one of many – paved the way for point number two from John Mullane. More points followed and Eoin Kelly, delightfully set up by Tony Browne, fired over another. Six points up; everything going right. Tipp came back into it with pointed frees before Dan Shanahan missed a great chance at goal and then Tipp's Lar Corbett was lucky not to be sent off for a bone-crunching charge on Eoin Murphy. Seamus Callinan had Tipperary's first score from play in the thirty-second minute and as Diarmuid Kirwan blew the whistle for half-time, it was 0–10 apiece.

The Waterford players charged down the tunnel. The subs were already there to applaud them in, something arranged by Davy as a team thing.

One of the back-room staff didn't want Waterford to fall foul by being first back on the pitch for the second half. He pleaded with the Croke Park match-day official who organised which team went back out first and convinced him of the merits of their argument. Too many times, Waterford had been left standing out on a pitch, left hanging out to dry.

The team talk started quietly. The players were quiet. They knew Tipp were there for the taking. They got energy drinks on board and gobbled down Jaffa cakes and bananas.

Davy knew this was the sixth time these players had been in this position, an All-Ireland semi-final. He calmly spelled out what needed to be done – to keep creating space, continue to work very hard and cut the supply of ball. Players spoke of how they were not going to throw it away like they had in previous years. Brick Walsh told them not to panic, that the plan was working. Then Davy's voice rose enormously, almost begging the players to keep applying the pressure, telling them that he knew some of the Tipp lads (possibly from his days managing LIT) and that they'd crack. He was roaring and screaming. It was time for battle again.

The subs clapped them back out into the coliseum. Tipp had been out there a few minutes already and Waterford fans give their team get a massive cheer. A slight drizzle was falling.

Sitting high up in the Cusask Stand was Seamie Hannon, who only a few months earlier had been a selector on the Waterford team. He'd come to Croke Park discretely and, pondering the first half, thought Waterford were not playing so well. If this game had been played a month earlier, Seamie thought, he wouldn't have come. He was still very sore about what had happened. He and former manager Justin McCarthy had felt very hard done by.

Down below, Davy had told the players not to shoot from bad positions near the sidelines as Waterford had lost too many games that way. Kevin Moran did everything to put two balls over from such positions but they went wide and he thought he was going to be taken off – but he was playing a blinder, one of his best games, just like the others.

Ken was having a great game at centre-back and Seamus Callinan, Tipp's star-of-the-season so far, was not. Ken's brother Eoin was playing great as well. But it looked like Tipp were at last gaining the upper-hand. Enda McEvoy of the *Sunday Tribune* scribbled in his notes that Waterford, 'need a goal'. And then in the fifty-sixth minute, there's a high delivery from Jack Kennedy and Dan Shanahan hit it on one-handed. After the initial save, Brendan Cummins in the Tipp goal had no chance against Eoin Kelly from the edge of the square.

The Deise cheering hadn't even stopped when Callinan put the ball in the Waterford net direct from the puckout. Shortly after, another goal-bound Callinan shot was blocked by Clinton Hennessy, and substitute Michael Webster somehow failed to connect with another shot; the ball was cleared, Waterford were still alive, thanks in no small part to defender Declan Prendergast. With Ken McGrath majestic in his central defensive role, and Brick Walsh playing better having being moved up front, Waterford dug deep. Jack Kennedy's heroics questioned the wisdom of leaving him out of the starting fifteen in the first place. The players had been moved around like chess pieces to create space up front but tactics alone weren't going to win this game.

We're not going to lose another semi, we can't, was the thought in each player's mind, We're going to win.

When Paul Flynn came on, Eoin Kelly told him they were going to the final, no matter what. That refusal to die – to keep at it rather than give up and trudge off yet again as nearly-rans tested their characters like never before. No, this is our day, stick to the plan, don't panic, ball over the bar, work, work, work – typified none more so than by Moran, Molumphy and Brick hoovering up possession. They were level again as the fourth official gave notice of three minutes of additional time. Tipperary's usually reliable Mullinahone maestro Eoin Kelly sent a crucial sixty-five wide, while Waterford sent over two points.

Declan Prendergast and the Waterford defence rowed in with a few crucial blocks, then Tipp dropped in one last ball but Aiden 'Ringo' Kearney came out with the sliotar. Diarmuid Kirwan blew the final whistle and pandemonium ensued.

Ecstasy.

Joy unconfined.

Eoin McGrath dropped to his knees and cried. Screaming players jumped on other screaming players. John Mullane and Davy Fitzgerald rolled around the ground, embracing passionately. Tony Browne was on the flat of his back looking up to heaven.

Those who had been with the team for years behind the scenes

– Doc Higgins, Jim Dee, Roger Casey and others – were all out on the field, roaring crying.

Eoin Kelly's fiancée Sharon got through security with their two-year-old son Sean (complete with 'Daddy' on his jersey) and jumped up on her husband on the pitch. Little Sean had a hurl in his hand and wanted to head for the goal. Like most players, Kelly was crying tears of unconfined joy. Fans were delirious. Waterford pensioners in the stands kissed the crest on their jerseys. Even Donal 'Donie' McGillicuddy, a camera supervisor with Observe Outside Broadcasting who were providing the facilities to RTÉ for *The Sunday Game*, and who was operating one of the main cameras in the Hogan Stand, jumped for joy in his Waterford jersey.

Gerry Fitzpatrick knew Kilkenny would be watching and thinking that Waterford players didn't know what the next step was. He wanted the first step in beating Kilkenny to be for the players to walk calmly off the pitch. Some hope. He hated ruining the moment but he ran out and tried to drag Eoin McGrath off the ground. There were others rolling around on the grass embracing one another.

We're over-celebrating, he thought, we have to stop. We're in the final – great; but if we lose the fucking thing, that'll be disgusting. He ran to Davy and shouted, 'Come on, Davy. Just get them in, get them out of here.'

Davy shouted back hoarsely, barely audible, 'Everybody is too emotional.'

As the players got back to the cool dressing room, there was utter relief and joy. They hugged and back-slapped. The back-room boys were delirious.

One of the more senior players noticed too many people in the dressing room. 'I was thinking, What the fuck is this? There's fellas jumping around the place and there were people in the changing room who had no business being there and straight away there's talk of tickets, suits, transport, family, where are we staying for the final … all this kind of stuff. You'd almost want to grab the former Cork manager Donal O'Grady or someone who has been through this and get him to tell you the list of things that shouldn't be allowed happen.'

The players started sitting down to take in what they had done. For a few seconds, some of them heard silence. Psychologists say it's a phenomenon replicated the world over when you achieve your goal.

Davy came in and tried to focus the lads on the bigger prize, saying his ambition was to get the Brick to come back in a few weeks time, walk up those steps and collect the cup. 'I've never been so proud in all my life,' he said, before heading out to give some media interviews.

John Costigan from the Tipperary County Board came in with trainer Eamonn O'Shea and both congratulated Waterford, saying they had been beaten by a better team on the day and for 'ye to leave no stone unturned to bring the Liam McCarthy back to Suirside'.

Davy came back and shouted for the lads to get out of the showers, then he spoke to them again, 'I'm as proud as I've ever been. We mind ourselves and don't get caught up in the shit [of celebrations] and we can beat Kilkenny and we'll come up with something to beat them.'

As the lads did a few warm-down exercises, Eoin Murphy was getting stitches from the blow he got in the match. When all the team had changed, Davy said, 'The job is only half done. Limerick came up here last year and beat ye and all they did was clap themselves on the back for three weeks. There's going to be none of that. And I want to remind ye, the night ye did what ye did [getting rid of Justin], how many people cut the shit out of ye around the country? Don't forget it. You can have your drinks tonight but anyone drinking tomorrow won't be here [for training] Tuesday.'

The sudden shock of winning and having been cocooned in the dressing room for forty minutes or so brought strange emotions to the players. The dressing room was their sanctuary. They had done something no Waterford team had done in decades. They'd made it to the final but they didn't want *this* to be their final.

Then, they headed out and the reality of the unreality hit them. Did they *really* understand what they had achieved?

A few went for drinks in the Players' Lounge, a room very close to the dressing rooms and still underground – with no windows to hint at the thousands of fans waiting outside. The gear went to the bus with Roger Casey. After half an hour of getting in the pints and bottles, the players emerged from the Hogan Stand entrance and the thousands of fans in white and blue converged in a wave of emotion. All any of them wanted to do was touch the players.

It was a release.

It was unreal.

It was magical.

It was incredible.

Everybody there would remember it until they had no memories left.

The team squeezed through the multitudes and went across the road into a cordoned-off area of Jury's where food and drink had been laid out. A glass partition separated them from the masses looking in, tapping the window, bursting to share the love.

Gerry Fitz was worried, thinking this was an excuse for the public to have a big party in Waterford for the next three weeks, whilst they knew the team still had one more step to go. Then, they piled back on the coach taking them to the train at Connolly Station.

'Put jackets over what ye're bringing on the train with ye, lads,' Davy said. Like other teams, the players had stashed a few beers for the journey home. Fans were waving, cheering, holding up babies to the windows of the bus.

At the station, the fans waiting to board the other carriages of the 7.15 p.m. special clapped them all the way up the platform. When they'd found their seats, the chanting and singing began immediately. They deserved their few drinks, they'd worked long enough for it and had been like caged animals for two months.

They'd gone farther than they ever had with Justin – or any team since 1963. They'd proved them-selves worthy and would go down in history.

They were heroes.

Mobile phones were beeping incessantly as the train pulled away. Jack Kennedy got at least fifty messages on his phone. He thought back to Doonbeg and that weekend which may just have made the difference between winning and losing.

The August sun was setting in a beautiful red sky over Croker, almost silhouetting their Deliverance Home, and they waved at the stadium in adulation, in reverence – it was no longer their grave-yard. Paul Flynn had always called Croke Park 'Our Lady', and the lads talked of how they'd see her again in a few weeks. Some wives and girlfriends were in the same carriage, others in the next one, and the train was being driven on emotion.

Eoin Murphy, the Bing Crosby of the team, started another song, his favourite being 'Stuttering Bum'. Then some of the lads sang 'The Galway Girl', the song used in the television advert for Bulmers in which Ken McGrath's fiancée Dawn (a part-time model) featured (Bulmers is sometimes referred to in the south-east as the Clonmel Chardonnay!).

Later, they all got off the train and were met by delirious fans, who carried Davy Fitz shoulder high out of Plunkett Station, to where Liam Cusack would have a free bar for them in the Granville Hotel.

They told stories about how they got to this point. They watched *The Sunday Game*. A few fell over, others went on to Ruby's nightclub.

They told each other how much they respected and liked each other, but reminded themselves that they hadn't won anything yet.

On the train back to Waterford, they had looked out the window at the darkening sky and thought of the journey they'd been on – the highs and lows, the sacrifices of friends and families.

They had brought such joy to thousands.

They had done it for their parish, their club, their county.

They were proud Waterford men.

And the journey – it was all about the journey. And what a journey it had been.

2

A JOURNEY THROUGH DARK DAYS AND DARKER NIGHTS

Waterford is 'a hurling county' – records show it was played here as far back as 1750 – with as proud a set of fans as you'll find anywhere in the country. And yet they are starved of success, famished and desperate for glory.

In half a century, only one All-Ireland title at either minor, under-21 or senior level has been carried high onto the hill of Ballybricken or into Grattan Square in Dungarvan. One measly, miserly, and yet marvellous, title in 1992 when the under-21s led by Peter Power did what no other Waterford hurling team had done since 1959.

1959! The last time Waterford won the senior All-Ireland title. In pubs from Passage in east Waterford to Ardmore in the farthest west, the copies of the match reports from that great day come from a time before man first went to space.

From that year to 2009, Kilkenny had won the championship eighteen times, Cork eleven times and Tipp eight. Of the nine counties that have *ever* won the All-Ireland senior hurling title, Waterford have fewer victories than the other eight.

The list goes on. Since Waterford's last win, Wexford have won it three times in 1960, 1968 and 1996; Galway in 1980, 1987 and

1988; Offaly in 1981, 1985, 1994 and 1998; Clare in 1995 and 1997; and Limerick in 1973.

Added to that, no Waterford club has ever won the All-Ireland club championship (which was started in 1972) and 1948 was the last time Waterford won only the second of their two minor titles.

It's not something in the water that has stopped Waterford from winning, because in other sports, such as women's Gaelic football, titles have been won by Waterford (five in the 1990s). This is the conundrum – why have Waterford hurlers failed to make it to so many big days and when they did make it, why did they fail to produce what was necessary to win?

So deep and painful are the defeats over the past half-century, that bringing Angela's ashes in an urn from Limerick to Waterford would be a wasted journey; you'd be so upset at the harrowing pain and the poverty of victories on the faces of depressed Waterford supporters that you'd have to turn back. Some Tipperary fans would gleefully slag Deise supporters, mimicking Deise with 'they shouldav' after every match!

Even though Waterford is a hurling county, for many years the hurling results were atrociously awful. There were, of course, sparks of brilliance, flashes of genius and heroic attempts – but they never caught hold, never burned long enough, were never able to win the day.

There were beautiful shooting stars that forced people to hold their breath in awe, spectators hoping it wasn't an illusion and that it wouldn't disappear, a night sky made extraordinary for a moment, before the darkness took her away into the void.

And, of course, the darker the night, the brighter the star.

But is it about making comparisons? For example, Wicklow footballers would be jealous of Waterford hurlers – who at least made it to a provincial final every decade or so. In the 126-year history of the GAA, Wicklow has *never* won even a Leinster senior football title. But the Waterford hurling fan doesn't compare his or her lot with lesser minnows in other codes; he or she compares their house and garden with the neighbours – Cork, Tipperary, Kilkenny and Wexford. It's understandable, then, that Waterford developed a persecution complex.

Waterford fans justly claim, though, that in their Munster championship matches, they may be drawn in the first round against Cork or Tipp and, having been duly beaten, had nothing to do but play a few league matches later in the year and wait for another day out the following summer.

Like the Limerick team of the 1930s, the Waterford team of the late 1950s were probably worth a few more titles, as Eamonn Sweeney has written in *Munster Hurling Legends*. The players were speedy, skilful, wispy and moved the ball quickly. The team had giants of men, such as Tom Cheasty, who the late, great commentator Michael O'Hehir depicted as powering through a Kilkenny defence with defenders 'falling away like dead wasps'.

The heroic imagery of those players from 1959 to 1963 should have been an inspiration for the players that followed but winning the Munster title in 1963 was to be a high point. Since then, the scenario for Waterford has been like getting a ticket to an exclusive party but being bullied off the dance floor with the prize of kissing the cup gone again for another year.

As the loyal Waterford fan bicycle-clipped it home past Ikes and Mikes on the Clonmel Road in the 1960s, or steered his Ford Capri through long-haired Killeagh in the east Cork of the 1970s, he must have wondered why he bothered. As he sighed heavily on the pillow after a few bottles of the local Phoenix beer in the 1980s, he dared to mutter those three little words so loved by Waterford fans, 'Maybe next year.' The day after the match, it would be back to work in the factory on the industrial estate and another slagging from the Kilmacow boys from south Kilkenny with their black and amber grins.

'Yiz might have thirty All-Irelands, but we have thirty factories!' is the only response the Waterford fan may muster. The Kilkenny lads come across the River Suir to work in Waterford but go home and win All-Irelands by the bucketload.

To understand what has happened in the past twelve years, we have to try to understand the past.

Waterford won the All-Ireland in 1959 and were beaten in the 1963 final by Kilkenny. Ten of the 1959 winning team were from Ballybricken in Waterford city, that small area encompassing Doyle Street, Keane's Road, Gracedieu and Roanmore: they started together, 'aged' together and retired together. 'It left a whole plethora of team vacancies to be filled that a county like Waterford simply couldn't do,' says journalist John A. Murphy from Dungarvan.

The relative success of those glory years were never built on and as Ireland grew up and partied in the late 1960s and early 1970s, so too did Waterford.

Some of those hurling for Waterford were superb, but it always seemed the team only had eleven or so good enough on any given Sunday. Back then, the 'Glass' blew big and strong and Waterford manufactured prize cuts and big, hard-earned wage packets. Other factories had to match Waterford Crystal's high salaries, and the city beat strongly as a manufacturing heartland. No need to worry too much, some thought, about losing a few matches, sure we have our jobs and our unions and our lifestyle. No need to exert ourselves with too much training, sure can't we just go and watch the local soccer team, Waterford Utd (the Blues), at Kilcohan Park in Waterford city, in League of Ireland games.

And they went to Kilcohan in their thousands. This never happened in Kilkenny or Tipperary, while Cork had a big enough population to sustain interest in soccer, Gaelic football and hurling. Most of the children in new estates that were built to provide workers for the factories played soccer and maybe a bit of hurling, but they saw that soccer could bring success and wealth.

Waterford's rich bosses competed with each other to see who could pay the most money to bring 'prestige' players to Waterford

Utd. The Blues had bags of money to spend on players and
managers – and they made sure it was spent. They attracted former
Manchester Utd stars such as Shay Brennan and even Bobby
Charlton! And they paid very high wages to attract other good
players, so Waterford's team became the envy of Ireland, winning
the league six times between 1965 and 1973. The players even
threatened to go on strike in the dressing room prior to their 1968
European Cup match against Manchester Utd in Lansdowne
Road. They wanted more money – and they got it.

In contrast, the standard of juvenile hurling didn't improve, with
traditional strongholds such as Mount Sion becoming more
important than ever in keeping the flame alive and dominating city,
county and behind-the-scenes. There was no animosity between
hurlers and soccer players; a lot of the senior players in both codes
were friends; but as Waterford was a small city, the pick of good
sportsmen was limited.

And in the 1970s, a few important things happened: the
famous 'Ban' on GAA members playing or going to soccer
matches and functions was lifted and more youngsters were
playing 'the foreign game'; and those religious Brothers in the
Mount Sion School who had fervently taught lads how to hurl
started to retire. As Martin Óg Morrissey, 1959 All-Ireland
winner and Mount Sion man, says, 'The Brothers started
disappearing and some youngsters didn't know where their
allegiance was, with soccer or hurling.'

And as any Kilkenny All-Ireland winner worth his salt will tell
you 'if you don't have it in the schools, you'll never progress'.

Frankie Walsh, the captain of the Waterford 1959 team, says he
can't say why Waterford didn't drive on in the late 1960s and 1970s
and he doesn't think the exact reason or reasons will ever be
known. 'That group in 1959 gelled together perfectly but it just
didn't happen after that. And when the responsibility for training
youngsters moved from the schools to the clubs, I don't think the
county board was ready for that or the implications.'

But those who had won in 1959 did continue to have influence on the players that followed them.

Seamus Power, holder of a 1959 All-Ireland medal, was the manager of the county senior hurlers in 1978, the year Tom Higgins was appointed the team's doctor, a position he held until 2009 (1978 was also the same year he set up his GP practice in Dungarvan). Doc Higgins had played rugby at school in Waterpark, the posh part of Waterford city, and, when he started with the hurlers, his idea of team talks consisted of 'a mild gee up' and 'out ye go lads'. But he hadn't experienced a GAA gee up! 'I never saw anything like the manic atmosphere in the dressing room,' he recalls. 'It was hell and fury stuff, lads hitting the table, and shouts of, "Go out and die for the jersey and leave your last drop of blood on the pitch." Seamus Power broke a hurley on the table and no one would give him another one as they knew it'd go same way, so he battled on with the remnants and sent the lads out. It was like a psychiatric outpatients unit – and I was told this was mild.'

But Seamus' team talks didn't bring victories and Joe McGrath, a larger-than-life character and businessman originally from County Down, took over in 1980. He worked for a multinational and trained the lads like mad.

'I remember they all lost weight,' says Doc Higgins. 'Jim Greene lost two stone, gave up fags and got his hair cut. Joe had an over-powering personality, very verbal and he'd dominate the entire dressing room.'

One day, Joe told Tom Casey to get his long, flowing hair cut because 'it's slowing you up'. The player duly did.

In the wider world of the GAA, Gaelic football had changed in the 1970s and 1980s with Kevin Heffernan and Mick O'Dwyer's new tactics and training for Dublin and Kerry respectively. Hurling and, in particular Waterford hurling, was years behind, though the county had some great players, such as Mossy Walsh, Jim Greene, Pat McGrath (father to a new son at the time whom they christened Ken) and Tom Casey.

The legendary Mount Sion clubman Pat Fanning took over in 1982 and with eight or nine good players, brought Waterford to two Munster finals! The psychedelic 1970s were fading away in a haze of strikes, defeats and beer, but here was Waterford in two Munster senior hurling finals in a row, 1982 and 1983, their first since the 1960s. The talk was of a revival, or the start of something great, but each time they were trounced out the door.

Meanwhile Kilkenny were continuing their winning ways and Waterford couldn't even get out of Munster.

'The art and the expectancy of winning is ingrained in all those chosen to wear the Kilkenny jersey but unfortunately the same cannot be said of Waterford,' Pat later said about these dark years. 'Down through the corridors of time, we have produced some of the greatest hurlers the game has ever seen but have sadly never been able to put a successful winning formula into operation. Unlike Kilkenny, we go into big matches hoping to win instead of expecting to win and this has been our Achilles heel. We have fallen at hurdles that we should have leapt in style; we have failed to crash this psychological barrier most counties like Kilkenny confidently take in their stride, and that is something that comes from having the profound belief of being winners. When we do succeed in breaking down that barrier, which basically is all in the mind, then those, in our hurling family and outside it, will realise that Waterford hurling has finally arrived.'

'We used to be hammered out the gate,' recalls Tony Mansfield, another former manager.

Cork humiliated Waterford 5–31 to 3–6 in 1982 and the following year the score was 3–22 to 0–12.

Doc Higgins remembers the 1982 game when Cork were hitting the ball over from all angles and some of the Waterford players afterwards in the dressing room were verging on a medical state of shock. 'I remember Greg Fives was shaking like a leaf, he was trying to light a fag and he could hardly hold it. The next year, then, the heart went out of team.'

Billy O'Sullivan, who played for Waterford senior hurlers for over a decade from 1988, says, 'The Munster championship is the most difficult to win. In the past, if you won Munster, you were nearly All-Ireland champions. So to get out of Munster was extremely difficult.'

Jim Greene says that, in Waterford from 1968 to 1986, there were only ever six or seven players each year good enough to compete with the best other counties would throw at them. 'We never had a full deck and never showed enough intent to get it right. We didn't have the right underage structures either. As for coaching? The joke in Waterford was that coaches were for travelling in!'

Mount Sion was the standard bearer for Waterford hurling, relying on an ever diminishing group of young lads who came up the ranks and learned their trade in that enclave of Christian Brother-taught toughness at the top of the town. Narrow streets where seven year olds would stare with hurley-narrow eyes as they sized up a penalty in the street leagues.

One such player was Sean Power. The man who would later play a very big part behind the scenes in Waterford's revival was born and hurling-reared on Canon Street. An important job for some lads was to keep sentry watch for the most feared guard in the town, 'The Boy Murphy', who would scatter balls, hurleys and coats if he and his bicycle came upon a street league game.

'An ongoing problem over the years,' says Martin Óg Morrissey, 'was that we never had an outstanding goalie for the Waterford senior team. And in the street leagues, nobody wanted to play in goals – and the boy who did go in goal was normally the smallest and maybe the weakest.'

Way over on the other side of the county, there were also lads learning to hook and block, but west Waterford was like a different world from life in the city.

As a young lad growing up in picturesque Ballyduff Upper near the Cork border, Maurice Geary went to nearly all of the Waterford games from the late 1960s. Most days after games, he'd be like many Waterford supporters, 'going around with your head down', trying to avoid any gloating Cork lads. But those two defeats of Waterford by Cork in the early 1980s were horrendous.

Maurice worked over on the Cork side of the border those summers. For most people in the Ballyduff area of west Waterford, their main shopping town is Fermoy, and many of their friends and work colleagues are Cork people. 'It was even worse than slagging. I can put up with slagging, but this was blatant sympathy, a kind of 'you poor fellow' sympathy. Those two defeats were the mother and fathers of hidings,' he says.

Fellow clubmate Seamie Hannon was one of the Waterford players who suffered those hammerings. Born and reared on the family farm two and a half miles from the Cork border, he now goes over regularly to some land he has on the border.

And as he's standing there, he listens to the gurgling of the famous little stream dividing the counties. The Tubbernahulla holy well (the 'Well of the Penitential Station') is close by. Cross the stream and you're nearly in Kilworth, where his mother came from. Waterford and Cork are so close and yet so far apart in terms of hurling histories.

Back in 1982, he thought they had a lot of training done, however, they didn't know how high the bar had been set, and froze a bit on the day and when Cork suss out a weakness, 'they go to town'. Training for the 1983 game consisted of lap after lap after lap of the field, 'a lap for every man on the panel – twenty-four lads, twenty-four laps'.

'We were flayed out and again didn't play on the day,' says Seamie. 'Waterford weren't up to speed at county board level and every other level, and the longer you go without making a break-through, the harder it was going to be.'

One of the training routines at the time to toughen lads up was having strong Tom Casey take penalties with three or four of the lads on the goal line trying to stop the ball with no hurleys; they'd be pleading with Tom in the dressing room beforehand to go easy on them, but he'd have to drive the sliotars at them, and the bruises on their legs, sides or arms would take a few days to show.

In the mid-1980s, Jim Joe Landers took over and he had the unlucky distinction of taking Waterford from Division 1 to Division 2 to Division 3 in the National League, a shocking embarrassment for a 'hurling county'. Fans remember him for his sartorial elegance, wearing a crombie or a sheepskin on the day of a match (and get a good slagging from some fans for such audacity!).

The camaraderie in the dressing room was good, and it would have to be because a proud hurling county like Waterford was, in 1986, now playing the best the country could throw at them – other proud hurling counties like Carlow, Mayo and Roscommon!

That's how bad things had got; it was the pits.

Then, there was a trip to play Kerry.

'Over the Healy Pass I remember,' says Doc Higgins. 'Everyone got sick on the bus – and we lost to Kerry!'

Then the Mayo hurlers came to Fraher Field in Dungarvan on 23 February 1986 and, yes, they beat Waterford too. 'An unbelievable result and shocking day for us,' says former player Jim Greene.

Twelve of the historic Mayo team were from the small village of Tooreen in the east of the county. The players made the five-hour journey in their own cars the day before and many of them hit the disco in Dungarvan that night. There was a total of three Mayo supporters at the game. Team manager Austin Henry gave a speech in the dressing room which is now part of Mayo folklore, 'Lads, ye are probably going to get the crap beaten out of you today but, sure, go out and enjoy it!'

Mayo played with the gale-force wind in the first half and with their marvellous Joe Henry at full-forward, and they went in 2–6 ahead at half-time.

'There was shock we were leading,' says Austin, who today works in Morocco but travels home regularly to watch Tooreen play. 'In the second half, lads put their bodies and lives on the line and our goalie, Dave Sinnot, who's originally from Wexford, was outstanding. It was a remarkable result. We celebrated on the way home and to this day, when we meet up, we still talk about it.'

Reports in the local papers in Mayo concurred:

'Mayo were like innocents been driven to the slaughter ... no one gave them a chance ... but they hurled with grim tenacity, heart, sheer willpower ... in the second half against the wind, Mayo concentrated on ground hurling and were more adept than their more famous rivals ... many breathtaking saves by Dave Sinnot in Mayo goal ... held on bravely till end ... most if not all of the Mayo players had the game of their lives ... Mayo 3–7 Waterford 2–7.'

For Waterford, it was despair heaped on despair. At this stage, a Waterford fan would have laughed if he could remember how. Very few went for the away games, such as the freezing cold, wet, miserable Sunday up to Bagnelstown for a league game against Carlow.

Doc Higgins and his wife Ann got the papers that morning and left their lovely warm home overlooking Dungarvan Bay to stand on the sideline in Carlow. With only a few dozen at the match, the doc questioned his sanity, especially when he saw a small man come in with a small dog. The man and dog walked around a bit, had a look at what was happening on the pitch, looked at each other and left. 'Not even the man or the dog could stick it!' recalls Tom.

But the insanity of the 'maybe next year' philosophy ran deep in the doc's psyche and when asked when he'd give it up, he told people he'd stick with it until Waterford won the All-Ireland.

There were other trips too. A nine-hour round trip on a clattery bus to Roscommon. 'Playing on a scandalous pitch with maybe a hundred or so there,' recalls Noelie Crowley, who started his decade-long career with the county in 1983. 'We were just unlucky in the 1980s. In the Munster championship, we were playing Cork and they had the likes of Jimmy Barry Murphy. He was ahead of everyone. His mind was working before he'd even get the ball. And we hadn't the training and we were always carrying a few players. The problem was for big games, we just didn't click on the day.'

Player welfare wasn't even thought about. 'You wouldn't even get a pair of socks,' says Jim Greene.

And if things weren't going right on the field, the best way to help you forget was to have a few drinks.

'We'd be driven to some league matches,' says Noelie, 'and on the way back the craic was great, stopping in pubs, some people recognising you and drinks being bought.' On one such day, Noelie remembers 'fellas puking out each window' of the car on the way home.

Myths developed and the night before a match, 'even though sometimes you'd be in a pub drinking a glass of orange, stories would go around that you'd be falling out of the pub,' he says.

'I'll tell you the truth, though, when I had a few drinks the night before a match, I'd play better,' says Noelie, adding that Frankie Walsh, a member of the 1959-winning team had told him 'never change a habit before the night of a match'.

Noelie recalls they were to play Cork in Fermoy in a league game in the 1980s on a Bank Holiday Monday. On the Sunday, Noelie cursed to himself, saying there was no way he was staying in. So he went down to Breen's that evening for a heap of drink. Very late, Garda Cormac Quinn gave him a lift home on the motorbike. 'He put the siren on all the way up home to my mother's house and told me to go to bed straight away as I'd a match the next day. I was very, very sick but I got man of the match and we beat Cork. That was the same day big John Quirke hit a goal for Cork with his hand from the twenty-one-yard line like a bullet.'

The rare victory that day was, of course, celebrated with a lot of porter – 'No one was off the drink then,' says Noelie.

Some players, 'particularly the Glass factory fellas', required sick certs most Monday mornings after a league game. One week the factory was nearly closed down as the cause of sickness on the notes was given as 'plumboscillance' – a completely made-up illness! 'Plumb' means 'lead' and 'oscillating' means 'to swing'; so the patient was in effect sick due to a 'swinging of the lead'! The mystery illness had never been heard of before and with fears that it could have been infectious, the unions nearly brought all the workers out on strike. When a company nurse rang to ask if it was infectious, the response was, 'It is out there!'

As some of the lads were out and about drinking, other young wannabe stars were honing their skills at those schools in the county which really made a big effort to develop hurling.

At eleven o'clock every morning in the primary school in Lismore, the principal Brother Dromer from Dublin and one of the teachers Sean Prendergast would call the children out onto the tarmac and continue the ground hurling, four-a-side leagues for First Class and up.

One goal was a doorway into the shed, the other was painted onto the back of the old woodwork room. With the walls all round it was hell-for-leather stuff, especially as the Brother wasn't too strict on the rules and would regularly stop for a chat with another teacher while he was supposed to be refereeing.

Other teachers would sip tea during their break and look out at some fantastic talents developing in what were sometimes ferocious games. And, as they watched, the teachers wondered if lads such as Dave Bennett, Sean Daly, Tom Feeney, Kieran O'Gorman, the Sullivan twins and Dan Shanahan would go on to greater things.

Maurice Geary was games master at the Christian Brothers secondary school in Lismore, and the lads now came to him at the age of twelve with fire in their bellies and skills learned from those little leagues. And they were mad for the game – any time Maurice would be in Lismore for messages, he'd always see a hurley in the hands of Dan or any of the others. But Lismore was one of the few places where this was happening. And there was very little being organised at county board level to nurture this talent, no thinking outside the box, no ten-year strategic plan. Everything was geared towards the senior team maybe making a breakthrough the following year.

'It was a short-sighted vision that didn't help the progress of the game in the county at all,' says Maurice. 'Why did it happen? Probably the continuing lack of success.'

Other counties, such as Kilkenny and Cork, were developing programmes for improving young hurlers but, in Waterford, long-term planning was a mirage in the desert of despair.

At the time, many GAA officials were martyrs for tradition, believing what had worked for the previous eighty years would work for the next eighty. This was acutely reflected in what is known in Waterford as the east–west divide.

For a relatively small county with a population of around 100,000 and no major mountain range splitting it, Waterford has two divisional GAA boards – one in the east and one in the west, each with their own fiefdoms. And each with their own 'county' ground – Walsh Park in the city for those in the east, and Fraher Field in Dungarvan for the boys from the west.

'The greatest curse ever,' says Martin Óg Morrissey of the east–west divide, saying the main problem was at official and officer level. His view is backed up by Jim Greene, 'It definitely was a factor in hurling not developing properly. Each board was working towards dates for their respective divisional finals. There was no cop on. And it meant we didn't have proper underage structures across the county as there was not enough effort being put in by each board at that level. And you can't build a house by starting with the roof.'

In the 1970s, 1980s and 1990s, the minor or under-18 champion-ship was organised within each area, and the winners then met in the county final. This meant youngsters didn't get to mix and learn from the best of the county's players on a regular basis.

At the same time, senior county players weren't meeting that often, and, invariably, their clubs came first.

'For some lads, it was tuppence halfpenny looking down on tuppence,' says Maurice Geary. 'The lads from Waterford city could be looking down on their country cousins down the west, and for decades it was like that. When they came up here to play us, we'd ask them how did they find their way up here? For many in the east, the county finished in Kilmeaden!'

There were many in west Waterford over the years who wouldn't have been to Waterford city until they were teenagers.

'The city fellas were different, are still different,' said another former senior selector. 'They talk different, but that sort of hint of arrogance and swagger on the hurling field is sometimes not a bad thing, you think you're better and the country lads then need to buck up and improve and play better to beat them.'

Back in east Waterford, one 'city club', which wasn't really a city club, was Ballygunner. Formed only in 1954 by James McGinn, the master of the then small rural primary school, the club was quickly developing as an arch rival of Mount Sion. The master trained lads who formed the backbone of the Ballygunner teams that won the county title in 1966, 1967 and 1968 but when the conveyor belt stopped, he realised it was back to basics. So in the 1980s, he brought lads through at school, such as Fergal Hartley, Stephen Frampton, Paul Flynn and Billy O'Sullivan – players who would later owe so much to this one man's ambition, drive and vision. Their hurling skills were helped by the foundation of the Tony Forristal Trophy in 1982 where the country's best under-14 hurlers represented their counties – and most of the present-day hurling stars wore their county jersey for the first time at this tournament.

Billy O'Sullivan, who lined out as corner-forward for Waterford in 1987 at the tender age of eighteen, says the Mount Sion–

Ballygunner rivalry was like an Old Firm derby, 'It produced great hurlers, was great for Waterford and was healthy. It was never part of our make up that we hated Mount Sion when we went to play them but everyone lifted their game.'

Tony Mansfield, a trade union organiser from Dungarvan, was appointed manager of the county team for the 1987 season, and his organisational skills helped take Waterford up the divisions and, in 1989, they made the Munster final to play Tipperary, the first such final to be covered live on RTÉ television.

As both teams arrived in Cork, the Waterford players, in raggle taggle jeans and jumpers, saw Tipperary looking very professional in blazers and slacks. And Tipp manager Babs Keating had been building up Waterford in the papers that week as a very dirty team.

As the players waited for the referee to start the match, Waterford free taker Kieran Delahunty was decked before the ball was even thrown in.

'It went from bad to worse and we were well and truly beaten, twelve points in the end. It wasn't pretty,' recalls Doc Higgins.

Noelie Crowley got sent off that day, but still maintains his innocence. 'I didn't even hit the chap. The player is living in Dunhill in Waterford today and I've never spoken to him since.'

Looking back on it now, Colm Bonnar says, 'When Tipp were playing Waterford, we felt we were always going to beat them. From 1986 to 1998, we gave them some almighty hidings, even in Walsh Park and were always confident. That Munster final in 1989 was free after free but there was nothing too bad.' Tony Mansfield says no specific instructions were given before the match; but the players desperately wanted to win. In the mid-1990s, there were a few bad melees and there was no great love between the teams.

Damien Byrne also got sent off for Waterford that day for clashing with legendary Tipp forward Nicky English and Damien and Noelie each got a six-month suspension. Noelie christened

Nicky 'God', 'He was a good hurler but you couldn't touch him because, if you did, he'd get a free, he got extra special treatment because of who he was; like God you couldn't touch him.' Tipp fans would obviously disagree.

After the match, Fr Fogarty for Tipp was very irate saying their players had suffered a lot at the hands of Waterford, who, in turn, had to tell the world of the 'intensity' of their injuries. The sports cartoon in one of the evening papers a few days later had a Waterford player shouting 'Give Him Timber', but holding a tree instead of a hurley.

Tipp went on to win the All-Ireland and Waterford were left ruing yet another missed opportunity.

In the first-round match of the 1990 Munster championship, Waterford faced Cork and the tension in the Waterford dressing room was high. History repeated itself – a hurley was broken on the table during the pre-match speech, and there were shouts for more hurleys but none were forthcoming.

One of the players trying hard to focus was twenty-four-year old Sean Cullinane, only on the panel two years with no county underage experience.

Since his first game for Waterford, Sean had been collecting each match programme and he planned to continue this for as long as he played. That sense of pride and nervousness when he made his first start was chiselled into a mental and physical toughness as he became a regular in the full-back line beside Damien Byrne and Jimmy Beresford, 'two gentle giants, hard men, hard hitting' as he sees them.

Training at the time was laps and hurling, with no warm-up beforehand, just a few stretches, knees up to chest and out the door.

The attitude that 'Waterford can only win if Cork play bad' was pervasive and everything Cork touched that day turned to gold, goals and points. They were rampant. Whereas everything Waterford tried didn't work. With ten minutes to go, Sean was hoping – praying – that the game would end soon because the beating they were taking was another humiliating disaster. As the final whistle blew, Cork were seventeen points ahead. Another hammering. Waterford could take some comfort from the fact that they were beaten by the best that year – Cork went on to win the All-Ireland.

That summer, Sean and new players, such as Stephen Frampton, wondered, once again, if Waterford's day would ever come.

Frampton got on to the panel in 1988 as an eighteen year old and was one of the few county players also going to college. Hurling at all levels, all over the country, was more 'animal' in those days.

'Our first ever Fitzgibbon Cup colleges game was in Belfast against Queen's, a horrific, terrifying experience. Every sideline cut we had they were spitting and shouting and roaring at us. There were no fences or anything. We lost; probably terrified into defeat,' he says.

Stephen couldn't believe manager Tony Mansfield would have to say to grown men before a match, 'Make sure you have your laces right in your boots and your studs right.' He and others thought it would be a given that inter-county hurlers wouldn't have to be reminded of such details.

Sports science then was all about who could count how many laps of the field they'd done in a month.

Facilities weren't much more modern. The shaft of light from an open dressing-room door was sometimes their only light for winter training at Abbeyside in Dungarvan. Lads would hide in a ditch if they could find one. It would be like that most nights until the clocks went forward each March.

'It was accepted,' says Stephen. 'There might have been more technology in Tipperary or Cork but that's the way it was in Waterford.'

The sandwiches afterwards were made by Bridin Ní Christeoir from the Dungarvan club and were served with a cup of tea and

Telex bars – that was the sum of it. 'I particularly remember the Telex bars – they were lovely!' recalls Stephen.

There were problems on the field as well, as Mossie O'Keefe from Passage East remembers when he came on to the panel at the time. 'Club rivalry definitely played a part in the county not doing well. There were times when let's say a forward from Lismore in the west wouldn't pass the ball to me but would put it to another Lismore man instead.'

The hurling was a lot slower then than now, and Mossie remembers forwards in particular having to stand in close when marking very hairy hurlers from opposing counties, 'because if you didn't, they'd leather you'.

Mount Sion man Shane 'Shiner' Ahearne says, 'You were delighted to be playing for your county and they'd still treat you like shit. The attitude was, 'If you don't like it, we'll get somebody else to play!' From both players and management, it was very unprofessional.'

And the results showed – the only consistency about Waterford was their inconsistency.

There may have been splutters of hope, but they always ended in tears, and then the tears started drying up, the heart didn't ache any more, and all was numb.

Would there be any hope around the corner?

3

FUN AND GAMES
IN THE EARLY 1990s

When a team's going well, mistakes are sometimes pushed behind
a curtain; when things go badly, everything is brought out for
minute dissection and discussion. And that is the way it was in
Waterford in the early 1990s when internal politics and disunity
was a boil ready to burst the county board.

'They were caught in time warp,' says one former player.
'Inward-looking fellas were getting into power just to have power
and stay in power. The county board was split down the middle,
and the eastern board was split with the western board. It was a
total mess.'

With cliques and people pulling in all different directions,
enemies were quickly made.

Some felt the Mount Sion influence was too powerful and went
out of their way to try to change it. Others thought and acted
differently. All the shenanigans were to have an effect on the
players, some of whom were the nucleus of what could have been
a very good side in 1991.

That year, Joe McGrath, the manager from the early 1980s and
now working in Cork, was called back to manage the senior
hurlers. He reinvigorated the setup and organised things such as

aerobics for the lads in Clonea Strand Hotel, where the sight of players – particularly the older players – trying to follow the lead of the female instructor in leg warmers while jumping around to pop music was something that had to be seen to be believed.

But his organisational skills and hard training, coupled with his insistence that, for the first time, players were to be treated properly off the field, was the spark of something new. Players thought he was six years ahead of anyone else, acknowledging that some of his training drills in and out of the cones had never been heard of in Waterford.

Aged nineteen, Brian Greene (son of former player Jim) came on the panel in 1990. 'I remember Joe had us training in the rain and our faces would be in the wet ground for the push-ups. "Pray for rain," I think he used to say. He brought a blackboard into the dressing room, the first time that was ever done! And he tried to give us some self-belief because we had none whatsoever.'

Joe wanted players to change their habits, and told them after one league match that they'd never win anything while they were drinking. Some players found it hard to change. 'We might not win anything in the bar,' said one of the players, 'but it's a nice place to be!'

Joe's enthusiasm even reinvigorated the supporters club and, for the first time in years, players started demanding meals after matches, with chicken and chips sometimes provided in Lawlor's Hotel in Dungarvan.

However, at the same time, a row developed over the rates of Joe's mileage expenses from Cork and because of the festering county board politics, the issue was allowed to become exaggerated into something major.

'Some players didn't give a shite about it, some were upset and there was talk of getting rid of him because those who had brought Joe in were part of one side of the county board!' recalls a player.

For some of the younger players, the row was enough to shatter their illusion of progress and unity.

At a players' meeting in Dungarvan, fourteen out of the panel of thirty who were there voted that Joe should go. For various reasons, others weren't present but this would be seen as a fore-runner for 'player power' – something which would raise its head many years later with Justin McCarthy.

Some players had wanted to keep Joe, having found a new sense of purpose, but they had felt intimidated and weren't strong enough to stand up and vote against. An acrimonious county board meeting the following week endorsed the decision but, by then, animosity had found its way in amongst the players themselves.

They went down to play Kerry in the first round of the Munster hurling championship and with five minutes to go, were just a point up, though a few late scores put some respectability on the scoreboard and Waterford won by six.

In the dressing room before the next match against Cork, Damien Byrne and others pleaded with everybody to put all the rows behind them and play with heart. The players did and nearly pulled off a famous victory but, in the end, lost by three points.

To this day, some players feel ashamed of how the entire Joe McGrath episode was handled, leading, as it did, to the break-up of a potentially very good panel. Another long summer of heartache and no inter-county matches for Waterford followed.

The county board appointed Georgie Leahy, a big man from Glenmore in south Kilkenny, as the new manager. He had brought that small rural club to win the All-Ireland club championship, an amazing achievement but, begrudgingly, some Waterford people thought the team was so good on its own, anybody could have managed them.

'Georgie was big, bluff man, a very nice guy,' says Doc Higgins. 'When he came to Waterford, he had a limited team and he was trying to do his best. They did a modicum of training but didn't kill themselves.'

'I got a fair response from the players and had no real problems with them,' says Georgie. 'Training was slack for a few weeks but I didn't have much trouble with any of the players. There was one evening we went up to Wicklow to play Wexford at the opening of a ground and we just about got fifteen players, but there was club championship on that day as well in Waterford.'

But he was trying to make things more professional, he says. Brian Greene was taken off in a league game away to Antrim after playing a trick on Georgie in the hotel room the night before. 'I felt I was being scolded for what I had done,' says Greener. 'So I decided to give up! My retirement was announced on radio the next day at the age of twenty-four! Lads slagged me after that I had more comebacks than Frank Sinatra! I never really found Georgie's team talks inspirational, it was "hasn't he two hands and two legs, there's no difference between ye and the opposition" – and we needed inspiration.'

In the 1992 National League campaign, a young Mount Sion player made it onto the panel. Tony Browne looked promising, following in the boots of his father and grandfather. He was eager to do what was needed to ensure Waterford progressed, but, the older players found it hard to change their habits. Something Tony and the other younger players found hard to understand.

The Friday night before Waterford were due to play Cork in the league, Fergal Hartley, one of the Ballygunner youngsters, was told he'd be making his league debut on Sunday at corner-back. He went to Geoff's pub in the city centre with a few friends, drank a few glasses of 7-Up and water and decided to head home around 11.15 p.m. Walking down past 'the Kentucky' the K-Fried Chicken, he saw one of his team-mates, an older player, the worse for wear. 'He's sitting down against the wall outside the Kentucky with a snack box! He can barely get the chips into his mouth. I didn't know him that well because I was only after coming onto the panel but I was thinking to myself, My God, is this what it's all about?'

Dietary habits in most other counties were nothing like they are today but this, recalls Fergal, was ridiculous.

The panel somehow pulled together and, in May, played Clare in Thurles, Anthony Daly's first time as Clare captain. Only 8,000 spectators turned up. The match ended in a draw but even fewer attended the replay in the rain, which Waterford won by two points, 0–16 to 0–14.

'I think Meaney scored for Waterford near the end,' says Anthony Daly, 'and I gave him a shot when he was coming back out. So at the end, Kieran Delhaunty said to me, "Stick to your fucking traditional music", or something like that, which looking back now, was a good one.'

Alongside the senior campaign was that of the underage teams and there were some excellent players coming in under the radar. The minors (or under-18s), playing in their first Munster final since 1968, got a draw against Tipperary with a last-minute goal from Paul Flynn and then went on to win the replay, 2–10 to 0–14.

Kieran O'Connor, who was commentating on the match for Waterford Local Radio, remembers the Paul Flynn goals well. 'The last goal in the drawn game – time was ticking down it looked like we were going to be beaten and 'here we go again' and he got a goal out of nothing. To draw we needed a goal and young Flynn delivered.'

Waterford fans had something to celebrate for the first time in decades.

Meanwhile, the under-21s had a magnificent two-point win against a fancied Clare team to win the Munster final in a pulsating game. Davy Fitzgerald was in goal for Clare and this would be the only All-Ireland medal to elude him (he'd won the minor All-Ireland three years earlier). The team included promising players such as Brian Lohan and Seanie McMahon and their manager was former Clare player Ger Loughnane. Their defeat at the hands of Waterford would steel them, but what would victory do for the Waterford under-21s?

'Waterford under-21s were a really good team in 1992,' says Davy Fitzgerald. 'It hurt Clare very much. In fact, it still hurts. But it made us want more, to be even more dedicated. You often see unbelievable players on the way up at minor and under-21 level and you wonder if they want it as much when they are at senior. You'd wonder if they get the same buzz. And when you win a minor or under-21 title, you are exposed to serious social events. It has happened also to Galway and Limerick.'

After beating Antrim in the semi-finals, both the Waterford minors and under-21s were now in All-Ireland finals. The minors played their final in Croke Park and, for many Waterford fans, it was their first time in GAA headquarters. Some got lost on the way through the streets of the capital. Even though they were beaten by Galway by six points, many felt this could be the start of something great.

The under-21s included players who had graduated from the Lismore academy of mini-school leagues, from Mount Sion's grit and Master McGinn's coaching at Ballygunner. Their manager Peter Power had also done a lot of work in the schools in Dungarvan, and some players say he had a totally different thinking from other Waterford managers. 'It was like they're all doing that, I'll do this!' And he didn't focus on laps, he focused on first touch.

His team was pitted against Offaly in the final and the venue was Nowlan Park in Kilkenny. Sean 'Growler' Daly from Lismore scored three goals and the game ended in a draw, 4–4 to 0–16.

Fergal Hartley hadn't slept great the night before the match, and he asked goalie Ray 'Lay Lay' Barry what he did to relax before a big game. Lay Lay told him to come down to The Farleigh pub in Passage East and, like him, have just two pints of Smithwicks on the Saturday before the replay. Fergal did, slept great and went on to be man of the match.

The replay was tight but, somehow, the boys did what no other Waterford team had been able to do for a long time – they held their nerve and secured victory, 0–12 to 2–3. It was Waterford's first All-Ireland under-21 hurling championship title. (Little did people know that seven of that defeated Offaly team were to go on to win All Stars, so hungry were they for success at senior level.)

There was joy unbounded in Waterford. And that was only the start of it. Everyone expected that most of the team would perform for the next ten years.

The homecoming included an open-top bus from the station with fans witnessing a trophy coming over the bridge for the first time in decades to a stage and massive reception on the hill at Ballybricken.

However, when some of the under-21s were called up to the senior panel, they couldn't believe the setup. Peter Power had trained them for their All-Ireland win with hurling, hurling and more hurling. Peter said under-21s should be fit and told them: 'You can have fifteen Carl Lewises on the team and get to the ball first but if you can't pick it up, it's worth nothing.'

He had also introduced a word that had been alien to Waterford hurling – tactics!

On the senior panel, though, things were different.

'There was no such thing as playing to our strengths,' says Lay Lay Barry. 'There were no tactics, just get the ball and hit it. For the under-21s, we had tactics, starting right back at the puckout. It's no disrespect to Georgie Leahy, but if he was talking in the dressing room, a lot of lads would be talking to someone else. Some of the young fellas were a bit cocky but we were never told how to handle that under-21 victory. No one ever sat us down and said, "Look lads this is a stepping stone to a Munster final in five years time."'

And how long did the celebrations go on for? Five months?

'Five years! Everywhere you went people were throwing drink at you,' he says. 'We went all the way round the county, especially to each club that had a member on the under-21 panel.

I remember one Monday night we were up in the small village of Tourin; the community centre then was like an auld cow shack; the people were great; there were crates of beer and an auld record player playing just Irish waltzes; we were told to get what we wanted; we didn't mind what was on the records after a while.

'I don't think some of us got sober for about three months. Every morning, you were getting up and going to local schools, then straight to next pub, five or six pubs a day, and then somewhere that night. There were bottles everywhere. Cappoquin – I think we spent a week up there, using it as a base. The setup at senior level was awful. If you didn't train, you didn't train, you were never asked why. It was a shambles and you could come and go as you wanted.'

If a Cork or Kilkenny hurler had won an under-21 All-Ireland medal, he wouldn't brag about it because the guy who comes round the corner could have five under-21 *and* senior All-Ireland medals at home.

But what's seldom is wonderful – and 1992 was wonderful for Waterford.

The feeling was that four or five of the under-21s would automatically make it to the senior panel, and maybe the same number of minors in a few years time, and this coupled with the ten or so 'good lads' on the senior team, would *automatically* mean that Waterford would win an All-Ireland senior title within two or three years! Hey presto!

If only it was that simple.

Waterford had a good defence but needed someone who could provide the finishing power the team lacked. On a beautiful summer's evening in May 1993, Paul Flynn was training with Ballygunner when long-time club member Charlie Lapthorne asked him if he could be in Walsh Park on Thursday evening at seven o'clock for training with the seniors. His county debut beckoned. A few weeks later, Flynners was lining out against Kerry in Walsh Park for his first championship start, and he'd just turned eighteen.

Flynners was a confident, even precocious, young man. He was a very good soccer goalkeeper, so good he was playing for the senior Villa team in Waterford when he was only fifteen, he even made the Irish under-15 squad and got trials with Luton and Aston Villa, going over to train with well-known goalies such as Nigel Spinks, Les Sealey and former England great Peter Bonetti. (He hadn't known who Bonetti was until he rang home to ask his father. The next day Flynners slagged Bonetti at the Luton pitch about England losing the World Cup and the young Waterford man wasn't called back to Luton for any other trials!)

Flynn had stopped growing at five foot nine inches, too small for soccer goalkeepers at the time and decided instead to concentrate on hurling. And now here he was – ready to play for Waterford in the last Sunday in May 1993.

Expectations were high after the under-21 win the previous year. It was the first round of the championship and Kerry hurlers hadn't won a game in this competition since 1926!

But Kerry had already trained 120 times, something they'd never done before, and their manager, John Meyler, was an astute man and had been a great hurler for Wexford in his day. He had watched Waterford play Kilkenny in a tournament a week earlier, had made ten pages of notes and told his players in training, 'We're going to beat Waterford, lads!'

'I always felt Waterford would underestimate us,' he says now.

Some of the Waterford under-21s had been asked to join the senior panel in January 1993, including Lay Lay, the young goalkeeper who was quickly becoming renowned for his shot-stopping abilities. He had played during every game of that National League campaign but when the Kerry game came around, Lay Lay and Ray Whitty were dropped from the panel for no reason and older players Pat Curran and Ray Sheridan were back in.

The day of the match, Paul Flynn was excited to have his first championship start. The county board was excited – it could be the start of a new era – so excited (with financial help from Waterford Crystal), they had got everyone on the squad blazers and trousers from Mackey's on the Quay to parade their new-found sense of confidence. The players had been measured up the week before and each player was to wear their new suit to the match and then home afterwards.

Board chairman Eamonn Murphy told them to be in Breen's before the match where they were given tea and sandwiches. He told them, 'Lads, I'm after buying ye new suits, whatever ye do, don't get beat today.'

He'd also arranged for a photograph to be taken before the match for the local papers. So they all went up to Walsh Park and as Kerry arrived, the Waterford players were having their picture taken in their shiny new, navy blazers, white shirts, red ties and grey trousers.

In jeans and T-shirts, the Kerry players – 'some of us were like lads coming in from cutting turf', recalls one player – had a good look. John Meyler thought that Waterford couldn't be focused on the game if they were having such photos taken. Waterford centre-back Sean Cullinane thought he saw some of the Kerry lads laughing, and for a man who didn't 'do' suits, he felt very uncomfortable with it all.

Waterford half-back Stephen Frampton was nervous and felt he shouldn't even be playing because he had broken his arm the previous November and was only just back.

Waterford Local Radio wasn't even doing a live broadcast of the match as everyone was expecting it to be a non-event. When commentator Kieran O'Connor saw the navy blazers, it reminded him of when Tipperary did something similar in 1990 before they played Cork. Cork had gone on to beat Tipp, but surely an ambush wouldn't happen today? His brother had been involved in 1957 when Waterford beat Kerry in football, but the reverse would never happen, not today.

But Billy O'Sullivan, the team captain, knew their preparations had been poor. He'd been very disappointed at the way training had changed from Joe McGrath's time and, just before they ran out of the dressing room, he remembers Georgie Leahy said to him, 'You're gone cat [rubbish] and you're coming off today.'

'I was gobsmacked and even though I was captain, he wouldn't let me lead out the team,' says Billy. Though George doesn't remember saying those words today.

Up on the bank watching the match were Lay Lay Barry and others from the victorious under-21 panel who weren't playing against Kerry. 'Jaysus, lads, ye should be out there,' commented some supporters.

'There was no reason why I was dropped,' says Lay Lay. 'Georgie Leahy had an old core, Damien Byrne, Noelie Crowley, Jimmy Beresford; and he put Eamon Cullinane in the forward line with Jimmy, so three backs were playing in the forward line, which shouldn't have been happening.'

In the Kerry dressing room, John Meyler told his players to go at Waterford from the start, 'Sure they're having pictures taken lads in new suits! They don't even think we're here today!'

A single coach had brought up the Kerry supporters that day – all twenty-five of them!

The match started and Kerry fought for everything. Waterford went into an early lead with a goal but Kerry put Mick O'Shea on Noelie Crowley, tormenting him incessantly. Kerry were still in it after twenty minutes and realised Waterford may not have been able to get it going. At half-time, Kerry were only a point down, 2–8 to 2–7.

Waterford went six clear in the second half but, amazingly, Kerry came back. Christy Walsh scored a great goal for the Kingdom and D.J. Leahy got a fluky goal from a long-range free. Everything was going right for Kerry and they were scoring points from near impossible angles. Suddenly, Kerry were ahead and Waterford were useless, apart from Paul Flynn who scored

3–2. The fans couldn't believe what was happening. Waterford tried for an equaliser but failed.

Then Terence Murray from Limerick blew the final whistle, it was all over: 4–13 to 3–13.

'When that whistle blew, we couldn't believe it. We were looking for holes to throw ourselves in,' says Sean Cullinane. 'Waterford used to find it hard to beat the weaker teams but this was a total embarrassment. I didn't want to talk to anyone.'

It was the worst result in all the long list of bad results in Waterford's hurling history and the lads got terrible abuse as they walked off the field. A few supporters threw stones and cans at the netting over the narrow tunnel which takes the players towards the dressing rooms.

Lay Lay Barry and others shouted at Georgie Leahy, 'You should be ashamed of yourself, Leahy. Young fellas here should be playing.' But Georgie kept going – 'It was just one of those results, a once off,' he says – and the following year, he was retained as manager.

'It was unbelievable,' recalls Kieran O'Connor. 'This was the Kerry hurling team! And we had guys who had won All-Irelands the year before beating a great Offaly under-21 team. The fans were disgusted. There was no back door; we were out. And then the under-21s were beaten by Limerick in Walsh Park, so we were gone in that too.'

Waterford All-Ireland 1959 winner Austin Flynn went into the dressing room and told the players they had no excuses, they should have won.

And the lads had to put back on their new suits when they were leaving the ground.

Shane 'Shiner' Ahearne was so disgusted that he didn't even have a shower, just put on his clothes and was ready to leave, red mist in his eyes. Jimmy O'Gorman, one of the selectors, asked him where he was going, but was told, 'Jimmy, get out of my way or I'll put you and the door out.'

In the Kerry dressing room, the players were hooping and hollering; they tried to drag Johnny O'Connor, the RTÉ radio reporter for the day, into the showers before county board vice-chairman Liam Cotter led the players in a rousing rendition of 'The Rose of Tralee' and afterwards John Meyler went on the supporters' bus to thank the loyal band of twenty-five who had witnessed the remarkable result.

Noelie Crowley went home and took his suit off as quickly as he could before joining the others in the Bridge Hotel, 'where the fans couldn't find us'.

The post mortem brought up all the problems – questions over at least one player playing soccer the week of the game, training, lack of training, drinking problems, everything.

Things weren't very good on the field for the next twelve months, but, off the field, some lads had a great time. Away games in the league through Tipperary always entailed a stop on the way back in Chalkes in Clonmel. The sessions were good. Georgie Leahy wasn't a drinker and many times, he became driver for Lay Lay Barry (now back on the panel) and others. And times were so different – if a player smoked, he would have no problem walking into the dressing room on the day of a league match with a cigarette in his mouth.

Waterford were relegated again to Division 2. 'Some forwards would rather score four points for the paper and the team get beaten instead of running, taking a few tackles and giving ball to someone else for a goal. We had a lot of individuals,' says Lay Lay.

But there were some promising developments, with Tom Feeney, a young back from Ballyduff Upper, joining the panel, and later a young Brian Flannery, who had moved to Waterford and transferred from Tipperary joined too. But the old problems persisted: some county players on a Thursday night after training still stopped off for a big burger and chips from Genoa's chipper or the Causeway in Abbeyside.

'I went on panel at the end of 1993,' says Tom Feeney, 'but the place was in chaos. Georgie tried his best and was a passionate man but there was no passion in the setup; players could sometimes tell management they couldn't make training and "okay" was the response. And then when we were playing other counties, there was sense of awe about the players on other teams.'

In the 1994 championship, Waterford were pencilled in to play Limerick in the Munster semi-final, having got a first-round bye, thankfully avoiding Kerry! On a Friday evening, ten days before the game, training was in Erin's Own ground in Poleberry. A few players were injured and some were missing but, from a panel of around twenty-five, only nine players togged out! After a short run, all they could do was have a small game of backs and forwards – where six backs marked six forwards and somebody out in midfield put the ball in – but they didn't have enough players. In the end, Lay Lay had to come out of goals to mark Shay Fitzpatrick, the physio, and Cha O'Neill from the supporters' club, who was standing on the sideline, had to go in goals!

Fergal Hartley was thinking that things couldn't get any worse, believing it was not from the lack of effort on manager Georgie Leahy's part.

The following Friday night, numbers were back up in Walsh Park for what was the last training session before the big game. Afterwards as the players showered, there was no sign of the sandwiches. Suddenly, a van pulled up from the Kentucky Fried Chicken in town and out came trays of snack boxes. One for everyone on the team and more!

Nothing was spared in this cordon bleu meal for high-performance athletes and everything was catered for. 'It was like something you'd see at half two in the morning,' says Sean 'Growler' Daly, who got his nickname from a lion T-shirt he had worn once as a child. 'Thirty lads tucking into snack boxes!'

They boys ate the food in the dressing room, which was now pungent with the smell of chicken and chips. But nobody said anything, they just ate. Then Georgie announced the team, giving no explanation to individual players about why they were being dropped, saying he was 'going for experience'. Some of the younger players were again denied their chance.

Even with the shambolic training, Limerick only beat Waterford by four points and Offaly went on to win the All-Ireland. Georgie Leahy's two-year stint as manager was over. 'I was asked to stay on for another year, but I decided not to,' he says.

In the winter of 1994–1995 and when training was on in Dungarvan on Tuesdays or Thursdays, some of the boys heading back to east Waterford would stop in Dunphy's roadside pub in Newtown and down four, five or maybe even six pints. This was after training! And they'd play cards with the few locals there and be home by 11.30 p.m.

'Every Tuesday or Thursday,' says Lay Lay, 'match or no match. We weren't told not to do it and knew no different.'

Tradition dictated that when a team won the All-Ireland, the visiting side for a national league game lined up before the match and clapped them onto the field, and the same happened when Waterford (with a new manager Tony Mansfield) went up to play Offaly in Birr. Many of the Offaly lads, no strangers to celebrating themselves, had been on the lash since their September win. A lot of the Waterford lads had faced many of the Offaly boys in the under-21 final two years earlier.

Outside the small tunnel under the stand, Waterford lined up to form a guard of honour for Offaly. Fergal Hartley could see the Offaly boys in the tunnel, waiting to run out, and there amongst them is John Troy. 'As the team is running, he's getting the last couple of drags out of the cigarette and then he stamps on it and out he runs!'

The game was held the day after the Waterford County Club final, where Mount Sion had just beaten Passage. Lay Lay had got to bed around 5 a.m. and he and team-mate Barry Walsh got collected around 9 a.m. for the drive to Offaly.

Lay Lay says, 'There was a man announcing things over the tannoy system at half-time. He praised me and Barry for being there, mentioning we'd lost the County final. Billy Dooley from Offaly started slagging me that we'd lost a County final. I said to Dumbo, one of our backs, "Next time, laave him in." He did and I got the ball, dropped it in front of him, pulled and he didn't fall; pulled a second time, still didn't fall; a third time, he fell; panned. Brendan Kelly, their full-forward who had a head like a television, came for me but Dumbo stopped him. I collected my hurleys and was already walking off before the ref sent me off. Their fans started slagging and I started bowing to them; some of them threw bananas and fruit at me. Tony Mansfield gave me some bollocking. Afterwards, Johnny Pilkington from Offaly came to me and said, "Don't mind that, don't worry about what happened." One of the Offaly player's neck was completely covered with love bites. I suppose they'd been on the beer for month or two celebrating the All-Ireland. They were real rock and rollers.'

Somehow, Waterford went on to win Division 2 and Peter Power came in as manager, bringing in Gerry Fitzpatrick, who tried to introduce some modern physical-training methods. But proper weights programmes and diets which were then part of rugby and soccer squads and athletics still hadn't permeated the psyche of the GAA.

'I tried to introduce a weights programme,' Gerry says, 'but I was met with fierce opposition. Most of the players weren't really into it.'

And the fun off the pitch continued. One weekend saw ten players staying up drinking in Dungarvan after a league match, hitting Tommy Power's pub at 9 a.m. ('where a heap of auld farmers would buy us a heap of drink') and getting a doctor's cert at some stage later in the day.

The team found it hard to get a 'style' on the field, with many players from the west playing a more physical game, carrying the ball more (football is big in west Waterford) and in some ways it was like two different counties.

Lay Lay Barry says players still weren't passing to the player in the best position. 'Some lads from the east wouldn't pass it to other lads from the east, never mind about lads from the west! A Mount Sion player might pass it to another Mount Sion player but not to a Ballygunner player. You'd spot it in training. Then the reverse would happen. This was going on for ten years. And a fella would sometimes rather put it wide than pass it, an attitude of, "Well, if I don't score, no one else will."'

Sean Cullinane, though, says the east–west divide was overstated, especially in the backline as backs would pass the ball to the person in the best position if they had to get out of trouble.

But sparks of brilliance were emerging. In training, Paul Flynn was hitting penalties from twenty-five yards to improve his aim, and his natural ability, vision and cuteness amazed others. But could he have done more? One former team-mate says, 'He'd score 1–6 some day when he maybe could have scored 1–10, he was happy with it.'

In 1995, Tipperary beat Waterford by twenty-one points in the first round of the championship in Cork: 4–23 to 1–11. Another disaster of a day and another championship over. A big row during the match involving a lot of players had ramifications even though nobody was sent off. Peter Queally from Ballydurn was due to graduate from Garda Training College the following Thursday but was called in on the Monday morning by his superiors (some of whom were not Waterford fans!), told his behaviour wasn't acceptable and he wouldn't be allowed graduate.

'I couldn't believe it,' Peter says. 'I was involved in the melee but nobody was sent off. I think it was one of the first times players were judged by television replays. My family was very disappointed as we'd hotels and restaurants booked and I had to wait another three months to graduate.'

Team matters off the field hadn't got any better and player welfare was a misnomer.

'We trained in January 1996 in Abbeyside one night really hard, an absolute ball breaker of a session,' remembers Fergal Hartley. 'It had started to snow but the showers afterwards were cold. Then we went in and there was a burka boiler where we made our own tea and were given a ten-penny Touchdown bar that you'd give to a child. I'll never forget it. We were after killing ourselves for this. Things got a bit better after we complained to the county board.'

That summer, they were being hammered again by Tipperary but late scores made it seem a respectable three-point defeat – the same day a seventeen-year-old Mount Sion player made his championship debut. As he arrived at the pitch, Ken McGrath was thinking, This is the biggest crowd I'll ever have played in front of.

Going out on the pitch, his team-mate Bugsy gave him a massive slap on the back to wish him well; Ken can still remember the pain!

McGrath's father was watching him run out, pride in his chest. Pat started playing for the county in 1972 and his sons got hurls early in life. Ken's first and only helmet was green and he had it till he was around fifteen but forgot it for a challenge match and hadn't worn one since. He was fearless, dynamic and an absolutely gem of a hurler. 'He was like Wayne Rooney when he was on fire,' says Sean Cullinane. 'You'd just give him the ball and he'd score; he was beating teams on his own and you knew he was something special.'

Before the Tipperary game, Tony Mansfield, who had been a selector in 1995 but had become outright manager in 1996, had told Lay Lay Barry 'not put too many balls down on Ken' because of his inexperience, but Ken won loads of ball and defied the odds. That year, he would play for Waterford under-18s, under-21s and seniors! Tony thought they could have beaten Tipperary that day if they'd had the players together for another week 'to sharpen their skills', but the setup at county board level meant it hadn't been possible.

Another debut at the Tipp match was Roger Casey, who looked after the hurleys, sliotars and gear, and he knew every sliotar was sacred.

'The most you'd be going to some matches with would be six balls so you couldn't afford to lose a ball or two. We used to chase balls when they went behind the goals in Walsh Park – all the time, we had no choice, we had to. We even got on to the guards who used to be behind the goal to stop young fellas taking them. We'd have to get on to the county board and they'd have to pay a garda or a steward to try to get the balls from the young lads.'

On and off the field, Waterford was still mentally and politically weak. During matches, players gave away needless frees instead of having the belief to chase down opponents.

Elsewhere, the hurling world was changing, a revolution was happening. In 1995, many of the Clare team, whom Waterford had beaten in the under-21 Munster final in 1992, won the All-Ireland, and, in 1996, Wexford captured the title. Traditionally weaker counties were achieving success, but Waterford was floundering in a sea of continuing despair. 'Clare's win was a kind of watershed,' says Fergal Hartley, 'with their running up hills and mountains and all that.'

Tony Mansfield stepped up the training. 'Without any deference to people, we had some good players but we hadn't strength and depth, maybe only seven or eight players as good as Cork or Tipp had.'

Underage coaching was still very weak and very few players from the 1992 under-21 team were progressing – and now the only way up was to demand more and more sacrifices from players if Waterford was to have any chance of catching the other counties. The facts spoke for themselves: in seven summers from

1990 to 1996, Waterford played ten championship games, they lost seven, won two (one against Kerry) and drew one.

In 1993, 1994, 1995 and 1996, they only played one championship match each summer. Each defeat was a nail in the coffin.

Sure why would anybody bother?

4

GERALD ARRIVES

By 1996, county board chairman Paddy Joe Ryan knew something serious had to be done.

He had been working with Justin McCarthy in the oil delivery business for many years, and had asked the former Cork great nearly every year since the' 1980s if he would train Waterford. Justin had always declined, and 1996 was no different.

Paddy Joe then rang Limerick's three-time All Star winner Eamonn Cregan to see if he'd do the job. Eamonn had managed Offaly against his native Limerick in 1994 when Offaly had won the All-Ireland.

'I'll never forget what he said to me,' says Paddy Joe. 'He told me that after what he had suffered after Offaly's victory over Limerick, he said he'd never manage another county team but Limerick! I was talking with Justin McCarthy after that and it was him who suggested Gerald.'

Gerald McCarthy was one of the greatest hurlers to have played for Cork, winning five senior All-Ireland medals and training the county team in 1990 when they won the All-Ireland. Like most Cork hurling supporters, he had a respect for Waterford, from the days of Tom Cheasty and the 1959 team which was full of hurlers who had style but who were tough enough to withstand pressure.

'It astounded me that Waterford teams had no faith in themselves when they played Cork. Their record against us was terrible and they thought they were beaten before the start. We knew we'd get a tough game, but always thought we'd have enough to beat them,' he says.

Paddy Joe rang Gerald and met him in Clancy's bar beside Gerald's trophy shop in Cork city centre. They discussed the situation and Gerald took a week and a half to make up his mind. 'I had seen some of the players – Browne, Hartley, Frampton – and knew they were superb. I thought I'd go down and help them out as best I could.'

Gerald went to the Waterford County Club final on 16 November where it was announced at half-time that he was to be the next county manager. Fans wished him well but they knew he had a mammoth task.

Shiner Ahearne was asked to become a selector and trainer. 'Gerald had a great track record, a good handshake. He'd look you in the eye when talking to you and we knew he was going to be a good manager. He was fond of his hair as well!'

Gerald's first meeting with the players was in Lawlor's Hotel in Dungarvan. Forty players turned up, and phrases like 'a new beginning' and 'let's all go the extra mile' were used. Gerald told them they'd aim to have a good campaign in the national hurling league that year, target a Munster final win the following year and aim for the All-Ireland in year three. Ambitious to say the least.

Players such as Ken McGrath were impressed. 'He had five All-Ireland medals and was a legend in the game. It was exactly what we needed at the time.'

But all the players weren't there to hear it. Ballygunner had won the County final and were training for the Munster championship and they had had a training session arranged for the same night.

Roger Casey liked Gerald from the minute he met him. 'He

was an out and out gentleman who treated me and the back-room staff the very same as the players. He wouldn't hold a players' meeting unless we were in the room.'

The GAA has always been part of Roger's life. The day after he married Kay, he brought her to the All-Ireland final for their honeymoon (they got tickets from a friend). It was a very wet day in 1974 and Limerick were playing Kilkenny – it was so wet that the dye from the paper hats the supporters were wearing ran all over their faces and clothes!

Under Gerald, training demands increased, with more sliotars, poles and cones which other counties had been using for years. No corners were to be cut, especially on the field during training.

After two weeks, the Ballygunner lads still weren't training with the county and another meeting was called, that the seven Ballygunner lads were told they had to attend.

Fergal Hartley was captain of Ballygunner, a club which desper-ately wanted to win the Munster Club championship. 'We were focusing on beating Clarecastle, not on the Waterford campaign the following summer so we thought there was no need for us to be there. Maybe it was disrespectful but, in protest, we turned up almost twenty minutes late for the meeting. Gerald McCarthy gave us a bollocking. I told him we were preparing to win the Munster Club as it would bring the county on. He said unless we were committed, he was going.'

Standing in his tracksuit in the cold dressing room of Fraher Field, Gerald told them he wasn't expecting them to train all the time, but that they couldn't just alienate themselves from the whole panel. Eventually they agreed – Gerald's enthusiasm and vision for the future won them over.

Working in Ballincollig in Cork, Tom Feeney sometimes got lifts to training in Gerald's Merc. 'One day I rang and told him I couldn't make training. He told me that lads not going training had to stop because we were going to do something this year. So we made massive commitments and bought into the argument. We trained extremely hard and players really started gelling. And he started putting players in their best positions.'

Some players did leave the panel when 'proper' training got underway. The Friday night pints were gone, replaced instead by body fat and bleep tests every six weeks on Clonea strand – and twenty laps of the field some nights for a warm-up!

'I was surprised at how unfit they were but the players responded very well and barriers had to be gone through,' says Gerald.

Some evenings there were players on their knees pleading for mercy in the Showgrounds, the open area just beside Fraher Field. Fitness, both physical and mental, increased dramatically. The supremely fit Sean Cullinane would sometimes lap lads twice before the session was over, but everyone kept going.

The players found their new boss ruled with an iron fist, though it was inside a glove, and he was fair.

'We knew he was a serious man,' says Dave Bennett who was twenty-one at the time. 'He wasn't coming from Cork for the spin. The training was animal stuff, real tough. I was in Cork studying at the time and he'd give me a lift to Waterford and, after the training, the minute I'd get back into the car leaving Dungarvan, I'd be asleep. It was two and a half hours of pure savagery, running, laps, everything, you name it. We used to do these half hour races or thirty-five minutes with twenty to twenty-five laps involved and we basically had to keep going.'

Equipment was still limited and conditions primitive so chin-ups were done on the doorframes of the women's toilets at the back of the stand in Fraher Field.

A few years earlier, Joe McGrath had the players running laps and Paul Prendergast and Peter Queally used to tear off but would get a bollocking from the senior players. There was a certain degree of annoyance about what they were trying to do! But now, under Gerald, they had an obstacle course set up in the Showgrounds which took fifteen minutes to complete.

Sean Cullinane and Billy O'Sullivan would lead and nobody gave out, nobody bollocked. A small but important change in attitude.

There were also humorous moments as the players' exposure increased and they got more and more phone calls from reporters. Some would get hoax calls from pretend reporters. One day, Garda Peter Queally (stationed in Pearse Street in Dublin) got a call from another guard, a chap from Cavan. They set to ring a team mate from the landline Dublin number with the guard pretending he was a reporter with *In Dublin* magazine. He had a list of lifestyle questions, such as what's your favourite biscuit and who is the worst hurler you played against. The team mate fell for the joke. Another day, Queally himself pretended to be a reporter and rang Gerald McCarthy, who also got caught out before totally off-the-wall questions were put to him. McCarthy promptly told the reporter to 'fuck off' and hung up.

Special speed work, aerobic and anaerobic exercises were introduced for other nights too.

Fergal Hartley says, 'The criticism Gerald got in Cork in later years I'm baffled with. Everyone here had huge respect for him. Maybe it's the thing in Cork — I mean it moves on all the time and maybe he hadn't moved on but certainly — at the time, for us — he was miles ahead of anything we'd come across.'

And on the nights they hurled, Paul Flynn was making the ball talk, practising again and again at the end of training, putting a bend on the ball, driving it at full speed with top spin so it would dip at the exact right moment into the net. 'Paul Flynn was twice as good as people think he was,' says Brian Greene.

Player welfare took on a new meaning too. Gerald organised sponsorship for two pairs of boots and tracksuits for each player. His name convinced others to come on board, with Waterford Foods putting around £20,000 into a one-year county contract, small money now but massive at the time.

'It was all so new to us,' says Stephen Frampton. 'We were getting gear and we never got gear before. This was my first pair of boots from the county board – four years after I started on the panel. It was great. When I started, we got a pair of shorts and a pair of socks for the championship match, which we could keep and you'd make sure you swap your jersey with the other team because the county board would ask for it back if you didn't!'

Meanwhile, a young chap from the west was called onto the panel. Dan Shanahan was already playing up front on the Lismore senior team and loved the county scene, but he fell out with Gerald because of 'the foreign game' on a bitterly cold, late January evening in 1997.

'I was training away like mad with the county hurlers and one Sunday morning, I played soccer for Lismore. The following Wednesday on the old pitch in Dunhill, I trained my arse off. The selectors and Gerald came up to me and I'll never forget what he said, "Dan, we don't think your giving a 100 per cent commitment. We'll call you back next year if we want you." Obviously he hadn't taken much notice of my training but I suffered the consequences [of playing the soccer game] but I didn't hold it against him so I just took it on the chin and went back to my club.'

Leaving the ground that night, Dan was gobsmacked and the enormity of what had happened began to sink in. He had missed hurling training that previous Sunday morning to play the soccer game but the implications were as rude an awakening as any seventeen year old could get. 'It was the biggest mistake I ever made in my life playing soccer that day because I suffered the consequences.'

Gerald hadn't told them *not* to play soccer – but Dan remembers it was probably just taken for granted. Could this be the end of his county hurling career?

On the field, Gerald tackled the giving away of unnecessary frees. 'There was a lack of faith in players' abilities because when a player got past, they'd slap him with the hurley, give away a free and it was over the bar. Waterford weren't a dirty team but they didn't know how to put the man under pressure instead of fouling.'

Things had to change off the field as well. In January 1997, for the first time, the Waterford players went on a weekend training camp (to the Clonea Strand Hotel in Waterford).

Players started arriving on the Saturday morning, with varying expectations – some believing there was a good chance of a piss up.

The panel trained for two hours on the strand, doing 'bleep' tests as well where players had to run between two given points beating an ever-increasing electronic 'bleep' machine as they ran. They may have been able to cod the selectors but the bleep test couldn't be codded. Lay Lay Barry and most everyone did well and, that evening, dinner in the hotel was followed by a meeting where players were asked their views on what was good or bad about the current setup.

Liam 'Chuck' O'Connor (originally from the Erin's Own club) raised a thing which has been going on for years with some players – he hated to see them after a game standing on their Waterford jersey while they dried themselves. Other things were said before Gerald told them they could have a few drinks but weren't allowed leave the hotel, which had been closed to visitors (unbeknownst to the Waterford players, a victorious camogie club team from Wexford were staying for the night).

The handy poker school got going – Mick O'Mahony, 'Growler' Daly, Lay Lay Barry, Peter Queally, Paul Prendergast and a few others. Gerald went to bed around midnight, reminding the lads they are to be on the strand for 7.30 a.m. for training.

Players drifted off to their rooms and, as the poker wound up just after 2 a.m., the camogie girls came in from a nightclub. Lay Lay, Growler and Peter Queally stayed up, chatting. 'Sure we had great craic,' says Lay Lay. 'Thirty young ones and a few fellas! What time did we go to bed? Some of us didn't!'

Peter Queally went up to his room around 6.30 a.m. but

didn't want to go to bed because he knew he'd never wake up for training.

At 7.20 a.m., Billy O'Sullivan and a few others were on the way out to the strand when they saw Lay Lay and Growler still up. 'Fuck's sake lads, put away those bottles and go and get changed!'

Lay Lay went up, togged out and somehow went training, hiding in the middle of the bunch of lads. Queally was there too. Lay Lay only managed not to get sick because the drink hadn't started to wear off yet. Growler didn't go and when the lads returned for breakfast, he knew he could be in trouble. He then got a phone call from a jockey about a horse 'that won't be bet' running at midday in the point-to-point meeting in nearby Dungarvan. Growler told Lay Lay he was going to the races and Lay Lay said he'd join him. They were best friends, soul-mates, still drunk and, sure, weren't they indispensable to the team?

The others were due to go to Abbeyside to play a challenge match at 2 p.m. Lay Lay reckoned Gerald couldn't drop himself and Growler – his reasoning was that he was the goalie and Growler had scored three goals in the under-21 final. 'He can't get rid of us.'

Some of the lads told the two not to go, but Growler had phoned his sister Bernadette, who arrived and took them to Dungarvan for the races. Their horse won at 20–1 (each had £20 on it) and another horse they picked in the next race, Bob Tracy, also won at 5–1. They had just won £600! Some people at the races asked them if they were supposed to be in Abbeyside, but they replied, 'We've been let out for an hour.'

The two boys didn't know it, but Gerald had sent selector Mossie Walsh out to the races. Mossie saw them but didn't approach them, instead he just reported back to Gerald.

It was now too late to go training and Lay Lay and Growler got a lift to Cappoquin where two members of the county board, Paddy and Anthony Walsh, ask them why they'd come up.

'We made up some story that there'd been a row,' says Lay Lay.

'I met Barry Walsh later at home and asked if Gerald had said anything, and he said he hadn't apart from that there were two lads missing for the match. We just presumed we were dropped from the panel, it was the biggest mistake we ever made. McCarthy was actually waiting for us to go training on the Tuesday night and I was later told that if we'd gone and apologised, it would have been grand, but we didn't go. We were embarrassed more than anything. I rang Shiner three weeks later to see if we could go back but he said it was too late then, "If you had turned up that night you'd have been okay." He never actually dropped us and we had no contact with him afterwards. I still regret it. The money from the point-to-point is well gone now and for years afterwards whenever Waterford lost, some fellas would blame us for letting them down, saying, "We'd have an All-Ireland only for you."'

Growler would later be asked back, but was gone again in 1999. Lay Lay, one of the best goalkeepers ever to wear a Waterford jersey, would also get to come back for a few months under Justin McCarthy, but it was too late by then.

Changes on and off the field were helping but not quickly enough and, in the spring of 1997, Waterford were beaten by Dublin at home and didn't get out of Division 2. Gerald's great three-year plan was going take a bit longer.

As part of the new thinking, Gerald started demanding things the players had never got before – such as an aeroplane trip to an away league game to Derry. He nearly resigned when he was refused at first, but he got his way in the end.

Another flight had to be taken when they went to Ruislip on Valentine's weekend to play London in a league game. Peter Queally had brought over some bangers which he had come across and was going to use them in the hotel the night before the match for a bit of fun and frighten the lads. He didn't get a chance, though, because after at a team meeting in the hotel on the Saturday night, Gerald had told them they would all be going to bed early. However, some of the back-room team stayed up and had a great singsong.

The next morning, WLR rang and some of the players went on air to tell their wives and partners that they loved them and missed them. It was also the day Doc Higgins nearly got killed. 'I was standing on the sideline,' he recalls, 'when I got a ferocious pain in my back and it radiated round to the front. I thought I was having a heart attack. I said to Shay Fitzpatrick the physio, "I'm finished." He looked down and said, "God, Tom, there's a brick here." It seems somebody had thrown a red brick from a garden behind us and it had hit me right between the shoulder blades. I was sore but didn't need hospital treatment. I'm lucky it didn't hit me in the head.'

That evening, they were back in Cork quite late but Gerald asked Doc Higgins and then treasurer Tony Morrissey and Kieran O'Connor to join him for a drink in his club, St Finbarrs – or 'the Barrs' as it's better known. The lads wanted to go home but he was insistent. He knew what was ahead of him and he needed some support.

'It dawned on me that this would be the first time Ger would be back in the clubhouse after what you could say was a big game with Waterford, even though it was only a win over London in Division 2,' says Kieran O'Connor.

They obliged and, of course, the Cork lads in the clubhouse were great at sarcasm. Up to a dozen of them got up at different stages and went over to Gerald, saying, "Great victory over London, Gerald boy! Jaysus, imagine beating a city with 6 million people, great stuff."'

In their first championship game of the summer of 1997, Waterford played Limerick, who had been in the All-Irelands in 1994 and 1996 and were double Munster champions – top dogs in the province.

Ray Whitty was in goal for Waterford and conceded two goals early on. Heads started dropping, it could turn into another hammering.

Gerald told Shiner to 'get the fuck round the other side of the pitch and tell them to get their heads up'. Shiner was fast and did as he was told, encouraging players, urging them to keep concentrating and fighting. He hadn't noticed that Gerald had decided to take Ray off; substituting the goalie with the first half not yet over was a brave decision.

'Ray was a fine goalkeeper but I took him off as I was more looking to the future,' says Gerald. 'It was a very tough decision and I wasn't blaming Ray for anything. He took it in the spirit it was meant. I'll never forget the look of fright on young Brendan Landers face when he was called from the bench to go in goal; the poor fella was almost shaking. He had a mad stare in his eyes, and I thought, God, I wonder if this lad is really ready for it? But he was.'

As Shiner came back around the pitch, he met Brendan 'Cider' Landers coming against him with his hurley, heading for the goal. Neither of them could really believe it. Shiner remembers the full-back line were concerned about another ball going in. Ray was devastated. As Shiner was coming back to the dugout, Ray's brother was shouting at him from behind the wire, obviously very annoyed.

In his parents' sitting room in Lismore, Dan Shanahan was watching the match on the television. 'I remember watching the game. I'll never forget it. I knew the lads. When Ray was taken off and Brendan, my club-mate, was coming on, I said to myself, "I could be there."'

Waterford lacked a spark and even though they were very well prepared, they still didn't have that deep belief that they could win – Limerick were too strong and experienced for Waterford and went on to win by six points.

Even though they were defeated, at this stage, a nucleus of friendships were developing on the panel, with Paul Flynn, Dave Bennett, Fergal Hartley, Stephen Frampton, Tom Feeney, Ken McGrath and Tony Browne all in tune with one another.

'There was great bond developing between us, especially those of us who had hurled underage from minor in 1993 onwards,' says Dave Bennett. 'We knew each other a long time. A bond is hard to describe.'

What had happened under Gerald was that county loyalty was taking over slightly from club loyalty. The edge when clubs such as Ballygunner play Mount Sion is intense, but Hartley and Frampton said it was left on the field and players from both clubs got on great with each other at county level. Their only regret in 1997 was that if Gerald McCarthy had been asked to manage the team in 1993, they might be a lot further on by now.

Brian Greene was back on the panel and training very hard. Sometimes his club-mate Gary Gater would collect him on his motorbike for training, but one Tuesday evening he couldn't. Greener tried ringing but as most people hadn't yet got those new mobile phones, he couldn't get through with his apologies. Gerald announced the team to play Laois in the league and Brian was dropped. After training in Walsh Park on Thursday, he asked if he could say something as he felt put out. Gerald started shouting, laying down the law, saying Greener had some cheek and that he'd talk to him next door. They went into Dressing Room Number 2.

'It was fiery,' says Greener, 'and both of us had our say. I think he was even going to drop me off the panel and I told him it wouldn't be the last he'd hear of this as I'd go public. There was a lot of shouting and he went to push his way past me to get out but I didn't budge and pushed him back. He hit off the wall.'

The players were listening to it all and the thump on the wall.

'Jaysus, lads,' said Ken McGrath, 'go in there and stop them killing each other.'

'There were no punches thrown!' says Greener, 'and we later made it up. We even hugged in the dressing room after the Tipp championship game that summer!'

From October 1997 to Christmas, each player was given an

individual weights programme for the gym, again something that hadn't been done before. And when team training resumed in November, some evenings would involve weights from 6.30 p.m. to 7.30 p.m. in St Augustine's College in Dungarvan; before hopping in the cars, without having changed, to the Showgrounds beside Fraher Field to run until around 9.30 p.m. It was savage stuff and was the regime two or three nights a week.

Ken McGrath says, 'I remember been fairly fit in November that year and you'd never normally be fit then. We used to put on a bit of weight but then we'd work it off. We trained before Christmas and went training the day after St Stephen's Day. I'd enjoy my Christmases, and Stephen's Days would have been a big day for the city lads, the rest of the lads weren't as sick as us. I remember dying going up and down the sand hills in Tramore on 27 December. In bits we were.'

Peter Queally recalls, 'The training over Christmas didn't stop our social lives, didn't alter it much, we got sick but still drank. I suppose it wasn't the most professional attitude.'

Training on the sand dunes was overseen by Gerald with Shiner shouting the instructions. Some of the dunes are sixty feet high and it was up and down incessantly.

They did this every Sunday morning for six weeks, with the famous statue of the Baldy Man of Tramore looking down at them from across the bay.

At the same time, the selectors felt something more was needed if the team was to make some kind of a breakthrough. They racked their brains to think of what. Then Greg Fives heard about what Tommy Lyons had done with the Offaly footballers – a diet! But not any kind of ordinary diet, this was none other than the Neutron Diet!

Shiner went to a clinic on Canada Street in Waterford that specialised in it, led by Kate O'Brien. They agreed a deal, costing a few thousand, and the county board were convinced it was necessary. Every player would be blood tested to see what foods and drinks they could or couldn't take. Some of the panel needed a shortcut to losing weight and improving their fitness levels even more. The players were told about it, they were to start in January, and to prove to them the belief the management team had in them, they would all go on the diet too.

So that Christmas of 1997, the players knew they would need the growing bond of loyalty, solidarity and friendship even more as they embarked on a new journey, not knowing where it would end.

5

1998

On bitterly cold Sunday mornings in January 1998, a group of thirty or so lads could be seen scaling sand dune after sand dune on Tramore strand. Two hours of torture, sometimes in howling wind and rain. After which, these boys were hungry!

The Neutron Diet is designed to shed weight and increase energy and one of its rules was no drinking any kind of alcohol. After their blood tests had been analysed, most players were given a list of twenty-five things that they couldn't eat or drink. After six weeks, they were allowed to start having the bottom item on the list for three days and, if there was no reaction to it, they could start having the next on the list the following week, and so on.

Sean Cullinane is a big eater and loves his cups of tea. 'The worst was giving up the tea,' he says. 'There's tannin in it and I just gave it up totally for eight months. I gave up everything on my list for six weeks. I loved white bread and we were allowed to make this special brown bread. Linda made it once but it was like eating sawdust. Tuna in brine was the only thing from a tin I was allowed. I was working in the foundry in town and the lads would be getting chips from the canteen and dangling them in front of me. Food after training was a basket of fruit in the dressing room.'

Sean was fifteen stones three pounds in January and went down to twelve stones twelve pounds by April and his body fat went down to 3.5 per cent (Brian Greene's was just 4 per cent and others were just as lean). Some of Sean's friends thought he was dying, but he felt absolutely fantastic. 'What it did in a match was help when you'd make a burst or get a heap of slaps, you'd be out of breath as normal but now you'd be ready to go again after only ten seconds. I was still hitting the ball as far as I'd more muscle.'

Going to matches, the main topic of conversation for the players was how best to make a stir-fry. 'It's debatable whether the Neutron Diet was scientifically credible,' says Fergal Hartley, 'but it was very tough and everyone did it very honestly. I remember going to work, then training in Dungarvan, arriving home at 11 p.m., preparing breakfast for the following morning and lunch for work because you couldn't eat anything in the canteen. Everything had to be cooked in certain oils; it was just hardship. I was allowed to have two squares of dark chocolate a day, which I didn't particularly like but it was like my life depended on having these two squares of Bournville. I used to have one after my lunch and one after my tea – it was like being in prison!'

Never before had a Waterford team given up alcohol, but these players all stayed off it for six weeks, bringing them closer together – and they started winning matches.

And Gerald decided to make a call to a chap in Lismore. 'No hard feelings, Dan?' was the central message.

Dan didn't do hard feelings and he thundered back into the panel and he and Gerald got on great. The others were delighted to see the prodigal son return – and, of course, they slagged him about the soccer, especially Paul Flynn, who was now one of the main characters in the dressing room.

'Myself and Dan used to play an awful lot on each other,' recalls Brian Greene. 'I remember Gerald asking me to take it easy on Dan, and you had to because if Dan didn't hit a ball Thursday night before a match, his confidence was shot to hell. Dan thought I was going to hit him for twelve years, and I think I might have only hit him once. Sometimes, he'd be nervous. If I caught the first ball on him, I'd have a great game.'

The team won the South Eastern League competition, held before the start of the National League proper – something they hadn't done before – beating Cork in the final before a big crowd in Walsh Park. The players now approached games with vigour and confidence, and they were no longer giving away as many needless frees.

'Indiscipline comes with not being fit,' says Peter Queally, 'and it's the same at club level – when you're not fit, you are going to get narky and foul.'

In previous years, Waterford had been between 66–1 and 100–1 to win the All-Ireland. But the odds soon shortened.

The league victories continued and, in their seventh week, before they played Laois, Gerald told them, 'Listen, lads, it's no accident we're winning matches and we're off the drink so, if ye beat, Laois, ye can have a couple of pints.'

Laois didn't know what hit them! Waterford trounced them and the lads enjoyed their pints that night.

In April, the weekend of the Grand National at Aintree, the players were taken on a Friday evening for a weekend away to the Kiltiernan Hotel. Pat Flynn, Paul's father, drove the bus, but he wasn't, by his and the players' admission, the best driver in Ireland. He didn't know he had grazed a car with the bus outside Gorey until the squad car pulled them over. The rain fell in Wicklow that night and Peter Queally got a bright idea. They were only supposed to have one night – Saturday – for socialising, but the boys started to think that it would be great to have a few on the Friday! The only problem was that they were due to play Offaly in a challenge match on Saturday morning at the Garda Club at Westmanstown near Lucan. So, knowing the staff there, Peter Queally rang and got the groundsman to ring Gerald to say the pitch was unplayable and the match was off! And because they had all been such good boys over the past six weeks, Gerald told them drinking was allowed that Friday *and* Saturday – the diet was officially over! And then the bar and the nightclub beckoned!

'We were all going around with pints of Bacardi Breezer orange,' says Brian Flannery, 'and the selectors looking at us saying, "Fair play to ye", thinking we were on orange! They must have known the following morning because trying to stay up on the cycling machines in the hotel gym was an almighty effort for us!'

On Saturday, Roger Casey was dispatched to the bookies in Bray with £400 from the lads to put on certain horses in the big race, which was won by Earth Summit, the 7–1 favourite. Nobody had him.

Some went to Druid's Glen for a round of golf, others got taxis to Johnny Fox's pub in the Dublin mountains. After a session in both places, they met back in the hotel for the disco and enjoyed themselves so much some decided to hit the artificial ski-slope at 3 a.m. And to bypass hotel security, some women picked up in the nightclub were hoisted onto the roof of golf buggies to get into the rooms!

There was a lot to talk about on the drive home the next day!

Waterford were now in the semi-final of the National League, an important milestone and, in it, they beat Limerick, with Micháel White getting a superb goal. Waterford played so well that Marty Morrissey, reporting for RTÉ Radio, said, 'You can have your Clares or Wexfords but this is one of the best displays of hurling I've seen in years.'

Waterford were now in their first national final since 1963. Each player was given a pair of Puma Kings – the first pair of boots they'd ever got from the county board. Off the field, hurling was at last becoming trendy, with players being asked for autographs in supermarkets.

However, before the final against Cork, which was played in front of a massive crowd in Walsh Park, Fergal Hartley's brother died at the age of twenty-eight. Fergal still played – and played quite well – but his head was understandably all over the place. Although Waterford played strongly, Cork were edging it.

'I think there was a bit of a hangover from the league final, which was only the week before, when we played Kerry in Tralee,' says Dave Bennett.

With only twelve minutes to go, Waterford were in danger of losing. Gerald McCarthy told Doc Higgins, 'We're in trouble here.' He shouted at Shiner to go around the pitch to encourage the players on the far side. The Waterford fans who made the trip were worried. 'Shiner, ya baldy bollocks! What are ye doing? We're going to lose this fucking match!'

Luckily for Waterford, Dan Shanahan's speed, accuracy and enthusiasm proved crucial and he scored a late goal to secure victory.

Next was Tipperary in the Munster semi-final in Páirc Uí Chaoimh, a place in which Waterford hadn't won a big game in years. Stephen Frampton had been in the hospital in Waterford with his wife Anne Marie who had given birth to their first daughter Emma that night. He got little or no sleep and was wondering on the bus to the match how he was going to play, considering the fact that his calf was also bandaged from an ongoing injury so that he had to wear a big heal-support-insole in one boot.

But in the dressing room, the players were really confident they could win. They finally had something other Waterford teams hadn't had for ages – deep belief. The tackles were fair but ferocious – fans still talk about a thunderous shoulder Stephen Frampton gave to John Leahy. 'We were at each other during the game as he was mouthing and niggling, stuff about family and things like that,' says Stephen. 'He was coming through with the ball and I hit him a shoulder and he was flat out. I cleared the ball and there was a massive roar!'

In a man of the match performance (still disputed jokingly by Frampton!), Paul Flynn scored ten points and Waterford won 0–21 to 2–12.

All Fergal Hartley wanted to do was make a beeline for the dressing room because he felt something was just not right because of his brother's death. So even the best of victories was put in perspective.

This was a massive coming of age. For the first time, the hurling world could see Waterford had a very talented bunch of players who were serious contenders, having for so long been the joke of the Munster championship. They won because of a culmination of factors: the training, the self-belief, skilful players coming good at the right time, management making the right calls, determination and heart. All those factors which had been in the negative in the past were now reversed. It had been an almighty turnaround but the job wasn't finished yet.

The GAA had introduced a big change that was to play an important role in the development of Waterford. If a team now got to the Munster final and lost, they would automatically qualify for an All-Ireland quarter-final berth – the famous 'back door'. The winners would go straight through to the semi-final, but it meant one way or the other, the Munster final wasn't going to be Waterford's last game of the year.

Shiner and a few other selectors went to see Clare play Cork in the other semi-final. 'We believed the Clare players were trying to bully Cork,' he says, 'and that some on the Clare bench were breaking rules and regulations. The Cork chairman, Frank Murphy, was saying to his selectors to stay within the rules and there was a bad atmosphere. On the field, Clare were dirty and they hit so often they couldn't be done for everything.'

Davy Fitz said it was one of Clare's greatest displays, hitting Cork with fast, hard hurling, and he also believes that 'subconsciously, we felt we would beat Waterford'.

Clare had beaten Cork playing on the edge of the rules and Waterford, outsiders against this great team, decided to go toe-to-toe with them. 'We were best when the game was played at a high tempo, but we didn't want to be dragged into a physical dogfight,' says Gerald McCarthy, who felt Clare were somewhat complacent going into the game because the Clare manager, Ger Loughnane, had been quoted in the papers saying that Waterford were 'the best coached team' in the country.

Since their last championship meeting in 1992, Clare had gone on to win two All-Irelands – Waterford had won nothing.

On the day of the match, Brian Flannery's taxi to the team bus pick-up point was late and the bus left without him! He managed to ring Shiner to get them to stop and the slagging as he got on broke whatever tension there had been. A garda motorbike escort from Urlingford was needed because the roads were so busy.

'And when we drove up Liberty Square in Thurles, the place was going absolutely mad. We went past Bowe's pub and the fans literally rocked the bus; it was an unbelievable feeling, some-thing none of us will ever forget. But when we arrived at Semple Stadium, it was head down and concentration time. For days before, we were hitting every ball in our minds and this was the real thing.'

The Munster council had arranged a special ceremony for the victorious Munster final winners of 1963, who, by chance, were Waterford! Legends such as Tom Cheasty and Martin Óg Morrissey and others lined up and were greeted with cheers by fans.

Roger Casey's wife Kay washed all the jerseys and felt such an affinity with the team, that she'd put a note in the jersey bag. When the bag was opened in the dressing room in Thurles, Gerald read it out: 'Wishing you all the best of luck in the Munster final and God bless, from Kay.'

Gerald then got down on one knee in front of each of the starting fifteen and spoke quietly and privately with each player, no shouting. Then, he gave the team talk. 'We won't be bullied on the line, ye won't be bullied on the pitch,' he said raising his voice a little. He wanted Waterford to be the first team to stand up to Clare, even if they were All-Ireland champions.

His message in training had been that some players were in the comfort zone, 'I don't see too many coming out with your knuckles and eyebrows cut; ye have to suffer that to get out of the comfort zone.'

Waterford had some 'young' players, including forwards Dan Shanahan (twenty-one), Ken McGrath (twenty), Dave Bennett (twenty-one), Paul Flynn (twenty-five) and Micháel White (twenty-one).

Peter Queally was in midfield with Tony Browne, marking Ollie Baker, who was in his prime. 'He was very, very strong, fast and quick; there was no mouthing, it was just all speed.'

On the sideline, psychological battles were also going to be fought. Waterford took what would normally be the Clare dugout and decided that wherever Clare manager Ger Loughnane and his selectors gathered on the sideline, Waterford selector Greg Fives would stand behind, beside or even in front of them.

When the match started, this tactic annoyed the Clare management team who weren't used to this type of thing. They started shouting and cursing at Greg to 'piss off away' but, two minutes later, he was back annoying them again, pretending they weren't there.

On the field, Tony Browne was performing heroics and players, such as the underrated Brian Greene, were flying. All the players put their bodies on the line. It was a tough physical game but not dirty, with neither team backing down.

'I suppose as well we were shocked by Waterford's physicality,' says Anthony Daly.

'They were in our faces from the word go and never let the intimidation up,' wrote Davy Fitz later.

P.J. O'Connell was sent off for Clare for a high tackle on Tony Browne. At one stage, Gerald grabbed linesman Pat O'Connor by the shoulder. 'Jaysus, Gerald, take it easy,' said Pat.

Ger Loughnane would say that Gerald went onto the field three times and verbally abused a different Clare player each time.

Anthony Kirwan scored 2–2 and Paul Flynn 1–2, with Flynners blasting a twenty-one-yard free to the net minutes from time and the last point from Kirwan levelling the scores as the game went into injury time. It was a torrid, tough, magnificent battle.

Time was just about up when Willie Barrett awarded a free to Waterford a hundred metres out. The management team called to Flynn to come out and take it. He was already on his way. Nine times out of ten, he'd convert a free like this, even though the distance and conditions were very difficult. In the stand, Waterford legend Tom Cheasty was sitting beside former Waterford manager Tony Mansfield. They could feel the slight breeze going across the park. Stephen Frampton could almost see himself going up to get the cup.

Flynn stooped and lifted the ball but knew instantly that he hadn't lifted it as well as he normally would. He struck it when it was slightly out in front of him, and, as it went towards the goal, he thought, There might be a bit of a tail on that.

Gerald McCarthy was directly behind him and was full sure it was going over. It had plenty of length and height.

It's going over, it's going, only another ten metres … but then a gust of wind combined with 'the bit of a tail' pushed the ball out to the right, just past the post. Players, fans, selectors, thousands just couldn't believe it. Willie Barrett blew the final whistle shortly after and a classic had ended in a draw, 3–10 to 1–16.

In the dressing room, Gerald was very disappointed but also happy that Waterford had proved themselves. He patted Paul Flynn on the back; he was not one to criticise somebody who had tried his best.

They went to the Park Avenue Hotel in Thurles, then owned by Waterford man Derek O'Connell, for food and drinks, with hundreds of Waterford fans. Everyone was on a high even though the match had been drawn. Suddenly, Derek came in. 'Lads will you quieten it down, there's a bit of a problem.' His wife Eleanor had died and she was being waked upstairs. As more and more fans arrived shouting and roaring, they were greeted with loud shushes.

Before the Munster final, Clare had no history of animosity with Waterford (in the way they had with Tipp, Cork and Galway) but now demons needed to be created to exact revenge and ensure Clare survived. All the talk of Waterford being a 'good' team was gone, now the talk was about how dirty Waterford were. It was clear the Clare tactics were going to change.

'We felt they out-Clared Clare the first day,' says Davy Fitzgerald, who had been in goal for Clare. 'There was a lot of stuff said and done the first day, and we said we were going to fucking give them enough the second day. But I never had a hate for Waterford.'

The Clare players were seething after the match was drawn and promised themselves that the replay would be different. The day before the replay, Ger Loughnane spoke with them on the field at Cusack Park, laying down the law and, in particular, accusing Seanie McMahon, Brian Lohan and Colin Lynch of backing down!

'He called us a bunch of cowards,' wrote Davy Fitz in his autobiography, 'and not one player was exempt from his wrath. Waterford had treated us like dirt, Loughnane informed us. Not one of the players said a word but his tongue lashing had the desired effect.'

Tony Considine had set about firing a few broadsides in *The Examiner* newspaper about Gerald's behaviour 'so that everyone, especially the referee, was aware of it for the following Sunday', recalls Ger Loughnane.

Referee Willie Barrett says the first game was tough but fair, 'I reckoned the replay was going to be tough but I wasn't fully prepared for the onslaught.'

Ger Loughnane says, 'I did emphasise that I didn't want any wildness but everyone was prepared to give their life for Clare to win.' He did berate Colin Lynch 'that he had let himself down, that he was a better player than Browne and that he was lucky enough to have one more chance to prove it', and also lambasted Alan Markham.

Waterford had a light training session on the Tuesday night and spoke about what had happened. At training again on Thursday before a large crowd, the feeling in the camp was good and they were confident of beating Clare in the replay that Sunday. But this time it was going to be dirty, very dirty. 'Clare had been saying in the papers we had been playing dirty,' says Gerald, 'just to give them the right to come out and fucking hammer us. We were prepared for it, and they were too.'

Ger Loughnane described this clash 'as war without bullets' and in his dressing room, he held up the county jersey and told the players that they had shit on it the first day and that if anyone was going to allow that to happen again, they should stay in the dressing room. He stared into each player's eyes; they were his soldiers, they weren't afraid. Loughnane wrote about the build-up in this autobiography: 'The cup meant nothing. This was personal. Waterford were not going to be allowed to humiliate some of our players they way they had done the previous Sunday. We wanted to put them down.'

In the Waterford dressing room, Gerald told each player to stand up be counted on the field but to 'keep our discipline at all times'.

Waterford didn't want to be dragged into a dogfight and the dressing room was tense, very tense. Nothing was said at any stage about the players taking out any of the Clare lads, Stephen Frampton remembers that clearly.

Because of the shenanigans in the first game, each county had been told only their respective managers were being allowed to patrol the sideline, the selectors would sit in dugout. Gerald decided to be in the dugout with his selectors for the start, but if Clare broke the rules, they'd all be out.

As he went out on the field, referee Willie Barrett was met by two Munster Council representatives, who said to him, 'Before you throw in the ball, make sure there's no selectors standing on the sideline.'

Full-back Sean Cullinane had pulled his hamstring and even a week of acupuncturist work had failed to get him right. Tom Feeney was at full-back and Sean went down behind the goal to encourage him. The wet conditions didn't help, but Tom played well.

After the national anthem, the players took their positions. At one stage in the first game, Stephen Frampton had been on young Alan Markham and now Markham was coming over to him again. Without warning, and with the normal pre-match handshake forgotten, Markham hit Frampton a slap with the hurley into his ribs.

'Jesus, Markham. What's the fucking problem?' said Frampton. 'We're here to play hurling, now fuck off.'

Frampton could see all the Clare players were wound up, 'absolutely wound up' – he knew a lot of the Clare players and supporters as he goes there often (his wife Anne Marie is from Kilrush). 'Clare people at the time thought Loughnane was the be all and end all,' he says. 'And they didn't care how the match went, just the result. I'd be old fashioned, thinking there's the right way of winning and the wrong way of winning. Everybody expects a tough physical game but we were not expecting Clare to come at us like that.'

Brian Flannery also got hit before the ball was thrown in. 'I got the hurley into the ribs; I hit back; I think every one of the fifteen Waterford lads was hit before the ball went in. There's no doubt it was orchestrated; the agro definitely threw us.'

Anthony Daly shook hands with Dan Shanahan and, when he saw it, Ger Loughnane went up to Daly, roared at him and Daly hit Shanahan. Dan went down, got up, hit Daly back with his shoulder so Daly was on the ground.

'We wouldn't have needed Loughnane to shout at us,' says

Anthony, 'Dan had scored three points off play on me in the first game and he was fair game, in fact all the Waterford players were as we felt very aggrieved. It was unbelievably intense. My older brother Martin said he'd never been at a game so tense, it was like you could feel it dripping off the stand.'

Clare's Jamsie O'Connor had gone to shake Brian Greene's hand but Brian was still sore about the first game when Jamsie had been spectacular. 'I shoved away his hand and there was pushing and I stuck out my shoulder when his hurley came at me and the hurley broke. Our faces were an inch away from each other and I was shouting at him, "Get another one!"' says Brian.

With the ball still not thrown in, Loughnane and his selectors emerged from their dugout, shouting and roaring.

Willie Barrett saw what was happening and left the four midfielders (Tony Browne and Peter Queally for Waterford and Colin Lynch and Ollie Baker for Clare) on their own in the middle and ran over to try to shoo the Clare lads back into the dugout.

'I told them to sit down but they just ignored me!' Wille says. 'Sure what could I do? A few of them were big men! Looking back now, I should have just thrown in the ball and got the game started and not worried about the sideline.'

But they weren't budging, so Gerald said, 'Right boys, all out!' Now, they were all on the sideline. A steward told Gerald to get back in, to which he responded with a gentle, 'Fuck off, we're staying here.'

At the same instant, the four players left in the middle started shouldering into each other, praising each other's family lineage.

Gerald was looking out and thinking how everything that was happening was completely premeditated from Clare. He didn't think Willie Barrett was going to be able to maintain control. Players had to look after themselves.

'I looked behind and saw what was happening,' says Willie, 'and

I said to myself, "Jaysus, Willie, get this going or it could get worse."'

Brian Flannery says, 'Thurles is such a big pitch, you are very much out on your own. It's man on man; you against your opponent; nobody else to save you. You can't hide.' Particularly on such a day!

Willie Barrett decided the best thing was to get the match underway, as that might stop the players trying to kill each other. He threw in the ball and all hell broke loose, as Gerald McCarthy remembers it: 'Colin Lynch went for Browne, who had scored three points in the first game, and let fly with the hurl three or four times, hitting not the ball but Queally and Browne, and then Ollie Baker – one of his own players! It looked horrific. He had to go.'

Ger Loughnane would later write in his autobiography that: 'Lynch let fly three or four times but only hit Ollie Baker on the heel!'

Davy Fitz has even another view of the event, 'Colin was wired, he pulled wildly but he did not strike anybody.'

Waterford fans, apoplectic at Lynch's antics thought he must, at least, be booked, but, no, just a free to Waterford. Willie Barrett says, 'I saw Colin pulling and pulling, there was a lot of pulling. I wanted the game to get underway but I had to blow for a free. So I blew the whistle slowly and gave a free to Waterford.'

Players don't normally get sent off in the first few minutes of a game, so it's always the best time to lay into the opposition.

'Clare certainly had more intensity than the first game,' says Peter Queally in one of the greatest understatements in hurling history, 'but those things don't really register when you're playing. I can't say I recognised a huge difference as I was totally focused. I didn't even feel Colin flaking, I didn't get angry and I didn't take it personally. But I wasn't going to stand back and look at a row. I got involved.'

Doc Higgins ran out to Tony Browne, who was now horizontal,

and, as he did, he saw two others going down. A few seconds later, a fourth. He can remember thinking it was an orchestrated assault on the Waterford players.

He went to Tony, then, without getting excited, roamed around to see who else required treatment. There were no serious injuries, so all that was needed was a quick rub and a few words in the players' ears, 'Get back on your feet. Don't be pussy footing around!' He was never one for mercy in such situations!

The Waterford players had no faith in the referee to sort out the mess. 'He's lost the fucking plot,' Stephen Frampton said to no one in particular.

'Maybe we [the officials] weren't as focused as we should have been,' says Willie. 'To this day, it's one of the biggest regrets of my hurling life. It was so volatile. Those first nine minutes – I never refereed anything like it before or since. I watched it on the telly the next night and had to turn it off.'

Everybody was back on their feet but on the sideline, Clare were also trying to win a battle and Doc Higgins said he could see shoulder charges from some of the Clare selectors. There was no hassle though from Dr Padraig Quinn, his compatriot in medicine on the Clare side – they left each other alone.

A few minutes later, Roger Casey was on the twenty-one-yard line with the forwards' hurleys and he could see a melee between Brian Lohan and Micháel White. What was going on was a lot less than what Lynch had done.

'I think Lohan fouled and White retaliated,' says Willie, 'and I thought, Time for action, and I sent both of them off.'

Micháel was walking down the sideline when Gerald came up to him, 'Where are you going?'

'I'm sent off,' was all Micháel could say.

Gerald started scratching his head, he hadn't seen it. He was thinking what a massive loss Micháel would be because he was such a fast player and Waterford's game was built on speed. Twenty-year-old White was so upset at being sent off he went to the dressing room and cried. 'I'm after letting everybody down,' he told his father Mick who had come in to see him.

'You stood up for yourself. Now go back out to the lads,' his father said.

After the melee, Waterford players stood tall.

Roger was looking on, thinking, They're dying for each other, something they never really did before. Nobody stood back hoping somebody else would do the work. They were now in the hurt zone.

Then Lynch and Browne were booked for hitting each other with their hurleys.

The hurley carriers from both sides had words with each other, each telling the other to kindly 'fuck back to your in front of your own dugout'.

A Clare player went down with the ball but Gerald thought he'd dived and indicated a diving gesture to the ref. Ger Loughnane rushed over to him like a shot, shouting, 'Are you fucking accusing our players of diving?'

Gerald thought, This man is mad to get something going, and shouted back at him, 'Cool it down, Ger. Cool it down.'

'I never felt it was going to get that physical, where Ger would be prepared to take me out,' says McCarthy.

But Clare started pulling away. The fighting at the start had given them a psychological advantage and Waterford's fast game was being stymied. Clare had gone out with a plan and were winning the war.

Late in the game, Shiner was running behind the Clare goal when a shot hit the post and dropped over for a point. But the umpire waved it wide. As Willie Barrett started running in, indicating he was going to give the point, Shiner shouted abuse at the umpire. He had started to move away as Gerald arrived over, and not having noticed the ref was going to change the decision, started verbally abusing umpire as well. The ref took a note in his book and Gerald's actions would have serious repercussions.

And then Liam Doyle for Clare slid over the endline at the town goal with the ball. Shiner was still there, believing a sixty-five was going to be given, but the umpire (Mikey O'Mahony from Ardfinnan) waved it wide. Clare goalie Davy Fitz went over to get the ball and said, 'Fuck off out of here, Shiner. You shouldn't be here anyway.'

'Fuck off you, ye little fucker,' came the response.

As he was walking away, Shiner was given a clip on his ear. He turned around – it couldn't have been Davy, he was too far away, so he presumed something must have been thrown by the Clare fans.

Clare closed out the game and, with three minutes to go, Loughnane said to McCarthy, 'Sure the game is over now.'

McCarthy responded, 'O ye're by far the better team.'

Waterford were beaten by a massive twelve points.

'We simply blew them away with power hurling,' says Davy Fitz.

After the game, the Waterford dressing room was like a morgue, with players completely despondent. Gerald McCarthy confronted Willie Barrett and told him he should have sent off Lynch in the first seconds, thinking that that decision probably cost Waterford the Munster final. He told his players they were good enough to win but, most importantly, that they were still in the championship.

Paddy Joe Ryan, chairman of the Waterford county board, even though he felt disgusted at what Clare had done at the start of the match, went into the Clare dressing room and said, 'Ye're the best team I've seen for a while and I hope ye win the All-Ireland.'

Loughnane wrote that he believed that when Waterford came near the big prize, they lost their discipline. Even though they played 'on the edge', Clare had an excellent disciplinary record under Loughnane – in the twenty-two matches he was manager, there were only two sendings off, both in 1998 against Waterford.

Everyone headed back to the Park Avenue pub and, as they are having their dinner and a few tasty pints, the bus carrying the victorious Clare team with the cup up front passed the window. Everyone felt sick and they dropped their heads and ate more spuds.

Later that evening, back in the Briar Rose pub in Waterford, Jim Flynn from Ferrybank told Shiner he'd seen the incident of the clip on the ear.

'The umpire fecking hit ya.'

'You're joking me?'

Later, Shiner got a copy of the match from RTÉ's Bill Lalor of *The Sunday Game* to check, and it was true. Cheeky bugger, he thought.

Mikey O'Mahony had done what probably no umpire had done before or since; he didn't tell anyone about it and died in 2006 still only in his early fifties.

'Mikey was the youngest umpire I had on that day,' says Willie Barrett. 'A lovely, quiet chap who never fell out with anyone. He was always happy. I hadn't known he had done that to Shiner!'

A big change in Waterford's attitude occurred that night – the players didn't go out mad drinking. They had a few pints but were home early – and they were thinking of the next game.

On Monday, the papers mentioned the fighting on the pitch but it wasn't until *Sportscall* on RTÉ Radio 1 that evening that things began to blow off, the callers were full of venom for Clare. The game – and Clare's attitude – dominated the sports pages for days afterwards, and disciplinary hearings for weeks, though Clare were very aggrieved about the way matters were handled.

It was a life-changing experience for Willie Barrett. 'That game more than any took so much out of me. I was really cut up. If only Paul had pointed that free in the first match, it would never have happened! I went out to France on the Wednesday to get away from all the furore and to see my daughter Yvonne and I walked the fields around Lyon for ten days thinking about it.

I felt I hadn't been strong enough in the replay and learned a huge lesson that day. I decided life went on and I trained like a man possessed the next winter to get back into refereeing, which I did.'

Waterford, however, had more pressing matters as they only had a week to prepare for their All-Ireland quarter-final against Galway.

They travelled up by coach and stayed in the Berkeley Court. On the Saturday evening, Pat Flynn took them by coach to Croke Park, heading up O'Connell Street because that was the only way he knew. Somebody remarked, 'That's where Nelson's Pillar was', to which the late Tony Morrissey, the county board treasurer, replied, 'Good job it's not there now cause Pat would hit it!'

The players got to Croke Park and walked out onto the pitch, many of them for the first time in their lives, a surface that hadn't changed too much since the last Waterford team played there in 1963. They couldn't believe how uneven it was, not completely flat. Looking around the stadium, they realised it was going to be a dream playing there.

Best of all, there was no pressure on them. The twelve-point defeat to Clare had lowered expectations and nerves. But Waterford had players of steel, such as Sean Cullinane (who was match fit again) and Hartley and Frampton, and they knew Galway didn't rate them.

It would be Waterford's third big game in three weeks – a fact that would become relevant again in 2007.

On Sunday morning, most players went to the special mass arranged for them in the hotel being said by Waterford priest Colin Fives, Greg's brother. Then it was a light meal and up to Croke Park.

Amongst the dignitaries in the Hogan Stand were Senator Ted Kennedy and Jean Kennedy Smith. On a dry day, with no breeze, referee Dickie Murphy flipped the coin and Galway decided to play into Hill 16 end (which had mainly Waterford fans).

Peter Queally, the battler, was playing midfield with Tony Browne, the artist, a double act par excellence. Waterford were to play it fast and wide. Tony had so much energy, he dominated proceedings from the start, winning the first free inside a minute and giving one of the best performances of his life. He did everything right and, a few minutes in, put over a sixty-five (the first of his seven points and the first Waterford hurler to score in a senior championship match in Croke Park since 1963).

Most midfielders would stay inside the sixty-fives and, if he was your ideal midfielder, then Tony wasn't your best role model that day, because he did everything he wasn't asked and more. He was like a magnet for the ball. To say he was phenomenal would be an understatement. He was, in fact, the biggest single reason why Waterford won. He put over a sideline cut from under the Cusack Stand and was absolutely magnificent to watch. Then he did it from the other side. He was a total athlete and a born hurler rolled into one – a unique combination. An elegant, speedy, natural wing-back who had no fear and tremendous ability. One of this greatest assets was that he never complicated what he was trying to do.

That summer, there had been some controversy over the painkilling injections he was getting for his ankle from Doc Higgins. 'Tony was the under impression we were injecting his ankle joint when all we did was put a bit of local anaesthetic on a ligament, an outer ankle ligament, to take the pain,' says the doc. 'There was some stuff in the papers that we were injecting steroids into his ankle which was an absolute load of rubbish. There was talk of going after the papers but we decided to ignore the fuckers.'

Sean 'Growler' Daly got Waterford's goal, Paul Flynn put over five points and Waterford won 1–20 to 1–10 and were in the All-Ireland semi-final (which would be against Kilkenny) for the first time since 1963.

After the match, the players went down to a reception in Croke

Park, but it was nearly over by the time they got there. They wanted the bus to stop on the way home for a few drinks but Gerald thought they should get back to Waterford. He came up with a compromise.

'Tell ye what lads,' he said, 'we'll go through Naas. Write down what ye want to drink and we'll get it for you. The county board will pay for it!'

Roger was sent into the off licence and thirty trays of drink were brought on but, by the time they were passing Moone, everyone needed to relieve themselves. Just past the village, they stopped and did their business in the bushes. Gerald was the last off and before he could get back on, bus driver Pat Flynn (Paul's father) pulled the bus away up the road.

So the most successful manager for Waterford in years was left standing there with a can of cider shouting, 'Ye fucking bastards, come back!'

He couldn't catch the bus and stood with his can and his thumb out, pretending to hail a lift. The first car that came by was a Waterford supporter's, who nearly threw his children out so excited was he to give Gerald a lift. Gerald laughed, declined and walked up to the coach where the party continued. Future coaches would only be commissioned if they had toilets on board!

The first training session was the following Wednesday and it got the drink out of the system with twelve three-quarter laps of Walsh Park at sprinting pace.

The excitement was mounting and nobody was getting over-awed. The national media focused on the Kilkenny–Waterford rivalry, with both flags flying from poles in the church grounds in Ferrybank on the county border. Vincent Hogan wrote in the *Irish Independent* 'that even God can't decide who he wants to win'.

The Waterford team headed up to Dublin on Saturday, 15 August and as they were passing Gorey, the radio crackled with news of a bomb in Omagh.

The team billeted itself in the Berkeley Court again, and with all the players safely tucked up in bed, the back-room staff enjoyed a mighty session in the bar down below with forty Ballygunner club members and Waterford supporters.

Some of the back-room staff had gone to Shelbourne Park for spot of greyhound racing and on the way go through the East Link Bridge, coach driver Pat Flynn (also known as 'Sliced Pan', a name he was given by Mary O'Sullivan because he used to collect bread in the shop on the way home from a shift in the Glass – his son was sometimes referred to as 'Small Sliced Pan') hit the barrier and the bus got stuck. Those on the bus had to get off to pull the mud guards off to release it. At the dogs, they took so much money from one particular bookie that he wouldn't take any more bets from them. RTÉ's Micheál Ó Muircheartaigh and his daughter joined in the excitement.

The next day, all the focus was on the match.

Kilkenny fans knew they hadn't one of their best teams, given their normally high standards, and the county didn't have the aura of earlier in the decade when they had won two in a row. But they did have stars such as D.J. Carey and Charlie Carter up front and were confident.

The Waterford fans were telling themselves that the Cats had been struggling in Leinster and were there for the taking.

One of the big talking points in the run-up to the game had been the touchline ban that had been handed down to Gerald McCarthy because he had broken the sideline rules and incursions during the replayed Clare game. He was allowed in the dressing room and on the field before the match with the players but for the duration of the match, he had to sit in the stand, which he felt was harsh.

Since arriving in Waterford, Gerald had been preaching about discipline and now he had to go to the stand when his players normally had him on the sideline like a sixteenth player. Both he and the selectors had discussed possibly flouting the ruling but he said, 'Whether you agree or not with a decision, you have to respect it.' He thought if he did break the ruling and they won the match, his penalty for the final would be even worse.

'Gerald not being allowed on the sideline – we played that all wrong. We should have told Croke Park to fuck off. Clare would have,' says Brian Flannery. They had a couple of difficult decisions to make with the selection of players in particular positions, decisions that many fans would later say they got wrong and which were crucial to the outcome.

Waterford had no experience of playing in front of a full house at Croke Park (at the time this was 66,500 because of renovations to the stadium) and some players found it hard to handle the pressure of the occasion. 'Just do what you've been doing all year', was the message.

As Waterford ran out onto the pitch, even seasoned Kilkenny fans couldn't believe the noise the Waterford fans made they were so excited. It had been an amazing summer for the fans, a great experience and magnificent, romantic journey. Some of them wouldn't even be too disappointed if they lost, so new and raw were their emotions.

But the players had only one thing on their minds – victory. Kilkenny had a relatively weak team but they had more experience of playing in Croke Park.

Waterford played against the wind in the first half and did well. Gerald McCarthy was in the stand near the front just behind the dugouts on the Cusack side, with selectors Greg Fives and John Galvin. They decided Shiner was to be their man on the sideline, and he spent the thirty-five minutes over and back, relaying orders to players. Shiner tried not to think of it as the loneliest place in the world because he had a job to do.

At half-time, in the dressing room, the Waterford players were confident. They had held their own in the first half.

'We really thought it was going to be ours as the year had been such a rollercoaster and we were going to have the wind behind us in the second half,' says Tom Feeney.

'I would have put my house on Waterford to win at half-time,' says Roger Casey. 'We had been playing against the sun and wind in the first half and we were only a point down.'

'Jaysus,' says Doc Higgins, 'some were feeling we're in an All-Ireland at long last. But we didn't know how crucial Gerald's touchline ban was going to be in the second half.'

Just before they went back out, Gerald told them that they were just over half an hour away from doing something special, something that no Waterford player had done in decades.

As the game resumed, however, things were not happening for Waterford and the fans were wondering why two full-forwards were being played in the half-forward line and why no changes were being made closer to the Kilkenny goal.

Gerald's philosophy was one in which he put a lot of faith in the players, in particular the inside players (full- and corner-forwards), because a Kilkenny corner-back could be beating the Waterford corner-forward for most of the match but all the corner-forward needed was one break and the sliotar could be in the back of the net.

That's the reason he was slow to move any of the three inside-forwards.

Waterford kept pumping in ball but an ageing Willie O'Connor was cleaning up for Kilkenny (he would later say he was hoping they'd stop putting the ball in as he was getting very tired).

Roger Casey was on the sideline with replacement hurleys if required and was wondering whether or not Gerald should come down out of the stand. He saw Shiner on the field and realised how hard it was to get instructions through to players as Shiner was trying to cover the entire field on his own.

Willie O'Connor was one of the most experienced corner-backs in the country and had been an All-Ireland winner with Kilkenny in 1992. Some people had said he was past it but the Kilkenny fans could see he was having the game of his life against young Micháel White and it inspired the rest of the Kilkenny team. 'Everything I tried didn't work,' says Micháel. 'If I went left the ball went right. I was taken off and was never so depressed at the end.'

Kieran O'Connor, commentating for WLR, said before the game that it wouldn't matter if it cost the Waterford county board £40,000, Gerald should come out of the stand as it would have given the players and the fans a massive lift. 'The Waterford hurlers without Gerald on the sideline would be like kids crying for help,' he said. 'He has moulded these players and his importance can't be understated.'

In the backline, Sean Cullinane was very worried; they were having a lot of the possession, but weren't putting points on the board. The lucky breaks don't come and, in their anxiety, Waterford players started crowding the square and the central lines and didn't spread the ball to the wings enough, as they normally would.

With fifteen minutes to go, D.J. Carey got a free. His marker, Brian Greene, always jumped up to try stop or deflect a free. 'I've stopped maybe two in 500,' says Brian, 'but I knew D.J. had a low trajectory with his frees. But he completely miss hit it and it went under my feet as I jumped.'

The ball went in around the square and dropped into Niall Maloney who put it into the net.

How such massive occasions can turn on such small matters!

Waterford reverted to old habits, driving ball after ball wide with the wind into Hill 16. Panic started to seep through the team and instead of moving the ball quickly to players in space, rushed passes were made and players over-carried the ball.

'It seemed to be everyone for themselves,' says one of the players. 'Shiner was running up and down on the sideline shouting all the time and instead of low ball into the forwards, we were hitting high balls. Everything was going up in the air.'

'I had started at centre-forward,' says Sean 'Growler' Daly, 'but with the chaos of everything, I was moved into the corner, Flynners was moved out, others were moved elsewhere. With less than ten minutes to go, it was panic.'

Shiner himself admits that Gerald not being on the sideline definitely affected the team.

As the game neared its end, Waterford were a point down. They chased everything, from one side of the field to the other. 'There was pure panic to get that last point,' says Peter Queally.

Some players were waiting for the ball instead of timing their runs and this played into Kilkenny's hands, suffocating the game. Paul Flynn took a shot from in front of the Hogan Stand and took some paint off the post as it went agonisingly wide.

Referee Pat O'Connor from Limerick blew up from the puck-out, having played only one minute of injury time. Waterford fans screamed that there should have been more, but it was too late. The game was over. Waterford had only scored three points from play in the entire match.

Across the field, players hadn't performed as well as they could have. Many sank to their knees, their tears falling between the blades of grass and into the soil of Croke Park.

In the Waterford dressing room afterwards, players were crying, sitting there in their gear with the tears falling down their cheeks and onto their jerseys and sweaty thighs. 'I had to do a television interview straight away,' says Stephen Frampton. 'People afterwards said I had spoken very well but a minute earlier I had been roaring in the dressing room!'

Paul Flynn was thinking that this was one of the best chances he'd ever have to get to an All-Ireland final, maybe the only one. He was thinking that if there had been another five minutes in the game, they would have won.

Sean Cullinane was crying, sitting beside Peter Queally. If somebody had told them beforehand that Kilkenny would only score 1–11, they'd have known they were in with a great chance. It was one of the lowest scores Kilkenny had put up in a championship match for a long time.

Roger Casey had never seen so many grown men cry. He could see tears plopping on the concrete and was heart broken for them.

Kieran O'Connor was coming down from his commentary position when he met RTÉ's broadcaster Jimmy McGee, who saw his despondency. 'Lads, if you think this is bad, imagine how people feel in Omagh,' he said. And it brought Kieran back to reality.

There was utter silence on the bus home down the coast road until Sean Cullinane bravely started singing and the lads joined in; Gerald turned to Pat Flynn and said he couldn't believe it, that they were the best bunch of lads he'd ever come across. They stopped in Gorey for cans and sang their way through the darkness, and the sadness.

Players and selectors came back into Waterford that night and the warmth of the welcome brought more tears, especially to Gerald McCarthy in his adopted county. 'We'll be back again next year', was the cry of many fans. But would they?

The players drowned their sorrows for a good few days.

'When I was a youngster, I had wanted to be in an All-Ireland final and win it,' says Tom Feeney, 'but I never really pictured it until that day after we lost to Kilkenny. It was only then you could really 'picture' that we could have been there.'

'It was sickening at the time,' says Brian Greene, 'but it's twice as sickening looking back on it now. Time only makes it harder to bear.'

Or as Waterford's Pat Fanning put it, 'The older one gets, the level of expectancy grows higher, hence disappointment becomes more acute.'

On All-Ireland final Sunday, many Waterford players watched the game at home, knowing they would have done very well against Offaly, a team they traditionally beat. Brian Whelehan won the game for the Faithful County after being moved up front and Waterford players thought how it should have been them up collecting the Liam McCarthy Cup.

Sometime after, a few of the players decided to go on their own holiday to Ibiza. Tony Browne, Ken McGrath and Anthony Kirwan flew out on the Saturday night, while Paul Flynn and Peter Queally went out on the Sunday. They had great fun, and even made a guest appearance on a Sky One programme about the fun to be had on the island!

At the end of 1998, Dan Shanahan was nominated for an All Star but the biggest accolade was an All Star for Tony Browne, who also got Player of the Year – the best hurler in the country and a reward truly deserved. A lot of recipients rested on their laurels but Tony decided he wanted so much more for Waterford, the county he loved so much.

But three doors had opened for Waterford in 1998 (as Ger Loughnane says) – the league final, the Munster final and All-Ireland semi-final – and Waterford hadn't enough leaders in each line on the field to march them to the medal table.

Meanwhile, that summer, a small seemingly innocuous incident had occurred on the field in Ballyduff Upper which would leave lasting memories for some. A group of six lads were pucking around on a Sunday afternoon, including fourteen-year-old Stephen Molumphy and his brothers Aiden and Denis. Little Stephen was in goal and the others were flaking shots at him. The boys saw a nice, big car pull up at the other end of the field and watched as a man got out. He took some hurleys out of the boot of his car and started to walk towards them.

'Do you mind if I puck around with you for a while?' the man asked.

'No worries,' said the lads, who were thinking that he must be at least fifty, sure he won't even be able to shoot.

But he was able to shoot. And encourage and praise the lads when they put in a good hand pass. The play went on for around twenty minutes, after which the man asked if any of them knew where Seamie Hannon's house was. They pointed up across the valley to a house on the hill.

'Thanks a million for the puck around,' said the stranger and he started to walk back to his car.

'Who are you by the way?' Stephen asked.

'Ahh, I played a bit with Cork.'

'Ahh, but we're Waterford,' they shouted. 'What's your name?'

'Justin McCarthy,' he replied.

6

THE END OF GERALD

In Waterford, 1999 began with the great expectation that the county would go one step better than the previous heroic year.

But sometimes you only get one chance at glory.

But you also only get one chance to party!

In January 1999, the team selectors and some of the county board went to Greenfields in Playa de Inglés in the Canaries – their first 'proper' holiday and a reward for how far they had gone in 1998.

Stephen Frampton shared with Kieran O'Connor, both were massive snorers. They didn't hear players come back from their first night out, banging doors and locking each other out.

The next morning, everyone was called to a meeting. There was a door missing from one of the rooms upstairs and the hotel manager said if it wasn't sorted, they would all be chucked out. The door was in bits with fragments everywhere.

So Gerald took on the role of Sherlock and got to the bottom of the mystery and discovered the damage had been done by two members of the panel, who were then unceremoniously kicked out of the hotel and forced to book into another one. Later in the week, as the players were walking past that hotel, they could see the two boys 'like convicts sitting out on their veranda six stories up' and there was cheering all round.

They all got together in the Irish Jockey pub nearby, where, by chance, Dungarvan man Willie White was playing. And, of course, they went to Kitty O'Shea's which was owned by John McCarthy from Cappoquin ('a good left-back in the 1960s'). John was thrilled to see the team and had tears in his eyes meeting them, in particular the big star Tony Browne, the Ryan Giggs of hurling.

As the temperatures soared, some players came down with a bug. Dan Shanahan, one of the excellent pool players on the panel, won a pool tournament back in their own hotel, the same hotel in which Tom Feeney nearly drowned.

The players had been having a few drinks poolside when Tom (who didn't swim) decided to cool down.

'I was terrified of water but wanted to go for a dip,' says the big Ballyduff Upper man. 'I had taken a few lessons but never mastered it. I looked down and thought it was no more than five foot deep but it was a lot deeper and when I jumped in I hit the bottom and thought, O my good Christ. It all happened in slow motion; I tried to get to the ladder but couldn't reach it. I went up and down again and started to panic. The lads were looking at me and saying, 'Jaysus, Tom's a real funny man!' I'm told Shay Fitzpatrick said he didn't think it was funny and he knew I was in trouble. I came up again and was shouting and then they jumped in and pulled me out.' Roy McGrath, brother to Eoin and Ken, was one of the heroes.

After a few nights out and hearty singing, lead by Gerald, the manager himself got a very bad bug, forcing the doctors to be called. 'He got very sick,' remembers Roger Casey. 'They were nearly not leaving him home and they had him wrapped up in tin foil.'

When they did get home, the training and the hurling continued.

Many people believed club rivalry got in the way of the county scene, but Stephen Frampton says. 'There was a huge amount of stuff written about that about how could Waterford ever be any good because we used to be beating the shite out of each other in the club championships. But it was absolute bullshit. I used to bring the two McGraths and Tony Browne up to training in Dungarvan and would have a pain in my side with the laughing on the way up. We used to absolutely leather the shit out of each other in championship matches but it absolutely stayed on the pitch and there was never anything else about it.'

Dan Shanahan, meanwhile, was improving as a hurler. But Tipperary were coming good and Waterford weren't able to take the next step. Gerald had now been with them for a few years and his original three-year plan had not been achieved and the initial 'buzz' associated with a new manager had dissipated. To be better than the best, Waterford needed to be doing more, not less, and some players had got big notions of themselves from the team's good run the previous year and weren't putting the work into training. These players were leaders on the field but not off it. Expectations had been raised but structures were not put in place to meet and realise them – and the players still seemed to doubt that they could win really, really win.

'I suppose people that are being cynical about the Waterford team said we couldn't do the big job and win an All-Ireland or whatever,' says Dan Shanahan, 'but I suppose we were unlucky because we then came up against a fantastic Tipperary side which had a couple of good years and then Cork started coming good again. On any given day, we could have beaten any of them but it just didn't happen and it's a shame because of the individuals that we had.'

But 'individuals' was the theme that was plaguing this team.

Looking after players off the field was still a hit and miss as well. In one match, against Wexford in New Ross, the players went to the Five Counties Hotel outside the town. They got basic chicken and chips, no starters or desert and when the waitresses came around with tea, she gave the players a packet of Marietta biscuits to hand around amongst themselves – and there was even talk of who would pay for the Marietta biscuits!

Pride in the jersey though was increasing. Years earlier, Roger had started to hang the jerseys on the pegs in the dressing room, but Gerald changed this and started to give them out, having a little word with each player as he did, telling them they were getting the jersey because they deserved it before wishing them well.

As Denis Walsh pointed out in his book, *Hurling: The Revolution Years*, in the history of hurling, the Big Three of Kilkenny, Cork and Tipp had never gone more than two years without winning an All-Ireland. But for most of the 1990s, the Big Three went five years without a title. Unheard of before then.

In the quarter-final of the 1999 championship, Waterford faced Limerick. Tony Browne had got a bad ankle injury just when Waterford needed him at full throttle. Not for the first, or last, time, Paul Flynn took responsibility and scored 1–8 out of Waterford's total of 1–16. Along with brilliant performances from Ken McGrath, Sean Cullinane and Fergal Hartley, Waterford held on grimly for the one-point win.

In the Munster semi-final, they came up against Cork in Thurles.

Waterford were favourites in a way as they were battle hardened and Jimmy Barry Murphy was playing a lot of young lads. In fact there were six lads making their championship debut for Cork – Donal Óg Cusack in goal, Wayne Sherlock, Mickey O'Connell, Timmy McCarthy, Ben O'Connor and Neil Ronan.

On the day of the match, Cork went to the secluded surrounds of Dundrum House rather than the busy Anner Hotel for their pre-match meal and chat. Mark Landers gave a talk showing the Celtic Cross and, as Brian Corcoran says in his autobiography, 'not even the best Waterford team in over thirty years was going to stop us getting to Croke Park'.

It was a frenetic game.

Jimmy wanted the lads to play hurling and if they lost, they lost, but they'd go into the next year more experienced. If they had lost, he would have been gone.

In the dressing room before the game, Gerald (who had a huge rivalry with Jimmy Barry which wasn't widely known at the time) said to the players, 'Do this for me, lads.'

Waterford started with the same team that had beaten Limerick, and it was close in the first half but Cork went in three points up. Tony Browne's ankle injury was hampering him – it became so severe that he didn't play again for six months.

Cusack remembers the Waterford support being very loud that day. 'Something like I'd never heard before,' he told Michael Moynihan in *Blood Brothers*, his book on Cork hurling.

At half-time, Jimmy Barry gave a great team talk, telling the players they only had thirty-five minutes left together unless they won, even though he'd been with many of them since they were minors.

Mickey O'Connell was having a marvellous game for Cork in midfield and scored eight points, with Landers beside him scoring two.

The game was slipping away from Waterford when Paul Flynn got a brilliant goal. It was Diarmuid O'Sullivan's first championship game for Cork at full-back, a forerunner of the massive duels he would have over the years with Flynners and other Waterford forwards. Joe Deane was popping them over for Cork (he would end up with a seven-point tally) and Stephen Frampton was very harshly blown up for a trip on Mark Landers when the game was tight near the end. On the sideline, Gerald thought Waterford were going to win but Cork outscored Waterford in the last twelve minutes by eight points to three, including a late Alan Browne goal for Cork, and they held on for a six-point victory, 0–24 to 1–15.

Behind the scenes, Cork were priding themselves on what would be known as 'the critical non-essentials', such as hydration, puckout strategy, logistics, morale-inspiring slogans, everything and anything that would hopefully give them that little bit extra over their opposition.

They had embraced modern psychological training techniques and this, coupled with a growing level of 'professionalism' in how their players committed themselves to preparing for games, had given them an edge. The pick of players they had was obviously enormous, and Waterford couldn't match the talent they had in depth.

When a team is winning, it's easy to extol the virtues of a disciplined philosophy, but Waterford weren't winning. And they weren't going to win unless they made that extra bit of sacrifice – a catch-22 situation.

The sacrifices were working for Cork because they went on to win the All-Ireland in 1999 in a dour final against Kilkenny. The year had ended early for Waterford when they didn't even reach the Munster final and, therefore, had no back-door matches. They hadn't progressed from the previous year. Frustratingly, 1999 was a year when no team stood head and shoulders above any other – it was another year when Waterford could have won the All-Ireland, and if they had won the previous year, a further win would not have been out of the question.

In January 2000, Jim Dee was asked to come onto the back-room team. From 1955 to 1978, he had hurled with Dungarvan and Kilgobnet, where he was from, and was part of the Kilgobnet team that had met neighbours Colligan in the mid-1960s in intermediate hurling in a famous match that had never finished. 'A lot of lads went to hospital and both teams got suspended for a year,' he remembers.

Having retired in 1999 after working all his life in Waterford Foods, Jim was asked by county board chairman Paddy Joe Ryan if he would become secretary to the senior hurlers. It took him a day to decide.

'The job involves every aspect outside of playing the fecking match itself!' he says. 'I organise training venues for the November and December sessions, such as Aglish and Clashmore up the west. You might get a phone call at 3 p.m. some afternoon saying a pitch is unplayable so you'd have to get another. I organise all the meals for after training also, asking the players what they want and then ringing the hotel or restaurant.'

So for the start of the new millennium, Jim Dee was in the dressing room on match days before any of the players and when they arrived, he asked where they had travelled from and how many miles they would be claiming for that night. He'd then ask if they wanted beef, chicken or fish afterwards and everything would be kept in a hardback A4 ledger book which Jim kept religiously. He'd count up the list (with management and selectors, there could be up to thirty-six meals to be ordered) and he'd then ring the hotel – same for all matches, home or away. And every day, he could expect to get at least ten phone calls from players about medical bills, hurleys, match tickets or whatever. And every night, he would go home and input the figures into his computer. First the late Tony Morrissey and then Michael Hogan would make out the cheques and Jim would hand them to the players, who really appreciated what he did.

Jim was very impressed with Gerald McCarthy.

That year, Waterford were again hopeful of doing well, but other teams were aware of their potential and didn't take them for granted. The limited success of 1998 was, in ways, backfiring on Waterford, and the other traditional top three counties (Kilkenny, Cork and Tipperary) had upped their training regimes considerably following their lean spell of victories in the 1990s.

Gerald knew he needed to freshen things up and, as the bells of the new millennium faded, his thoughts turned towards a new physical training regime. He brought in a thirty-six-year-old Tipperary man who had only finished hurling in 1998 (his last game had been against Waterford!). Working in Waterford Institute of Technology with a lot of young hurlers, Colm Bonnar had been using his degree in physical training to extol the virtues of new techniques.

'The players raised a few eyebrows when I came in first, but they said nothing,' says Colm. 'I think a conflict still existed partially with club versus county; maybe that's why they were quiet bunch. We got them fitness tested in Limerick University and I pushed them extremely hard; we had some desperately tough nights with 1,600-metre, then 800-metre, then 400-metre runs. Some nights we had fifteen 400-metre races, with an odd 800-metre one thrown in. It was all very new to them. I remember Tony Browne saying, "Jaysus, is this what you do in Tipp? No wonder ye're so fit." Then we did speed endurance runs, shorter distances.'

The players still lacked real belief though. One evening at training in Dungarvan, Colm stopped everything. "Fuck's sake, lads, what are we at here? We're only going through the motions. How many here think we are going to win Munster?' he said.

Nobody answered.

Then, slowly, Peter Queally put up his hand, then Fergal Hartley, and that was it.

'What are we about if ye don't believe we can win it?'

The process of changing a tradition was slow.

Waterford had a first-round championship match against a Tipperary side that had been rebuilding strongly. Waterford had to stop Tipp from scoring goals, so Peter Queally was brought back at wing-forward to play near Hartley in the defence. Queally mopped up a lot of ball but John Leahy had a stormer for Tipp.

The Premier County allowed the Waterford forward line very little space and it was a close, dogged game but Tipp were five points up at half-time and Ken McGrath, who scored three points for Waterford from his forward position, had to go off injured. James Murray from Tallow in west Waterford had his first championship start and his addition to the team was important but not enough, as Tipperary won 0–17 to 0–14. Waterford had stopped Tipp scoring goals, but had themselves failed to score a goal – and it was their lowest score in Munster since 1996.

Waterford were now back to their 'one game a summer' scenario and an impasse had been reached. Another year was over and the breakthrough hadn't come.

Gerald McCarthy said he was leaving – his original three-year plan was now in shreds. 'I told Paddy Joe Ryan I was going,' he says. 'I genuinely felt if Waterford were going to take next step, they needed somebody else. He said we've nobody in place, if you give us one more year, we'll get somebody next year.'

The players also wanted him to stay, so Gerald agreed to give it another year – but new blood was needed.

In January 2001, a nineteen-year-old Mount Sion player Eoin Kelly was asked to join the squad. As a teenager, he had been considered an amazing prospect and was on the under-21 panel for six years. It was during those years, that the club played Waterford in a challenge match in Ardmore and Kelly lost a tooth in a freak accident with Dave Bennett.

Eoin's first impressions of Gerald had been that he was a nice man who gave everyone a fair go – a good hurling man. Gerald had told him that if he played well in a challenge match against Galway (which was taking place two weeks before they were due to play Limerick in the championship), then he'd start against Limerick but, unfortunately, as he says, 'I had a stinker and came off after twenty minutes and didn't start against Limerick.'

When players compared what they were getting with those from other counties, player welfare remained an issue. 'We weren't really looked after to be honest,' says Eoin. 'That is compared with other inter-county teams, Kilkenny or Cork or Tipp. We were way down the pecking order. I suppose we were a small county and there wasn't an awful lot of money there. Gear wise, we were way down the pecking order. You'd see other lads coming to matches. They'd look like a team. They'd have the best of gear on them.

Colm Bonnar saw a different dynamic, 'It was leaders we needed in training and I always felt some players, such as Paul Flynn, could have pushed themselves more; could have been more of a leader. Paul was so talented; as good as Nicky English in skills.

Nicky had a great touch and great peripheral vision to bring lads into a game but Flynn could do anything with a ball in terms of striking. It was frustrating to see him not push on. I think Eoin Kelly was very influenced by Flynn at the start as Paul was his idol. We spent a lot of time trying to bond players as there was too much mistrust between some players. I would have heard and known things before I came in: Dan Shanahan was just a young chap and the rumour was a bit nervous under a high ball; also if you are up Flynn's hole, he's not going to like that and Kelly, if you are in his face, he could get frustrated. It was hard to get everybody on the same page.'

Paul Flynn says he put it in at training but believed that practising hurling skills, touch and technique was as, if not more, important as running laps.

Another young player was also brought onto the panel – twenty-year-old John Mullane from the De La Salle club in the city. He'd played for the county through the grades and his blistering pace was something Gerald was very impressed with. 'John had been flagged to us the year before. I found him a lovely young fella to deal with, very obedient and knew exactly how to be deployed in a game.'

Peter Queally remembers training in January 2001, with 100-metre runs and players being knackered after only five minutes. He wondered if not enough stamina work was being done, something which might come back to haunt them if they need to close out a game during the summer.

Waterford went to Cork to play Limerick in the first round of the Munster championship – a game they desperately wanted, and needed, to win if hurling was to progress at all in the county. The under-21s and the minor teams were not making any kind of breakthrough at their grades. Gerald says the players didn't know it was going to be his last year no matter what, but the players knew this was make-or-break with them and the manager who had brought them so far, and yet not far enough.

Gerald got the players to link arms in the dressing room. 'I want you to think of somebody in your lives, either with us or passed on, and dedicate this performance to them,' he said. Some of the players had tears in their eyes as they drove out onto the field.

Waterford started the match at blistering pace, with Mullane getting a point and Waterford's forwards firing on all cylinders. After only twenty minutes, they were eleven points ahead and cruising.

'We were playing some of the best hurling we ever played at that stage of the game,' says Ken McGrath, who would score four points. A goal from Seamus Prendergast, making his championship debut, and 1–4 from Paul Flynn, who was again performing on the big day, should have set them up for victory. Mullane pulled his hamstring and had to go off but Waterford were still leading comfortably at half-time. However, Limerick started to eat into the lead and drew level – and Waterford didn't have the stamina to keep going.

'We were lacking something big time,' says Ken. 'Ger was right there, he couldn't have done any more.'

Waterford's brilliant full-back Sean Cullinane recalls that as they were eleven-points up so early in the game, they may have taken their foot off the pedal. 'I know you shouldn't do it but it happens,' he says. 'And then they were always going to get their period for scoring.'

With nearly ten minutes remaining, Waterford were back in the lead and nine points up. Limerick had Brian Begley at full-forward and Cullinane had been playing very well against him. But a full-back's position is one of the most important on the field – akin to the goalkeeper, one mistake and it can change the game. Sean prided himself on being able to read a game very well and, in particular, always tried to get out in front of his marker to deny him possession.

Waterford were playing into the sun when a high ball came in.

'I was doing what I always do,' says Sean. 'Playing out in front but I lost the ball for a split second in the sun, suddenly it was gone in over me and Begley was behind me. I got caught, end of story.'

Begley bagged the goal and a second and Waterford were on the rack. There was still time for them to salvage a result but Limerick were in the ascendancy. Waterford seemed to die while Limerick drove on, winning 4–11 to 2–14.

Afterwards, players said if Cullinane couldn't get to grips with Begley, nobody could. The dressing room was like a morgue. Another season over before it had even started. Ken McGrath and others were finding it hard to believe they had lost such a commanding lead and had been beaten again in the first round.

Before they got into the showers, Gerald McCarthy told the players he had something to say. After thanking them for their marvellous efforts over the years, he told them he still believed they could go to another level, but that it would have to be with somebody else. He wished them well in their pursuit of glory.

'I enjoyed those five years in Waterford as much as anything I enjoyed in hurling,' he says. 'I was so proud of it, so delighted to make the acquaintance of so many friends and good GAA people.'

Now players such as Ken felt they were really at sea. 'I remember thinking we were kind of fucked to be honest with you,' he says.

Dan Shanahan, who had scored only one point in the match, was heartbroken with the manner of defeat but he understood why Gerald was going. 'He couldn't bring us any further. He was after bringing us 99 per cent and he just couldn't get us over the line.'

Players tried to comfort Sean Cullinane who was inconsolable. 'Even after all these years,' says Sean, 'I still hear about that game two or three times a week. It's unbelievable, the mentality of some people. I wasn't even having a bad game, just got caught that one time. You could play twenty-five great games but some would only remind you of one mistake. There are a small group of knockers in every county and there's nothing you can do about them, they are everywhere. They'd be saying, "Waterford are great and aren't the young lads brilliant", and then if you lose the next game, they'll be saying, "They're all crap!" They don't see the long-term thing.'

The Tipperary team, which had beaten Waterford the previous year, had now matured and went on to win the All-Ireland in 2001. Waterford fans could only look at their neighbours with jealousy and a resigned sigh.

At the end of Gerald's reign, Waterford were down to single figures in the betting stakes to win the All-Ireland – a great achievement but still not good enough. Something extra special was going to be needed if the journey was to carry on.

7

JUSTIN McCARTHY AND 2002

The dance floor of Davitt's Creation nightclub in Dungarvan is a place where, over the years, many young men and women have looked into each other's eyes for the first time, swooned and danced the night away. It's a place where romances have been born and rebuffed. Where lips have met and parting words shot.

And now it was the turn of another new romance – Justin McCarthy and the Waterford senior hurlers.

It was a Monday night in late 2001 and Justin had invited the Waterford panel to meet him on the dance floor.

The players had no say in who the new manager was going to be and all that most of them knew about McCarthy was his column in *The Examiner*. Some knew about his impressive record with various teams and that he had a genuine love for the game. There was a bit of a buzz as the players and back-room team gathered.

As he drove towards the venue, Justin believed he knew when the time was right to do something. The main reason he was going eastwards now was to help Waterford have their day in the sun; he had a soft spot for them and had been guest of honour when the under-21 medals had been presented to the victorious 1992 team. He wanted to get every Waterford player to improve even a little so that the entire team would improve a lot.

As he wrote in his autobiography, *Hooked: A Hurling Life*:

'There is a popular theory now that hurling is a young man's game. But why's that? Because there has been an over-emphasis on physical fitness. We won't be making that mistake in Waterford. I want our players to have a balanced lifestyle. Nobody is more fanatical about hurling than me but I have a life outside of it. I spend a lot of time with Pat and the children. I walk through the fields. I have a huge interest in photography, and yet I'll find the time to clean my car at least twice a week. We're focusing on quality rather than quantity. Come the championship, we'll be hurling fit.'

Justin's goal was to deliver at least one major trophy – he didn't say his *sole* aim was to win an All-Ireland. He was going to use Colm Bonnar to keep the players physically fit, and would maintain his own personal rule that when he called players in they were to respond quickly. 'The last guy into that huddle does thirty press-ups. Any guy who sniggers repeats the dose. I want them to know that every second in training is precious.'

Above all, Justin believed he'd been lucky in life in that when one door had closed, another had opened, which is why he says he doesn't become bitter.

Justin's autobiography was published in the spring of 2002. It might be expected that the players would be interested to know the philosophy of their new manager but, amazingly, very few of them read it. And Justin knew hurling: he was Hurler of the Year in 1966 (when he was only twenty-one) and had coached Antrim, Cork, Clare and Cashel Kings.

On his way to the meeting, Justin came across a road accident at Youghal, and the guard directing traffic was Peter Queally, who was now stationed there.

'You'd better not be late,' Justin said out the window.

'I'll try not to be,' was the reply.

As he drove into Dungarvan, Justin knew he could be making this journey many times. He had been thinking of the great work Gerald had done with the team. He had known Gerald from when they'd roomed together on Cork under-21 teams. He wouldn't ring him for advice, though, he had his own thoughts on how things were going to work with his new selectors, Seamie Hannon from Ballyduff Upper, and Nicky Cashin, whom he had met twice already in Dungarvan. They had hit it off very well, with Seamie thinking the new manager was a hurler to his fingertips and a 'no-frills man'.

Peter Queally made it to the nightclub shortly after Justin had been introduced and had started to speak about his own career playing and managing before speaking enthusiastically about his philosophy on training. 'Hurling fitness is a different fitness from swimming or cycling and match fitness is a different fitness to being fit.'

Justin was very laid back and spoke in a relaxed, assured, calm manner without raising his voice, saying he wanted to win every match, an indication that he'd be picking his strongest fifteen every time – a sign of things to come and a strategy that would have serious repercussions down the line.

Paul Flynn was listening intently. He had spoken with a few players who had played under Justin when he had trained Cashel Kings, and they said he was a fantastic coach but warned 'a year or two will run its course'. He liked what he heard about training with the concentration on drills.

'I had met him once or twice before at different things,' says Paul Flynn, 'and he presented us the under-21 medals. I suppose my first impression was that he liked to talk. He spoke for nearly an hour and thirty minutes the first night, and it was a very self-centred talk. But I was looking forward to it as he wasn't emphasising so much physical activity, like running laps. I hate running laps.'

It took a while for players to warm to Justin (who himself went to the Alley in Rochestown on Christmas Day 2001 and many other days to keep his touch in). With a new manager, the players started off enthusiastically and they put in the miles from the first training session in Clashmore on 10 January 2002 – that night, the total miles clocked up by players and management came to 1,195 – followed by 1,367 miles on 15 January and 1,407 miles 31 January, when training was in Ballymacabry (they had ten team sessions between matches and training that month).

Ken McGrath remembers, 'We had been used to Ger and a more physical training so we were a bit weary of it. That first winter we got through it and stayed in Division 1 of the league and began to see what Justin was all about and we started improving as hurlers.'

But there were casualties, such as Stephen Frampton.

He was still at the top of his game (playing in the All-Ireland Club Championship semi-final in February 2002) but received no positive signals from Justin about his future on the panel. He wasn't picked for a league game against Kilkenny, played against Meath (but played badly because he was so frustrated) and then trained hard to overcome an ankle injury to pass a fitness test before a league match against Clare.

'The jerseys from one to twenty-five were handed out,' says Stephen, 'and I didn't even get a subs' jersey. Then I looked at the programme and my name wasn't even on it. I had gone past annoyance at that stage and was embarrassed. Justin or the selectors never said a word. Later that week, I tried unsuccessfully to contact Justin, then I spoke with Colm Bonnar and he didn't know what Justin was going to do. Then Victor O'Shea was picked ahead of me for a tournament game, even though he was in America! I was asked by a selector to step in and I told him to forget it.'

For Stephen, it could be seen as a big regret now but, at the time, he felt it was the right thing to do. He had given fourteen years on the panel, but says he didn't receive a phone call from Justin, the management team or county board when he went.

'For some reason, we forgot to give him a jersey,' says Colm Bonnar, 'and forgot to put him on the panel. It was a very bad oversight for us for such an experienced player. He could have hung us out to dry but he didn't. It was always for the good of the team with him. I felt very sorry for Stephen.'

At that time, Sean Cullinane had three small children under the age of four and with work commitments, found it very hard to get to the 5.30 p.m. training sessions in Dungarvan (a new, earlier time decided by Justin). He was dropped and confronted Justin. 'Am I in your plans, Justin? If I am, I'll try to get off work to get to training. I've a problem getting to training but I don't mind doing it if I'm part of your plans.'

Sean says Justin just shrugged his shoulders, said nothing and walked out. After all his years service to Waterford, this is what it had come to. 'That's the last time I ever spoke with him or any of the selectors. I thought some of selectors might have picked up phone but no. I went home and didn't go to the match and that was it.'

'Sean's decision to leave was his decision,' says Colm Bonnar. 'Justin wouldn't have phoned him to try to get him back. Sean was one of the most focused Waterford players ever.'

Justin's training involved basic hurling skills, blocking and hooking in pairs that many players hadn't done since they were children – but in a two-hour session, some players wouldn't break a sweat.

'We never did laps,' says Brian Flannery, who had trained under top IRFU guy Dr Liam Hennessey. 'Liam used to explain what you are going to do and why; but never Justin. One night, he took over the physical training, and you had to go head over heels and fall into the ground; stupid 1950s mad stuff. I said I wasn't doing it, he stopped everyone else and told me to do it. I told him to fuck off and I walked off the field. I had a sore hamstring from the previous night's training. I rang him a few days later and got little soot from him. He almost told me I wasn't putting it in. I told him he had no idea what I did because five days a week, I went to the Woodlands gym at 7 a.m. and did a good session before I went to work. Even with half an injury, I'd still train or play.'

Brian made it back on the team but, like Michael Collins, felt he had signed his death warrant, 'I felt the first chance he got, I'd be out the door.'

Peter Queally was another player who had a problem with Justin, believing his training methods weren't going to work.

'Justin had a huge bonus in that Gerald had done so much with us in terms of fitness. If Justin had come in in 1996, I don't think we would have done as well as we did. When Justin came in, the lads didn't push themselves at the hurling drills. Then, there were fellas bickering and they weren't pushing themselves. You can do hurling drills at four different gears – lads were doing them at second or third because it was a lot easier. And discipline wasn't a big thing with him. He had a bit of a naivety about him too; he felt everyone was on his wavelength with regards the 'I love hurling and I'd do anything for hurling and I won't drink or I won't do this'. But it's not the case. Fellas need to be told, they have to be disciplined, to do drills a lot faster than they should be doing it.'

Other players remarked that when Justin spoke, he spoke very passionately about the team, with one saying he was 'an absolute fanatic'. Colm Bonnar says he felt the players wouldn't want to get on the wrong side of Justin. '"Don't ever cross me" was one message line I remember very clearly from him,' says one of the senior players.

Others, such as secretary Jim Dee, were very impressed with McCarthy's hurling skills and his dedication to trying constantly to improve players. Jim got on very well with him from the start and built up a great friendship. They started going off to matches together to watch other teams if Waterford weren't playing.

Dan Shanahan hadn't known Justin personally before he arrived but had heard he was a very good coach and hoped he'd get on well with him.

So with players dropped and the confusion of the new training methods, in January 2002, very few players actually believed they were going to have one of the most amazing summers of any Waterford team.

Brendan Landers had become the first-choice goalie in 1998 but McCarthy had more time for Stephen Brenner's puckouts. Brenner won the nod, and Landers decided to go, walked himself. 'I left after the league in 2002, even though I'd been there all along since 1997,' says Brendan Landers. 'Basically, Justin never even spoke to me. I don't know why. I never approached him but he never came to me to tell me improve on this, that or the other. It was sad leaving as I was still young but he wasn't giving me a chance for whatever reason. I felt it was his way or no way. And then what happened later in the year obviously hurt me not being there.'

'We had been training up in Clashmore under lights,' says Lay Lay Barry, 'and Brenner wasn't there. Justin said to me, "Here, Ray, there's two balls, you go down on that goal there, you are the only keeper here tonight." And someone said, "Sure, Brendan is here too", to which Justin replied, "Oh, if he is, tell him to go down there." The thing with Justin was that if he didn't take to you, tough.' The back-room staff also noticed big changes under Justin compared with Gerald.

'All he wanted for training was three dozen hurling balls, cones and poles and that kind of thing,' says Roger Casey. 'There'd be a players' meeting before we went out to play a league or champ-ionship match. He'd always ask me, hurley carrier Paul Kelly, the physio, the Doc and Jim all to leave the room beforehand. We felt very belittled. One night, Fergal Hartley said he wanted us at the meetings; there was a bit of silence and Justin said, "Well I want to talk without them here", so we had to go.'

Justin's honeymoon period didn't last long. The day after St Patrick's Day, Waterford travelled by bus to Parnell Park to play Dublin in the league.

Paul Flynn used to talk a lot to the referees, and during the match he jokingly said to Dickie Murphy from Wexford, 'You're having a bad match today Dickie.'

'When he missed a free,' says Dickie, 'I told him he wasn't having such a good game himself!'

Waterford lost, with most playing horribly. The players stormed into the dressing room and threw their hurleys on the ground and against the walls, and started shouting, kicking gear bags, and giving out to and about each other. Ken McGrath was particularly furious and continued shouting at Justin after he came in.

'There was a massive row,' says Brian Flannery. 'When we calmed down a bit, we sat down and told Justin we needed more physical training. He totally disagreed and said the reason we had lost the game was because of hurling mistakes and hadn't anything to do with fitness. And that was end of conversation!'

Many of the players shook their heads in disbelief. The bus had been full on the way to the match, but many decided to share lifts with the six players who had driven up and the bus went back with only around a dozen players. Many felt totally disgusted and felt an important psychological battle had been lost.

But Justin continued with the hurling drills and as the ground hardened coming into the summer of 2002, the players could feel their first touch improving. They were still fresh, as they hadn't to endure three months of hard winter flogging. Of course they'd trained, but not the same way as they had under Gerald. And training with a hurley and ball in hand didn't sap the players' brains or bodies as much.

At training, players had to try and judge what mood Justin was in. As Paul Flynn says, 'Every day was different with him. One day he could talk to you and the next day, he wouldn't. You wouldn't know with him, I won't say you were walking on eggshells, but you were kind of wondering what humour he was in.'

Twenty-eight-year-old Tom Feeney was getting to know Justin well and was an important part of the team in Justin's eyes.

Working in Cork as an engineer, Tom would drive to Castlemartyr where Justin would pick him up ('his car was always pristine, immaculate') and take him to training. Some evenings, Tom would do a five-hour round trip just for training. 'If you were in Justin's picture, you'd get top treatment; he'd do anything for you,' he says.

The players sensed the season was turning into a disaster and not many of them truly believed they were going to beat Cork. The management team felt it too, and in a gamble of mammoth proportions, on the 10 May with just sixteen days to go before the Munster semi-final, Justin took the players on a trip to Ballycastle in County Antrim. It wasn't intended to be a drinking weekend, but a bonding and get-away-from-the-routine weekend. What better way to sooth the pain from the 'Parnell Park fiasco'. But the players wondered about the benefits of travelling so far to play Antrim.

On the Friday, they travelled by train and bus, and players become even more annoyed, the whole thing was a mess. They'd been travelling since 1 p.m. and didn't arrive in Ballycastle until midnight but the welcome from the locals was as warm and generous as ever – Antrim GAA people really appreciate teams from 'down South' coming to visit them. Each player was given a massive mixed grill including a fourteen-ounce steak! The players were starving, ate for an hour and said, 'What will we do now?'

They all went for a stroll. Their intention wasn't to go drinking, but everybody was giddy. They saw a pub and, thinking it'd be closed in ten minutes, decided to go in for a pint – just the one! The four customers in the 'House of McDonnell' couldn't believe that thirty lads were piling in.

The pub, which dates back to 1745 and is owned and run by Tom and Eileen O'Neill. Originally from the Glen of Aherlow, Eileen served the boys into the wee hours and players had a right session and singsong. On the way back to the hotel (players can't remember the time exactly, but it was about 5 a.m.), Justin was looking out of his bedroom window on the second floor and he could see and hear all the lads outside, including a few lads up on a JCB tractor, pretending they were going to start it!

Justin didn't give out to them. He turned to his room-mate for the night, Colm Bonnar, and said laughing, 'Look at this craic!'

'The next day,' says Eoin Kelly, 'we were dying but we decided we'd sink or swim together and we'd a job to do; so we beat Antrim in Dunloy.' Some of the Antrim players said they couldn't believe the smell of drink off the Waterford lads.

'And that Saturday night we had our 'organised' night out; it was a good night but not as good as the first night which had been sort of spontaneous,' says Fergal Hartley. An 'early to bed' night at 3 a.m!

'We went sightseeing and a tour of the Falls Road on the way back,' says Tom Feeney, 'The whole weekend was fucking crazy … when Browne is on form, you can forget about it. And Eoin McGrath; brilliant.'

The atmosphere on the train coming home on the Sunday was one of the best the players could remember. And in training the following Tuesday night, even though some were physically worse for wear, the team spirit level had gone up 100 per cent – there was now a bond and a unity which hadn't been there before. Many players felt that if anything was going to 'save' their season, it would be this and nothing to do with Justin.

Waterford then went to Thurles to play Cork in the Munster semi-final and, deep down, many were worried they wouldn't have enough in the tank to beat the Rebels.

Peter Queally was sitting beside Brian Flannery on the bus to the match. As he looked out the window at the rain, he was thinking of their preparation, thinking it had been somewhat mediocre and that their form in the league had been patchy. He was also thinking about Justin's regular saying of 'Keep it handy, keep it tidy lads', and hoping they would have enough to see them through.

Brian Flannery turned to him and said, 'If we win this match, Justin will be the luckiest manager ever.'

Because of an injury to his shoulder from a challenge match against Dublin ten days earlier, Ken McGrath wasn't starting the game. But on the bus, he was 100 per cent confident that Waterford would win. It was a feeling he hadn't had before, that self-belief, and much of it came from Justin's 'touch' drills which he had been really pushing since April.

Waterford fans taking their seats in Semple Stadium were worried how the team would do without Ken.

Cha O'Neill, who was now a Waterford city councillor, couldn't find parking. Thinking about the time a few years back when he'd stood in goal at training, he drove up with his family to the gateman at Semple Stadium. He knew he'd have to use every trick in the book to get parked up in time for the throw in. 'I'm the Mayor of Waterford, I don't have my chains with me. Can I get in please to park?' he said.

The man looked at him, sighed and turned to his colleague on the gate, 'We'll let him in, even if he is the tenth person already who's claimed to be the Mayor of Waterford!' (Cha would later become mayor.)

Underneath the concrete stand, Justin gave his team talk in his normal, measured way, after which the players ran out to a tumultuous reception. Everything was ready and the game began.

Donal Óg Cusack in the Cork goal made a great save early on as the lead changed a number of times in what was turning into a thrilling game. Ken was introduced just before half-time. The Waterford fans went wild.

In the second half, Donal Óg made a mistake which, he would later say, cost Cork the game. Tony Browne sent in a speculative ball from midfield. It dropped between Diarmuid O'Sullivan and Donal Óg but skidded on the greasy surface into the net. Whenever Donal Óg plays Waterford again, there will always be some Deise fans who slag him about it.

The game was end-to-end stuff with nothing in it.

'It was a very tight game,' recalls referee Dickie Murphy. 'At one stage, I gave a free out to Cork when Dan fouled. I'll never forget what he said as he ran after me, "Dickie, I swear on my daughter's life I didn't do it, I never touched him!"'

Paul Flynn was giving an exhibition, particularly in free taking, and had put over twelve points when Brian Greene gave Ken McGrath a great pass and he hit it over the bar at the Killinan End for the winning score. For once, Waterford hadn't folded, the disappointment of the past three years had galvanised them and they won 1–16 to 1–15.

Later that summer, the Cork players would go on strike while Waterford would be winding up for a right bash at the title.

Dan Shanahan was wondering what his role on the team was going to be as he hadn't really figured in Justin's plans up to that point. Justin had brought him on as a sub in the Cork game when, of course, he wanted to start.

'I got the feeling that maybe I wasn't up to his pace of the game, or maybe I wasn't his kettle of fish at that time,' he says.

Tom Feeney had a major problem the week of the Munster final – an awful toothache. He told Justin at training his tooth was killing him.

'You need to get that sorted,' said Justin 'I'll ring my dentist.'

The following day, Tom got calls to confirm an appointment with Justin's dentist in Cork and the tooth was taken out.

On the Thursday night before the match, Justin brought in Martin Óg Morrissey, Tom Cheasty and Frankie Walsh to talk to his players. All three had been on the last team to win the Munster title for Waterford. McCarthy would say afterwards that this encounter made the difference between winning and losing. History matters in Munster hurling, where deeds of the past can influence today's players.

Páirc Uí Chaoimh, Sunday, 30 June 2002 – a day which will be long remembered by Waterford hurling fans.

Tipperary went into the game as All-Ireland champions and hot favourites. The last – and only – time Waterford had beaten

Tipperary in a Munster final was 1963. Now their manager Babs Keating (in *The Sunday Times*) went with the headlines of 'Tipp's Eoin Kelly Unmarkable' and 'Waterford Going Down By Ten Points'. Justin now had the ammunition he needed to raise his players, and he read them Babs' statements.

The players based in the city got on the bus in Waterford and it picked up the lads from the west in Dungarvan. They had a bite to eat in Lawlor's Hotel before they headed off. Just joining the panel was twenty-one-year-old Brian Phelan from the De La Salle club in the city. He loved the buzz and was particularly impressed with Dave Bennett's joke-telling ability. 'We all got on great with the players from the west,' he says 'They all say 'lad' down there and we'd joked about picking up their auld slang!' Another new player for the season was Eoin Murphy from the Shamrocks club in west Waterford. He would prove to be an immense addition to the squad and was keen to show he had what it took to play at corner-back and be one of the best in the country.

Before they passed over Youghal bridge on the way to the match, Justin McCarthy got the driver to stop. He then stood up, looked down the coach and said, 'We're not coming back over this bridge tonight, without the cup.'

Not one player shouted or roared and no one clapped – they didn't know if they should. So he said louder, 'Did you hear what I said?'

The players responded with a loud, 'Yeah! Yeah! Yeah!' and a massive cheer and clapping. They knew what had to be done and were eager to perform. Dan Shanahan was disappointed he was on the subs' bench, but was still hungry for action. 'We knew we were going to win,' says Tom Feeney.

They went to Midleton to puck around the ball, but because of the rain, they had to use the hall. When it was time to go, a garda escort got them to Páirc Uí Chaoimh in fourteen minutes.

Thousands of Waterford supporters had made their way to Cork in cars and buses. Ned Tobin, a huge hurling and Elvis Presley fan, crossed the bridge at Youghal, with friends such as T.V. Honan from Spraoi in the 'Ally McLoughlin's' bus. Halfway over the bridge, Larry Gogan announced on the radio that Elvis was back at number one in the charts with 'A Little Less Conversation'. For Ned, it was a good omen. Wearing a new Elvis T-shirt underneath his jersey, he'd later declare, 'I told you, King. I told you I'd bring you to a Munster final.'

It was the month of Roy Keane, Mick McCarthy and the showdown in Saipan, but for legions of Waterford fans crossing the Blackwater into Cork, the World Cup final scheduled for noon that day scarcely mattered. They travelled in hope unaware of their date with destiny.

Since leaving the panel a few months earlier, Sean Cullinane had been hoping for some miracle, hoping that they might ring but he didn't get one phone call from any of the management team asking him back. He didn't try phoning them either. As a reminder of how quickly former players become yesterday's men, he had to buy his own tickets to the match against Tipp. He was stuck in the corner of the stand, down low in against the railing. The tickets couldn't be any worse, but his heart was with the lads on the field.

Fergal Hartley didn't tempt fate by preparing a victory speech but his words in the dressing room before the match were magnificent, totally from the heart and demanding every player to 'do it for your family and friends'.

In every few rows, there was a Waterford fan or a former player with stories to tell of their love for this team, this county. There were the few who still remembered 1948, the players and descendents of 1959 and 1963, the wives, girlfriends and mothers who had given so much and the youngsters wearing replica jerseys with 'GAIN Feeds' emblazoned on the front.

Waterford played with the breeze into the town goal and points were exchanged before Paul Flynn lined up a twenty-metre free. He buried it and Waterford were ahead. But Tipp pegged it back, and were ahead by a point at half-time. Justin's half-time speech was measured, quiet, telling the players to continue doing what they're doing and be careful at the back.

'Remember lads,' said Brian Flannery, 'we're still a point down.' For Peter Queally, it was enough to dispel any sense of complacency. The second half would be a battle like never before.

The players ran back on the field, knowing this was as good a chance as they were ever going to get to win a Munster title. They had learned not to fear Tipp, but the players from the Premier County got two goals early in the second half to pull away. 'When their third goal went in,' says Fergal Hartley, 'I thought, Fucking hell, are we ever going to beat these guys?'

But Waterford didn't panic and with belief – and points by Mullane, Kelly and Flynn – drew level.

Then Tony Browne kindled the never-say-die attitude of the squad and ran through on a dropping ball, pulled it and it was in the net. A magnificent goal.

A quarter of an hour to go and Waterford were three points up.

The game ebbed and flowed and Flynn, with only fourteen minutes left and 1–6 to his name, was feeling good. He wasn't injured and things were ticking over nicely. He saw that Justin wanted to make a substitution. Micháel White was ready to come on. Who was going off? Then he saw. He couldn't believe it. No way, it couldn't be, he thought, he's taking me off.

As he sat in the dugout, he thought, This is Justin saying, 'I'm the new boss in town', more than anything else.

At that point in the match, Ken McGrath had scored seven points, Eoin Kelly three and John Mullane four – and the defence had stopped Tipp scoring again.

'I remember a Tipp player putting in a challenge on me with around ten minutes to go and it was very weak, a token challenge and I knew we were going to win,' says Fergal Hartley.

Dave Bennett was brought on with only a few minutes to go and also scored a point. Seamus Prendergast and Eoin McGrath had also got on the scoreboard.

Waterford were winning by eight points as Aodán Mac Suibhne from Dublin blew the final whistle: Waterford 2–23, Tipperary 3–12.

In Irish bars all over the world, people had been watching the match. In Paddy's Point pub in Torrevecca in Lassina, Gerald McCarthy and his wife Mary jumped for joy (as did most people in the bar) when the final whistle was blown. Some asked him for his autograph.

In a rural town in France, Eamonn O'Connor, brother of the WLR commentator Kieran, tried everywhere to find a pub that had the match on satellite, but had no luck. He had been getting updates on the phone from Cork and after he got the final score, he sat down on the roadside kerb and cried his eyes out.

Peter Queally went to exchange jerseys with Tipp's Eoin Kelly; Peter knew Eoin was on his way to GAA superstardom and he thought it'd be nice to have it. 'Naw,' said Eoin gracefully and thoughtfully, 'you'll want your own jersey in years to come; you should keep it because of today.' And he was right.

Fans ran onto the field in an outpouring of emotion people there will remember for ever. A steward grabbed captain Fergal Hartley and told him to go up to collect the cup. Fergal hadn't a clue what he was going to say!

It had been thirty-nine years since a Waterford man had raised the trophy, and Fergal Hartley climbed the steps to get the cup from Christy Cooney. In an emotional speech, he thanked Gerald McCarthy, Justin, of course, the back-room staff, past generations of players and all the thousands of fans. 'The real famine is over,' he said.

A quarter of a century earlier, Justin McCarthy had brought Clare to the 1977 Munster final only for Cork to beat them. Here was his redemption – here he was, taking a 'weak' county and making them champions.

Sean Cullanine, who only a few months earlier had been on the panel, was delighted for the players and for his county. And yet felt a bit sick that, after all the years service he'd given, he wasn't getting a medal. He went down into the belly of the stand and was in the dressing room when the players arrived down with the cup. Peter Queally and others hugged him and there were smiles all round.

The players then celebrated as they hadn't done in decades. It was like they'd won the All-Ireland, not just the Munster final. 'It was a natural thing to do I think because it was forty years since any type of victory,' says Paul Flynn.

Being heroes in a county is something special for any GAA player. 'When you feel loved, it's brilliant,' says Tom Feeney.

And Justin sometimes had a way of making the players feel on top of the world. 'John Carroll, who's he?' he said to Feeney as they got on the bus, in reference to the great job Feeney had done on the Tipp forward.

They went to the Imperial Hotel on the South Mall in Cork city for a meal. Maurice Geary, who had seen so many days of heartache, met his club-mate and Waterford selector Seamie Hannon. There were handshakes all round. 'I never thought I'd see the day,' said Maurice, and Seamie agreed.

The players told Sean Cullinane to get on the bus with them back to Waterford, so he did, sitting beside his old friend Peter Queally.

Justin had asked for the bus to be stopped at the bridge in Youghal. Before that, though, a stop had to be made at the garda station in the town where Peter Queally was now stationed. He had promised his work colleagues they'd stop if they won, so he walked proudly into the station, brought his work colleagues out and had pictures taken on the street.

It was dusk when they got to the bridge and everyone got off the bus. The traffic had to stop too, but nobody cared. There was a line of cars packed with Waterford fans behind the bus, hardly believing that they'd lived to see such a moment after all these years. Up to 400 supporters had heard about the plan and were waiting at the far side of the bridge, festooned with flags, white and blue everywhere.

And then with the cup held aloft, the panel, management, backroom staff and supporters walked across the bridge into County Waterford and a surge of emotion passed through them all as they met with the Waterford fans on home soil. Grown men cried and the hairs on the back of people's necks stood straight.

Doc Higgins, who had soldiered for so long with the team, had a lump of raw emotion in his throat. He loved every moment of the journey, had no regrets and was now part of this unbridled celebration of all that is great about Waterford. With tears welling up, Billy Costine drove the bus over the bridge behind the lads, a moment he will never forget.

Getting back onto the bus, Sean Cullinane passed by Justin and said well done but whether he noticed him or not, Justin didn't say anything back or even acknowledge him. Sean didn't care, this was a day of joy. When the bus got to Grattan Square in Dungarvan around 15,000 fans were there to greet them.

Over the next few weeks, players took the cup around the county to as many schools as possible, hopefully setting alight desires in youngsters that someday they too would go on and win for the county.

Seamie Hannon and Maurice Geary thought of Donal Kenneally, their Ballyduff and Waterford friend, who had worked for so many years in the building trade across the Cork border in Kilworth. They remembered Donal being in Semple Stadium in 1982 covered head to toe in Waterford white and blue – and the slagging he got from the Cork fans when he went back to work after that massive defeat. A few years earlier, he had fallen through a roof and broken his spinal cord – so they brought the Munster cup to his house. The absolute joy in his eyes and the thrill on his face when he saw the cup was something they will never forget; that's how much it meant to fans.

As Munster champions, Waterford were now straight through to the All-Ireland semi-final, where they were to play Clare. They had a six-week gap to fill.

'We didn't know how to deal with the six-week gap and it killed us. Possibly Justin didn't know either,' says one player.

Goalkeeper Stephen Brenner says it was like a roadshow going round the county, understandable in some way, but not the right preparations for an All-Ireland semi-final. In that first year, he thought Justin was very good, but this changed in later years when he felt the manager became a bit cocky. 'At training sometimes,' says Stephen, 'you wouldn't know if he was showing off. He'd be taking shots at the goal; he was still very skilful; but if he got a goal, he start shouting, "Whooo hooo", and that sort of stuff. He was an interesting man! At the end of training, he'd have the balls tidied up straight away, even though some lads would want to practice more. He'd say he was trying to keep us fresh but he'd hunt us in off the field. We thought he had to be centre of attention.'

Complacency also seeped into the players' minds with some of them thinking that, as Munster champions, they should easily get to the final and that another Munster team, especially Clare, was not going to stop them.

'And Justin had talked us up,' says Stephen Brenner.

The Friday after winning Munster was the first training session back and some players were playing club football championship matches the same night. The county's club teams had also been developing, with Ballygunner winning the Munster Club Championship in 2001 and Mount Sion going on to do in it 2002. All of which had helped players believe in their ability to win big games.

They had seventy-two team training sessions or matches under their belts so far that year and would do another twelve before the semi-final but would it be enough? They went up to Croke Park for a puck around on 24 July but nothing like a full 'dry run' of what they'd be doing on match day. Waterford weren't used to those long weeks between Munster final victory and All-Ireland semi. 'Our training in that period wasn't intense enough,' says Tom Feeney. 'We had played Limerick under-21s in a challenge match at the end of July and they'd nearly beaten us. It should have been a wake-up call for us but it wasn't.'

The night before the semi-final they stayed in the City West Hotel. As they went to bed, the players felt confident. Some slept well, others not so well. Brian Flannery was sharing with Seamus Prendergast. 'Seamus got to sleep before me,' says Brian, 'and he was snoring very loudly! I couldn't wake him so I got the double quilt and slept in the bath! I didn't sleep too bad but woke up kind of cramped!'

Stephen Brenner was sharing a room with John Mullane, and it took them ages to get to sleep as the room was too hot. 'Maybe not sleeping in your own bed the night before a match wasn't great,' he says.

Legions of Waterford fans were enjoying a great pre-match function in the Goat Grill in Goatstown, organised by the Dublin branch of the Waterford GAA supporters club, where they sang till late to 'Drops of Brandy' and were joined by some county board members.

Meanwhile, Clare were confident.

They had been knocked out of Munster, but had quietly come through the qualifiers and gained valuable match practice in beating Dublin, Wexford and Galway and were now coming good just at the right time. And they always had the feeling they could beat Waterford.

'It's a funny thing, but we didn't fear Waterford,' says Davy Fitzgerald, then the Clare goalie. 'We reckoned that if we really got stuck into them and fought them, we'd be in with a chance. We even knew that if Waterford got off to a flyer, we'd stick with them, keep working hard, keep fighting them.'

In the run-up to the game, Doc Higgins could feel something wasn't right. 'Waterford had such a complex about success,' he says.

'We were always struggling, always the underdog and we didn't have the tradition of winning or the confidence which goes with that. There seemed to be a fear of success, and fear is the big word there.'

The ultra-professional preparations of other counties (such as Armagh footballers doing complete 'match day dry runs' to time exactly how things would go) was not done with the Waterford hurlers – and, sometimes, small things matter.

Some of the Waterford players who went to mass that morning were disappointed that others in the wider travelling contingent (not players of course) were treating the weekend as if they were on a school trip to the zoo. 'All giddy and stuff,' says one player. 'It didn't seem right – and it was only a semi-final!'

They went by bus to have pre-match puck around at the Na Fianna club grounds but arrived late and a junior football match – pencilled in for after the Waterford team were to have finished – had already started.

'We had to get them off the field,' says one of the players, 'and our warm-up was rushed. And then the garda escort was useless as they stopped at every red light; compared with the Thurles gardaí, it was a mess. Then we went in the wrong side of Croke Park, missing our turn off and met the Clare bus coming against us. We felt they were saying, "Look at those stupid fuckers. They don't even know where Croke Park is! We're not going to lose to them." There were too many non-squad people on our bus and lots of waving going on. And then it seemed like very short period in the dressing room. None of it was right.'

'It was unreal when you think about it,' says Brian Greene. 'We had to pull into the side to let the Clare bus with its garda escort pass us. We could see them laughing at us.'

The county board and management team had six weeks between the Munster final and this match to make sure nothing went wrong. Shambles?

'We were all hyped up, mentally trying to focus on the game

ahead,' says Andy Moloney, 'and there we were on the bus, reversing and pulling in and giving way to the Clare bus. I was never so annoyed or embarrassed. It was all wrong.'

On the bus, Dan Shanahan was wondering what more he had to do to get on the starting fifteen. He'd been going great in training but wasn't starting again. For a player who was at the heart of things under Gerald, he would get only seventy-eight minutes of championship play in 2002 under Justin.

As the players paraded round the great stadium before the match, Andy Moloney looked up at the sea of Waterford supporters and flags. 'It's like something out of *Gladiator*. You feel such pride and I thought, This is where we're meant to be. It gives you such a positive feeling. I had trained hard and for the previous three weeks, was preparing mentally for the massive challenge of marking Colin Lynch at midfield. I was ready.' Compared to 1998 when the 'new' Croke Park wasn't finished, it now towered above the players. Some say it seemed massive, the stands were way taller and it was an entirely new experience which fed into their nervousness.

For the first time in modern era, Waterford had gone into the All-Ireland semi-final as favourites and now that tag was being justified. They were a better team than Clare but would they show it on the day?

Waterford got off to a great start with Eoin Kelly on fire and Andy Moloney and Peter Queally playing brilliantly in midfield. Colin Lynch dug the hurley into Moloney's ribs a few times and, as he gave one back, Moloney said to him, 'Come on, we'll drop them here now', to see if Lynch would fight it out there and then. But he didn't and Moloney had a stormer against the Clare warrior that half.

Waterford were a very 'verbal team' and shouted a lot of instructions to each other. On big match days, players say it's impossible sometimes to hear a man nearby.

At one stage, Fergal Hartley was running out with the ball when Clare players converged on him. From only around sixteen feet away, Andy Moloney was roaring at him but Fergal couldn't hear him. 'I actually stopped shouting because I knew he couldn't hear me. It's unreal out there.'

Near the end of the half, Queally was caught in possession near the Waterford endline and couldn't hear Brian Greene calling for a pass. Clare got the sliotar into Alan Markham and he buried it past Stephen Brenner.

The seeds of doubt were starting to spread. Ken McGrath had been playing at centre-half-forward and was nullifying brilliantly the influence of Clare's Seanie McMahon, who was normally Clare's chief playmaker. Ken had also got two points. There should have been no need for any changes but in the Waterford dressing room at half-time, an amazing thing happened.

'We were sitting there when Justin and the selectors came in and said I was going up centre-forward,' says Andy Moloney. 'Eoin Kelly was coming back to midfield and Ken was going out wing-forward on Quinn. I was shocked as I never really played centre-forward.'

Ken was being moved as Justin felt he could get more points on the board away from McMahon. Colm Bonnar says Ken was going poorly. They decided to move him because they wanted to get him more into the game. Colm admits they took a 'lot of shit for it afterwards'.

But the feeling was not good in the dressing room. 'I looked around,' says Brian Flannery, 'and I knew we were a spent force. I knew we were beat. It goes back to training and mental preparation and we knew training hadn't been severe enough to take us where we wanted to be. I looked around and we were out on our feet, we didn't have the work done.'

Going back out, Andy Moloney sensed problems lay ahead, 'Centre-forwards need to run over and back, not in and out, and read the game in a certain way and I wasn't used to it.'

Seanie McMahon began dominating and Ken wasn't getting the expected return on his new marker. The game started slipping away. Brian Greene could feel the anger rising; he wanted to be out in the half-back line, not stuck in at corner-back and he blamed Justin. 'He was after getting rid of Sean Cullinane and Frampton and as the second half went on, I was thinking he had to make some switches but he didn't. I was like a dog. I really think his inability to make decisions during the game cost us – he's not a great manager. I don't hold it against him that he was old school.'

The forwards were not winning enough ball and the backs knew it. 'In that second half, we had nobody stepping up to the plate,' says Flannery, 'we had very few capable of putting his hand up and winning a puckout. Our big players didn't perform. At one stage, I was looking up the field and couldn't see anyone winning ball from Stevie's puckouts.'

Then, Dan Shanahan came on. 'Me and Dan would have a great understanding,' says Stephen Brenner, 'but, that day, balls were just being batted down away from him. Nothing was working.'

Andy Moloney was so pissed off at what was happening that he organised a few positional changes on the field with ten minutes to go. Justin hadn't told the players to do it but they were desperate. They fought hard but it wasn't enough. Waterford lost by three points: 1–16 to 1–13.

The dressing room was not a nice place to be.

Afterwards, the players went for a drink in the Players' Lounge and Justin went down to the bus with driver Billy Costine to get something. On the way back up, they met Davy Fitzgerald in the lift. 'Jaysus, I thought we were fucked the way ye came at us at the start,' Billy remembers Davy saying, adding that Justin didn't really respond. What if they hadn't made those half-time switches?

'A few months later,' Andy Moloney recalls, 'selector Seamie Hannon said to me, "We should never have moved you."'

With a lack of independent team meetings, the players never got a proper chance to discuss openly with management what had happened in 2002 and what was needed to go further.

To ease their sorrow on the train back from the match, the players got a card school going – their favourite game that day and all other days on train journeys was AC Juicy. One of the lads was such a bluffer the lads joked he 'couldn't lie straight in bed'. 'Sometimes lads had to put in €100, especially after a few drinks. Lads would be crazy,' says Peter Queally. It'd been a crazy year.

Although they didn't reach the All-Ireland final, Waterford players had medals to show for their endeavours for the first time since 1963. Some had more, as Mount Sion players, such as Ken McGrath, Eoin Kelly, Eoin McGrath, Tony Browne, Brian Flannery, Brian Greene and Micháel White, had all picked up a Munster medal with Waterford, a Munster Club medal with Mount Sion and another county medal with Mount Sion – and Ken had received an All Star award, so a good year!

But by other counties' standards, not good enough.

8

THE UNKNOWN AND
YET DEFINING SEASON

A Munster hurling medal is a prized possession.

And after Waterford had won their first senior title since 1963, you'd expect the matter to be dealt with in a manner fitting their heroic exploits.

In early January 2003, the team was due to go on holiday to Morocco, a reward bequeathed to them by the county board, a small thank you for bringing such joy to tens of thousands of loyal fans. Justin had decided on Morocco after little discussion with the players.

But Peter Queally said the players weren't asked about where they would have liked to have gone, and the holiday had been organised the same week as the Ballygunner hurlers were heading out for their holiday in Majorca (a reward for their club exploits). There was also no discussion about wives or girlfriends going, so the recently married Peter (he had put off his holiday to November because of the hurling) decided not to go.

The Waterford players went on their holiday, while the Ballygunner lads headed out theirs.

'The place in Morocco was in the middle of nowhere,' says Kieran O'Connor of Glanbia. 'Everyone was cracking up; the Beach Club Hotel was lovely but there was nothing to do.'

Sean Power, who runs Harvey Travel in Waterford, believed a trip to 'the Western Kingdom' of the Sahara wasn't a good idea. 'Against my wishes, the manager took them to Morocco. He wanted to take them somewhere quiet, because there was another team in Lanzarote that week. There's no use sending lads on trips that the manager would like but they mightn't.'

To break the boredom, Kieran O'Connor got talking to one of the hotel staff and they agreed to have a Morocco v. Ireland soccer game the next day. With Kieran as manager and Pat McGrath, Ken's father, as his assistant, they had the highly pressurised task of picking a starting eleven.

Ken McGrath, an excellent soccer player, wanted to play but Mount Sion were due to play in the All-Ireland Club semi-final when they got back and everyone knew the club wouldn't want Ken getting injured. 'I want to fucking start!' was his plea. But Kieran didn't want to have to explain to Jim Greene, the Mount Sion manager, what had happened if he got injured!

The day of the match, taxis brought the players away from the hotel and they saw a football stadium, thinking, Wow, we're playing there? but, no, the convoy went a lot farther over dirt tracks and through extremely impoverished parts of the city.

After a team talk, the players and selectors sang the national anthem on a pitch that had no grass and which was full of lumps and bumps – but the Waterford boys, resplendent in white tops, shorts and runners, were all up for it. The local Moroccan selection tried fancy tricks but when big Seamus Prendergast (goalkeeper for the day) kicked the ball the length of the field, they gasped in awe. Meanwhile, John Mullane and Eoin Kelly, both superb soccer players, led the charge.

At half-time, Ken was still asking Kieran when he'd be going on. The game was the highlight of the week and Ken was on the sideline, seething. As the second half progressed, he still wasn't being played.

'He got thick and said, "I'm getting a taxi and going back to the hotel,'" remembers Kieran. But with fifteen minutes to go, they put him on and, with five minutes to go, Justin McCarthy was put on. 'He scored a goal and ran around like a child!' recalls Kieran. 'He told me he was never at a soccer match before, which tells you with him it was hurling, hurling and more hurling!'

Waterford (representing Ireland at soccer in Morocco) won 4–0!

The welcoming locals, delighted that men staying in the posh hotel would grace them with their presence, brought the entire entourage to one of their houses for Moroccan tea. 'The tea was terrible stuff altogether! Pure treacle which we all felt we had to drink,' recalls one of the players, 'but we had a singsong and sang all the Irish songs and they sang a bit.'

Back in the hotel, they had champagne to celebrate Waterford's 100 per cent international club record.

When they got back to Ireland, there was still no talk of when the Munster medals were going to be presented. A few months earlier, some players had asked if they could get them before Christmas 2002 – but that hadn't happened.

In the first week in February, as the lads were gathering for training in Aglish, Justin and a county board officer came in and handed out small envelopes containing two tickets. The Mount Sion players weren't there as they are training for the All-Ireland Club Championship.

'What's this for?' the players asked and were told that it was for the medal presentation, which would take place Friday week in a pub in Dungarvan. The players weren't consulted and, even worse, Mount Sion were due to play on the following Sunday, so they wouldn't be able to enjoy themselves.

As it was an occasion that may only come around once in a generation, all the players wanted it to be a special night. 'What about Mount Sion?' asked the players. 'They're playing the following Sunday. And we've the start of league the next week, so we can't even enjoy ourselves.'

Many found Justin's reply flippant. 'Ah, sure, just come along and enjoy yourselves, get your medals and have your Lucozade.'

Some players did discuss the medal presentation during phone calls, with many feeling a wrong was being committed. Should players have got together independently of management to discuss their issues? Maybe, but in Waterford, it didn't happen.

'Cork hurlers were doing it but not many other teams at the time; it wasn't really something that came up,' says Fergal Hartley, who was the Gaelic Players' Association (GPA) rep with Waterford hurlers in 2002 and 2003.

The GPA had been founded in Belfast in 1999 as the official autonomous representative body for GAA players. In its infancy, there was more time spent filling out membership forms rather than on-the-ground involvement of GPA reps.

After a discussion, some players rang the Mount Sion lads to let them know about the medal presentation. The Mount Sion players said they wouldn't be going, and Fergal Hartley would be missing too.

Peter Queally rang the county board liaison officer to tell him that the players wouldn't be going to the ceremony. Justin heard what was happening, and was told that Queally was one of those complaining most. The county board wanted the ceremony to go ahead as they had had the tickets printed and the preparations had been made, so it was up to Justin to convince the players to go – but they were not for budging.

'We won it together, let's celebrate it together,' was Justin's reasoning to the players, but he couldn't persuade them to change their minds. The medal ceremony was put off until October – fifteen months after the title had been won. By then, some of the players had pulled off the panel after falling out with Justin.

Other issues had started to arise too. The players had no proper hydration at training (only water when they wanted energy drinks, something they had had previously); on some evenings, the showers didn't work in Fraher Field; and, sometimes, there were only limp sandwiches after training. These were all things that the players felt Justin should have been taking care of, things that they shouldn't have had to bring to his attention. And they knew that in other counties, players were getting these things.

Brian Flannery says, 'Cork were fierce loyal to each other; we used to skit about the likes of Donal Óg and Seán Óg – but they were natural leaders, big personalities, when they led, everyone followed, and I don't think we really had that sort of unity or team loyalty.'

The right kind of leadership was lacking.

'A lot of the characters in other, more successful counties seemed to be less erratic and down through the years, some Waterford players were pretty erratic,' says Tom Feeney today. 'It's very simple really – go training, train hard, go home, go training again, and so on – but this hadn't been done consistently by everybody on the panel for the past fifteen years.'

'People in Waterford, including the players, weren't used to the newly acquired fame,' says Andy Moloney. 'There was no real code there and some of the lads were acting the bollocks. I found Justin brilliant on the coaching but him trying to deal with everyone on a panel of thirty was a problem. But I felt that if you wanted to chat with him about something, you could.'

A small delegation of players met a county board delegation, with Justin present too. The players aired their main grievance – that they felt they were doing Justin's job for him and that these matters were things that Justin should have been pursuing for them.

Colm Bonnar believes the success of winning Munster raised the bar, 'Intrinsic motivation is you hurl because you love it and have loved it from a young age. But then more things come into play, such as boots, training gear – the extrinsic things that can become very important, the things that go with success.'

Jim Dee, the secretary, was beginning to see a major difference in the management styles between Justin and his predecessor, Gerald. He knew that, under Gerald, if a young player had had a problem, Gerald would have just called him aside and had a quiet word in his ear to sort things out. But Justin, he thought, was not like that.

Jim knew first hand how things worked behind the scenes in Waterford GAA because he turned up to the training sessions and all the matches and was involved at the ground level (in the ten-year period in which he has been secretary, he's only missed two training sessions – and that was because he had to attend two weddings).

After their success winning the Munster title, 2003 should have been the year Waterford reached the next level. It should have been when they united, as the Cork hurlers were doing, and regrouped with greater intent. It should have been the defining season for all the right reasons.

But, even at the start, things were going wrong.

Justin spent a lot of time trying to turn some players who were natural footballers into good hurlers. He succeeded but at the expense of fitness levels, which were starting to drop dramatically. The players got through 2002 with the store of fitness they had from Gerald's time, but, with the new season, the pounds were being put back on. Waterford had a very poor league campaign but had won the first round of the championship by eighteen points against Kerry at Walsh Park. Michael 'Brick' Walsh made his first appearance in a Munster game for Waterford and the young Stradbally defender was noted as one to watch for the future.

Next, Waterford were to play Limerick in the Munster championship semi-final (a day on which the television cameras at the match didn't work so the match wasn't covered). But the feeling in the camp wasn't good and some of the players, including Peter Queally, the hero of so many games, were beginning to tire of Justin.

'He had this obsession with style,' he says. 'I remember we were in Kilgobnet in the hall when Colm Bonnar just wanted to do circuits. It was a very small hall and Justin said no, telling us to get into pairs and start hitting the ball to each other. We were like sardines. It was his mindset. He was asked to manage Waterford – he should have managed us. I don't think he got that clear in his head – managed, not coached. He is the best coach in Ireland; he loves his hurleys, loves the drills, is very enthusiastic, but there is such a difference between managing and coaching. Managing is so personal.'

'He used the same tone of voice for team speeches as if he was ordering a cup of tea,' says one player. 'A kind of high-pitched voice, very rarely shouting or losing it. And if he did, it didn't have a very telling effect. Some of the lads were constantly behind his back cutting him.'

Waterford struggled through what was a bad league campaign. They had their first full recorded meeting with a dietician under Justin on 23 April (such things were regular in other counties by this stage). And, even with fifty-six training and match sessions under their belt by May, things weren't great in the camp.

The modern inter-county hurler is under a lot of pressure to perform. He puts in an awful lot of time and effort and players from his club and supporters expect him to be superb. But many need to be told of their importance to a panel, with players at the periphery sometimes needing it more than anyone.

'He didn't talk to younger lads,' says one player. 'You could lose a bit of form after a year or so and you'd be dropped without explanation. Being on the periphery can be a very lonely place. That's one of the big areas Justin fell down on as he didn't go out of his way to work on a team spirit – it happened in spite of him. And we weren't being supervised as regards having drinks after matches … so we started going off again after matches and having the craic.'

'Justin wasn't great at locking doors and making sure we did what he said,' recalls another long-serving player. 'He said, "No drinking now, lads", but we all went off and drank as we knew we weren't going to be punished. Justin really believed in his head we wouldn't drink, instead of really enforcing it.'

Peter Queally, not one of the drinkers, was dropped for the Limerick game and was not one of the five subs brought on. Clem Smith wreaked havoc for Limerick, picking up man of the match, and Waterford were lucky to get a draw, 4–13 to 4–13.

Paul Flynn was the star for Waterford with three goals and three points. As they were coming out of the ground, Justin McCarthy told Kieran O'Connor from Glanbia just how good he thought Flynners really was, 'Shades of Ring, shades of Ring.'

For the replay six days later, Queally, 'The Enforcer', was asked back to do a job on Smith. Dan Shanahan was on the bench again – he was a sub in the Kerry game, in the drawn Limerick game and now again for the replay. He was thoroughly perplexed.

Even though Peter Queally's father was in hospital, dying of cancer, Peter was absolutely thrilled to be picked on the starting fifteen. 'I'll never forget that feeling,' he says. 'I was thirty-two and so happy to be given the chance. I rang my father and I was crying on the phone.'

He played so well Clem Smith was taken off after nineteen minutes and Queally handled his replacement Ciaran Carey just as well. Waterford lost Tony Browne through injury after only twenty minutes but the genius of Paul Flynn came to the fore yet again – at one stage he angled away from three Limerick defenders and instead of going for a point, drove the ball across Timmy Houlihan in the Limerick goal and watched it squirm under his body. Waterford won by two points: 1–12 to 0–13.

Training continued for the Munster final against Cork and the team went to Thurles on the Tuesday before the match to re-acquaint themselves with the surroundings. After training, sitting under the far stand, Justin named the starting fifteen and Queally wasn't on it. There was no explanation, no reason given, and Queally felt very low. It wasn't in Justin's make-up to tell players why they'd been dropped, but Queally felt his relationship with Justin had changed since the medal debacle.

After the training and the anticipation, after all the build-up, the Munster final on 29 June was decided on a number of small but vital decisions and actions.

Cork, under Donal O'Grady, were confident, having beaten Clare by eleven points in the semi and were spurred on by the fact that they didn't want Waterford to win back-to-back Munster titles – something that would have been a first for Waterford.

'We just wanted to win the game,' says Donal. 'There was no massive rivalry between us and Waterford at that stage. We might have used stuff that was said in the papers but every team does that and we focused mainly on how we would perform. Our preparation involved timing everything right, such as the time we'd arrive, bandages, warm-up, etc. Preparation was very important as it helped the players relax. We tried to be meticulous. I'd talk with every player and we'd go through scenarios; but the main thing was trust – trust in players and the game plan.'

Unknown to most, Diarmuid O'Sullivan for Cork had a virus, but, not wanting to give Waterford a psychological advantage, he was started on John Mullane. But the gamble didn't pay off and he was taken off early in the match. Mark Prendergast went in on Mullane and played relatively well on him.

Waterford had the breeze and went two points up, but Cork got a goal from Setanta Ó hAilpín. Waterford managed to come back and then Mullane got a great goal: 1–5 to 1–1 after twenty minutes.

Every time Cusack, in the Cork goal, went to puck out the ball, the chant from the terrace was 'Tonneeee Brrooowwwwnne' reminding the Corkman of the 'great' goal that had been scored the previous year.

Brian Greene was at full-back, even though he had never played there before in such a game. Cork brought back Timmy McCarthy as a third midfielder to block any ball coming through to Ken McGrath, who'd been marked closely by Ronan Curran.

'For that ten minutes when Timmy was brought back, I think Waterford hardly picked up on it,' says Donal O'Grady, 'and it helped stem the flow a bit as Waterford could have run away with it.' But Waterford added some more points to lead 1–9 to 1–4 at half-time.

But O'Grady wasn't worried – he knew there was a lot of game left and knew that Cork would stick to their plan. Waterford made a few positional switches at half-time – but they weren't changes that added any new dimension to their game.

Waterford had a lot of wides in the second half – and Cork had Setanta, six foot six of pure confidence! Declan Prendergast was doing well on him but when Setanta was given half a chance – bang, it was in the net!

But after Cork had gone ahead, Mullane got another goal after a short free to him from Paul Flynn. The game was going great. Dan Shanahan was on the subs bench, thinking this was most certainly a game for him and expected to be brought on.

But with the game slipping away, Justin took off Eoin Kelly (who had a bad game) and brought on Paul O'Brien from Tallow ahead of Big Dan.

The Cork experience started to show, and one of their corner-backs caught Paul on the wrong foot, drove him off the field towards the stand, got the ball and, launched it upfield. Joe Deane caught and buried it – another goal for Cork! Peter Queally was brought on for the last four minutes – but Waterford had already lost: 3–16 to 3–12. Paul Flynn was dismissed late on and Ken McGrath missed six frees.

The game is clocked up as another in which Waterford started well but faded away near the end. John Mullane's total of 3–1 was magnificent, but apart from four points each from Dave Bennett and Paul Flynn, there wasn't much to shout about. Justin had made five substitutions but they hadn't worked.

Before they went in, Big Dan walked over to Justin and selectors Colm Bonnar and Seamie Hannon on the sideline and said, 'What have I done wrong not to deserve to get a game?' He spoke in as calm a manner as he could, no shouting or roaring as others might in a similar situation. All he was told was that it was their decision. Dan told his manager that he respected that, but he needed them to tell him if he'd done anything wrong. Could they tell him why he wasn't given a run out? They couldn't.

As the men were talking, Dan's uncles were coming down out of the stand and they shouted over, 'Tell him to fuck off, Dan. Leave your hurley there and come back to Lismore.'

In the dressing room afterwards, Justin didn't say much. Cork captain Alan Browne came in to offer commiserations.

There was similar frustration for other Waterford players. Two days later, Queally was in a petrol station in Cork when he met Mark Landers from the Cork team. Landers told Queally that he couldn't believe he hadn't been playing, as they'd been targeting him as someone who could burst up things.

The following Wednesday, the team met in Walsh Park for training, and Justin took them over to the stand and got them to sit down. He talked for ages about what had happened on the previous Sunday. Yes, the players admitted, they had played badly, but some thought he was waffling and preaching and not taking responsibility for his decisions.

The only player who could really say anything to him on that particular evening was John Mullane and he spoke up. 'Justin, you'll have to take some of the blame here yourselves. You can't just lay it all back on us.'

The players felt Justin's answer was, again, somewhat waffly. Nobody else spoke, some were afraid to open their mouths because if they did, they could suffer like Queally had.

In training, Big Dan did what he does best – put his head down, trained hard and kept his mouth closed. The selectors didn't apologise or mention anything to him, but realised they needed him.

Like a good wine, Dan had matured. He'd done nothing but

knuckle down and work – and he loved training.

'I suppose at twenty-one, I was wild and that, a small bit wild. I just enjoyed a few drinks with the lads but I always had a head on me shoulders,' he says, noticing how the game had evolved since his younger days. He was very conscious of the fact that he hadn't figured in Justin's plans the previous year, only coming on as a sub in games. But then – and it was not something that was widely known – he'd been seriously injured with poly-arthritis in his knees, for which he had had to take steroids which, in turn, meant he had put on weight.

But now he was back, training harder than ever and his legs were getting better. Over the twelve-year period in which played for Waterford, he only missed nine training sessions, out of the hundreds that were held.

Next up for Waterford were Wexford in Nowlan Park, in a make-or-break game – but complacency had set in amongst the camp. Queally was back on the team but things weren't good. Waterford were favourites but had a fragile mindset, like Wexford. The Waterford and Wexford fans got on very well (there's no 'bad history' between them) and there was a festival-like atmosphere with a massive beach ball being passed over the heads of fans. Former Wexford manager Liam Griffin came down from the stand and pointing his finger at thirty-two-year-old Larry Murphy (who wasn't starting and was feeling like a broken man) saying, 'Today is your day when you come on! I just know it is!'

Dan Shanahan finally started a game for Waterford and was really unfortunate not to score at least two goals as Damien Fitzhenry in the Wexford goal gave an exhibition of shot stopping. Nonetheless, Waterford were 0–9 to 0–3 up after half an hour. Wexford defender Declan Ruth was so frustrated he threw the ball at Ken McGrath's arse and pulled hard. 'To be fair to Ken, he pulled right back at me!' laughs Declan now.

For many of the greying Wexford players, it was last-chance saloon. Larry Murphy did come on for an injured Adrian Fenlon.

His marker Tom Feeney said, 'Well howya, Larry? How's it going?' Larry caught a ball and gave it to Rory Jacob, who scored a goal just before half time.

Dave Bennett and Peter Queally were having bad games for Waterford. 'Justin was waving his curly finger at me and I was being taken off, gone after five minutes of the second half,' says Queally. He felt it was inevitable that he was going to be one of the first players substituted.

Unfortunately, Waterford's changes didn't work, and Wexford's did.

At one stage, Seamie Hannon and Colm Bonnar told Brian Flannery to get ready, and his name was being written out on the slip of paper when Justin just came up, shook his head and that was it. 'Why would you be a selector if you have no input?' says Flannery.

Even though Wexford were playing against a strong breeze in the second half, they were more hungry for the victory. They knew Waterford blew hot and cold, and everything was going right for them. 'I missed one ball and it hit me on the forehead and bounced down to Rory and he got another point!' says Larry Murphy.

'We knew with ten minutes to go we had it won; Waterford's heads went down,' says Declan Ruth. Wexford won 1–20 to 0–18. Larry Murphy and Liam Griffin embraced on the field, 'We were both balling crying!' says Larry.

Afterwards, Justin called all the Waterford players into one of the dressing rooms and started talking.

A mobile rang. It was Queally's. His mother told him that his father had been allowed home to watch the match but that his blood pressure had gone sky high and so he'd been rushed back to hospital. Queally started to walk out when Justin called him back. 'Justin, I'm just sick of fucking listening to you,' he said, and kept walking.

He realised he had been wrong to say it; he knew it wasn't the time or place, that everyone else was feeling just as bad. But he felt he had to say something.

Some players were happy somebody had stood up to Justin, others were disappointed with Queally's timing. But after the game in a nearby bar, players remember that some senior officials in the county board were saying, 'Jaysus, we'll have to get rid of him now.'

They all, including Queally, went out that night and the next day to drown their sorrows. That weekend, Paul Flynn backed Thomas Bjorn to win the British Golf Open; the Dane was three up with a few to go but stayed in a bunker for four or five shots and lost. It seemed when things were going badly, everything was going badly.

What happened next was a disorganised heave against Justin. Although it was never made public, a number of the senior and younger players were involved.

'In the 2003 Munster final,' recalls Brian Greene, whose father Jim had been mentioned for the manager's job before Justin was appointed. 'Big Dan and Brian Flannery were warming up for a lot of the first and second half but weren't brought on. We spoke to them in a dark corner in a bar after the match. Players wanted to leave the panel but we said hang around. I was thirty-two. Four or five of us then had two or three caucus meetings when we'd meet in Flannery's house.'

Says Brian Flannery, 'We discussed that we were going nowhere fast, that training wasn't hard enough, that, basically, Justin had to go and that under him it was a dictatorship, not a democracy.'

'I thought we'd shame Justin out of it but I should have known better. Everyone had their own reporter to talk to. But then Peter Queally's sister was killed in a car accident and nothing happened with it all,' says Greener.

Not all the players had been contacted about the attempted coup as those organising things felt everyone was big enough to make up their own minds. Paul Flynn says he didn't hear about it until five years later.

'The push to get rid of Justin wasn't that serious,' says Stephen

Brenner. 'It was for some players, but I couldn't see the county board backing the players and getting rid of Justin after him winning Munster in 2002.'

For Brian Flannery the malaise ran very deep. 'It shows the importance of one or two players setting the standards for others to follow and Justin would have been more divisive than anything. Our best players were not the natural leaders at the time. The guys with the foresight were not necessarily the best hurlers, the guys who had a bit of thought put into it. You compare that with the Lohans or Seanie McMahons in Clare; highly educated, big leaders, big personalities, when they led, everyone followed. I don't think we ever had that. In 2003, there was a chance for the team to go in a different direction; but it didn't happen; while some of the bigger players spoke openly that change would have been best for the team, they basically went for cover.'

Bank official Flannery is afraid that in twenty years time, when people look back, they will file this team as one of the best teams never to win an All-Ireland. 'There will be no twenty-five-year celebration, you won't see us walking out, being introduced to the crowd. That's the greatest tragedy. Given the team, the quality of players, it's reasonable to say that that's a poor return.'

Then some newspapers printed an article, mentioning the fact that Brian Greene and Peter Queally had removed themselves from the panel. Then, with Peter and his family in mourning and with him sitting at his sick father's bedside, people started phoning WLR, some saying that he and Greener weren't fit to lace Justin's boots.

'WLR was on and these wankers were ringing in, not even giving their names, cutting the fucking back off us,' says Peter. 'My father had only a couple of weeks to live. He was listening to this and there was silence between us. It tore my heart out nearly. After everything we had given and this is what it boiled down to.'

Once again that summer, Waterford had got to an All-Ireland quarter-final and the back-door system was working in Justin's favour. Waterford were nearly guaranteed to get to a quarter-final every year, as there are really only eight or nine teams in the country at the same level as them.

At the same time in Kilkenny, Brian Cody was developing a team full of big men who could catch the ball high or low, who could stand their ground, who weren't going to be pushed around and who could score lots of goals. Most importantly of all, Cody was astute enough to see when players were in decline, and had the talent at his disposal to bring in fresh blood at the right time.

'I could see stuff coming down the line and knew six or seven players were talking. And then Queally and Flannery and Greene got hung out to dry because they weren't asked back on the panel,' says Colm Bonnar, who remembers the frustration of Justin not having done enough physical training for the 2003 campaign. 'And some players were very flighty, you couldn't even get inside their heads; if they weren't settled off the field, how could they be settled on it? And the loss of Cullinane, Frampton, Flannery, Greene and Hartley in those years meant there was a big void in leadership.'

Justin survived 2003 and started planning for the following year. He knew he'd have to change the training regime because it wasn't working. He made enquiries and heard about a man who was working at the Waterford Institute of Technology, who had been involved with various Fitzgibbon teams, who was currently coaching a basketball team in Cork and who had previously worked with the Waterford senior hurlers back in 1995. His appointment of Gerry Fitzpatrick, he felt, might just turn things around.

Gerry had a plan and met the players in November. For the next two months, he put the players on personalised weights programmes, so they would be ready to start full training in January.

But some players, such as Brian Flannery, did not get the letter asking them back on the panel for 2004. He had seen the writing on the wall. 'Even though I had been hurling well, he hadn't spoken with me for twelve months. Sometimes that year, Justin would take the first fifteen to play backs and forwards and the rest of us would be on other end of field with Seamie Hannon. I knew I'd be better off at home watching *Coronation Street* because even if I caught balls in me mouth, he wasn't even watching; that was no way to train a team. Justin had great qualities in very limited circumstances. When these Waterford players are retired, we'll soon appreciate how good they were.'

Meanwhile the east–west Waterford divide hadn't gone away. At this time, GAA President Seán Kelly was leading the charge to develop grounds around the country further, as Croke Park was effectively 'finished'. He says a proposal was put to the Waterford county board that unspecified millions of euros would be ploughed into Walsh Park to develop at 35,000-seater stadium, but some in west Waterford wanted Fraher Field to be developed.

'There were similar disagreements in Galway about developing Salthill or Tuam but they sorted out their differences and Salthill was done,' says Seán Kelly, now an MEP.

But squabbling in Waterford delayed the matter and although they eventually agreed, it was too late, the money was gone. And to this day, Walsh Park, originally known as 'the Showgrounds' as it was a British army display ground, remains undeveloped.

9

2004 – GLORY AND HEARTACHE

Players in any sport can easily get into a comfort zone from which they don't see a way out.

Gerry Fitzpatrick's philosophy was not about getting the team fit for this year and then allowing them to go on the beer for three months before starting back at the same point next year. Every winter, he wanted to see an improvement on the previous year, so they would get better incrementally. He needed adequate time at each team training session for stamina, speed and agility work. None of these things had featured up to this point. The tests on each player were the most complex they'd ever had – tests for strength, stamina, speed, agility, functional leg movement, functional arm movement, posture alignment, flexibility and body fat composition.

'John Mullane is very quick but Seamus Prendergast is stronger so you can't say John Mullane is fitter than Seamus Prendergast because you're not comparing like with like,' Gerry says. 'It's about getting them thinking – John Mullane can never be as strong as Dan Shanahan or Ken McGrath but then it's highly unlikely that Michael 'Brick' Walsh can ever be as quick as John Mullane or Eoin McGrath. So there is no point in flogging a guy to be something that he doesn't have the potential to be and some things are not highly trainable, like speed. There is a percentage of speed that is highly trainable but strength is very trainable.'

The first thing was to make the team much, much stronger. They were working from a very low base where some of the players couldn't bench press 100 kilograms – but they all bought into the new regime.

Players such as Dan Shanahan could see the entire culture changing and could see the lads loving it. The physical aspects preached by Gerry complemented the superb drills practised by Justin perfectly. And the players were encouraged to go to Peter Kirwan's small 'rehab' gym out past Kilmeaden – a specialised gym based on American and Australian techniques with specialised equipment, a squat rake, glut ham machine (for lower hamstrings), a Jacob's ladder (designed by the New York fire brigade) and a lot more besides. Each machine helped players condition their muscles and put no pressure on the joints as they stretched and completed the exercises.

Peter also taught juvenile hurlers how to fall properly by rolling their shoulders first – the same way as jockeys are taught to fall from a horse. Simple but important stuff.

Justin also brought in a new selector, Kilkenny man Nicky Cashin, who saw a positive in the squad's psychology in that what happened in 2003 lowered expectations. The pressure on the players wasn't as great.

At the end of an indifferent league campaign, Waterford travelled to the capital to play Dublin, a team they hadn't beaten in eight years. Paul Flynn lived up to his reputation as 'the man for the talk'. In the first half, he combined well with Dave Bennett for a goal and cockily put the ball right into the corner of the net. Waterford were winning well.

At half-time, Justin praised the lads, 'Keep it going now, boys. Flynners, you keep it going there, lad, there's more goals in this for you.'

'Ara, take me out of the forwards and put me in wing-back,' Flynners said. 'I'm bored, put me back to wing-back, will ya?'

Justin looked at him aghast, not knowing what to say. He

shrugged it off. Flynn would say the same thing at training sometimes for the laugh.

Of course, Justin didn't switch him and without really trying
hard, they won handily.

Waterford played Tipperary in Thurles in the last league game
and found themselves six points down with fifteen minutes to go.
Flynn went for goal from twenty-eight metres out. Dan was on the
edge of the square, right in Cummins' way. Flynn hit it, it came in
over Declan Fanning's head, he got a touch and it landed low on
goal line, Cummins managed a touch but it wasn't enought.

It was in. Momentum restored. The game ended in a draw.

Waterford had qualified for the National League final, playing
Galway in Limerick.

One of the newest additions to the panel had been Jack Kennedy
from Ballyduff Lower. He had been playing very well but had
twisted his ankle and wasn't able to start against Galway. Dan
Shanahan was twenty-seven years old and had been involved in the
Waterford set up for many years. Since Justin had come in, he
hadn't started many matches – and felt he should have. Now he
was starting again, and he felt it could be a big chance.

However, on the day things didn't go according to plan (again!).
To begin with, the traffic was heavy from Waterford to Limerick
and they got to Claughan on the other side of the city from the
Gaelic Grounds at 3.15 p.m., too late for a proper pre-match puck
around. They all got off the bus, and then got back on the bus, and
had to have a mad dash across Galway with a garda escort. Players
on the back seat laughed when they saw a minibus from Dunhill
full of Waterford fans on their coat-tails. Galway had been in the
ground since 3 p.m., and were a lot more relaxed. Waterford were
not fully tuned in. They were not fully acclimatised and the walk
in the parade ended up feeling unreal for many players.

They didn't settle in to the match easily either. The players made
silly, elementary mistakes resulting in 2–10 of Galway's total of
2–15. Waterford lost by five points, but Dan had overcome any

dent in confidence he'd been suffering by getting 1–6 from play.
If Jack hadn't gone over on his ankle, he may not have had the
chance – that's how narrow a line it is sometimes.

Waterford had a week before they played Clare in the first round
of the Munster championship.

On the Tuesday evening, a practice match amongst the players
was organised and the dimensions of the field were brought in to
allow for more intense hitting. Gerry Fitz had everything geared
for the Sunday coming, not the Sunday gone.

Semple Stadium in Thurles on 16 May was a sea of expectation.
Davy Fitz was warming up in goal for Clare, mad for it after a two-
month suspension. Davy and Clare were ready for Waterford.
They thought they were going to grind Waterford down, as they
had done in Croke Park twenty-four months earlier. And it had
been years – six years – since Waterford had beaten Clare. Since
1998, they'd beaten Cork and Tipp and Limerick – but never
Clare.

Many of the players remembered the 2002 semi-final loss – it
had been bad. Was this their chance at revenge?

After a winter of excellent training, Waterford were like coiled
springs, hungry wolves waiting to play.

Eoin Kelly got the ball at the throw-in, passed back to Ken
McGrath, up to John Mullane, over the bar – fifteen seconds gone.
Dan drifted in as Tony Browne drove a long ball in, he fielded it
over Conor Plunkett and past Davy into the net. Then Dave
Bennett pointed a sixty-five and the score was an amazing
Waterford 1–4, Clare 0–0.

Next, a long ball from Bennett that Seamus Prendergast flicked
to Dan's big hands and he put away for his second goal. Davy was
seething.

Two minutes before the break, Tony Carmody was fouled and
Clare had a twenty-metre free. As Davy ran up to take it, a few
Waterford fans shouted abuse at him about his private life. Awful
stuff. But they were the type of spectators who were more

interested in the pints, the session, and the vodkas and Red Bull. Davy's shot was blocked but Tony Griffin got the rebound; and Niall Gilligan got a point to leave Clare only six down at half-time.

Waterford were flying in the second half and Paul Flynn was having a great game. Waterford roared on; Clare wanted to go home. Davy was still getting abuse, terrible abuse.

Anthony Daly was the manager for Clare and was thinking of making another substitution in a faint hope of salvaging some sort of pride. Such was the confidence of the Waterford players at this stage that Tony Browne, who was not too far away from him, shouted, 'Bring them all on, Daly! Come on yourself!'

'I could only look at him and I thought, Ya fecker, you're right!' says Anthony. 'It was just one of those games no matter what we were going to do, it wasn't going to work.' With such good forwards, Daly thought Waterford were electric and believed they should have won an All-Ireland, but felt 'the management needed to have more cuteness'.

With minutes left, a shot by Brick Walsh hit the post but Shanahan was there for the rebound – three goals in an hour against Davy Fitz! 3–1 from play for Dan – he really was on fire. A fine line indeed.

Waterford won by nineteen points (3–21 to 1–8) their biggest ever championship win over one of the other top four Munster boys. For Clare, this was as bad as 1993 when Tipp mauled them by eighteen points.

For Waterford, next was Tipp in the Munster semi-final.

Tom Feeney had been struggling with form and had made a mistake against Clare which had given them a penalty and a goal. A week before Tipp, Justin took all the players to the dogs in Cork but, beforehand at training, announced the A and B team, and Tom was on the B team. 'What tends to happen then is the shield comes down between you and management, they don't talk to you; it's all about the A team,' he says. 'Ken looked over at me and said, "What's that all about?"' But Tom knew, it was the first time in his career that he wasn't going to make the championship start. Declan Prendergast went in.

Later that week, another small thing reared its head which used to annoy some players.

'We wanted tickets to be sorted and given out at least a week before big matches,' says Stephen Brenner, 'but Justin would say, "If you're thinking about tickets, you're not thinking about the match." Tickets wouldn't be given out then until the Thursday night before a big game, which was a nuisance, another distraction.'

Sunday was a sweltering hot day in Cork.

Brendan Cummins in the Tipp goal had been practising saving twenty-metre frees, expecting at least one from Paul Flynn.

Stephen Brenner, Waterford's goalie for the day, was slightly nervous and, as usual, touched the crucifix around his neck that had been given to him by his wife Helena as a wedding present. He asked his late father Ger to look after him. 'I could leave in five goals and it still wouldn't affect me,' he told O'Connor in *Last Man Standing*. After fifteen minutes, he dropped a long ball before Declan Prendergast just got it off the line.

Then Big Dan got two goals for Waterford before Tipperary's Eoin Kelly, twelve metres out and being pushed wide, hit for the near post. Brenner tried to let the sliotar come in to his stomach, but the ball hit his hand and dropped into the net.

A few minutes later, he raced in as Declan Prendergast fumbled. Kelly shot from fourteen metres out, slow-motion stuff. Brenner was looking at it as it bounced in front of him. He went to push it around the post. He was waiting for it to hit the hurley – but it never did and hopped into the corner of the net.

He was furious with himself.

The game throbbed with entertainment and excitement. Waterford were eccentric, spontaneous, crazy! Mullane got a goal; Paul Flynn then shot for the top corner, only for Brendan Cummins to make one of the greatest Munster championship saves;

Morrissey kicked the ball into the net at the other end for a Tipp goal; Flynn and Ken went off injured; and, with a minute to go, sub Paul O'Brien drove home the winning goal.

Waterford were up by a point, the fans were delirious.

In injury time, Mark O'Leary missed a great chance, the Waterford backs fought like hounds for it and Tipp's Eoin Kelly was superbly blocked by Brick Walsh. At last, the final whistle blew. The Tipp players collapsed. Waterford had won by a point, 4–10 to 3–12 and were in their third consecutive Munster final, something they hadn't done since the great teams of 1957, 1958 and 1959.

Colm Bonnar, now part of the Tipp setup, remembers Paul Flynn was standing in front of the Tipp dugout after he'd been taken off. 'When the final whistle went Flynners ran up to me and said something, then ran across the field to celebrate! There could have been war, the Tipp lads on the bench were fuming, but I said 'Leave if off, lads.''

Brenner shook hands with Cummins as they left the field, 'Jaysus, that was mad stuff altogether!' Cummins agreed.

The issue of who was going to mind the net for Waterford was going to be crucial this season.

Some players felt that Justin was not good at bringing new talent into the squad, but three weeks before the Munster final, he arranged a challenge match in Walsh Park between his team and the under-21s, who had nineteen-year-old Wayne Hutchinson from Ballygunner in midfield, along with Liam Lawlor. Wayne had been on the under-21 team for three years and had ambitions to hurl for Waterford at all levels. In warm sunshine, he wasn't thinking about the possibility of being called up to the senior panel and he relaxed and played his own game – then Justin called him onto the senior panel.

Justin thought the lads deserved a break, so he decided to bring them back to the Marina Hotel in Ballycastle, County Antrim, for a weekend away.

On the Saturday evening, they played a match in Dunloy and, afterwards, a massive singsong started in the clubhouse with a band belting out the tunes. The six foot six giant of a club chairman was even wearing a Waterford jersey which he had paid £300 for at an auction, such was the romantic attraction of fans all over the country for Waterford to do well.

Players were called up to sing, with 'Everybody's Got The Right To Go Wrong' proving very popular.

One of the players blasted out a rendition of 'Go On Home British Soldiers, Go On Home'. Half the people in the pub looked incredulous, while others were jumping up, cheering and shouting. 'I was thinking, Fuck's sake, I hope we don't get shot here!' says Tom Feeney.

The bus took them the hour-long drive back to Ballycastle for the disco in the hotel and most of the players were worse for wear. The following morning on the way back home, they went into the O'Donovan Rossa clubhouse for soup and sandwiches around midday. Shortly after, Sinn Féin president Gerry Adams walked in with his grand-daughter and wished the players well against Cork. As the players were sat on the bus waiting to leave, Adams got on and said to them all, 'Best of luck now, lads. I hope you win. And that singing you were doing last night was fantastic I heard. If you're ever stuck for a gig come up to us!'

It made for great fun on the long journey home.

Back in training, Tony Browne was having trouble with his hamstring. He was very good at listening to his body and knew when work was needed on his muscles. Two days before any big game, he went out to Peter Kirwan to get a good rub, go through a series of stretches and talk shop. Physios are, in some way, like psychologists. And now in the fortnight before the Munster final, Tony needed more work on this body than before. Sometimes, he could be out to Peter twice a day. They even had breakfast together, porridge and fruit scones with jam and worked hard at getting Tony's hamstring ready for the big game.

Other players had different ways of relaxing. Eoin Kelly and John Mullane went to a Waterford v. Cork City soccer match, and the Cork fans were chanting at Mullane, 'Sully's gonna get ya! Sully's gonna get ya!'

The Friday night before the match, Cork goalie Donal Óg Cusack was giving a talk to the players at the end of training in the corner of the field in Páirc Uí Rinn. Legendary stories of bygone days abounded. 'Waterford must be overcome, so we won't have that pain deep inside our heads,' he said, referring to the pain which goes on all winter when a team loses during the summer. Cork were ready, very ready.

There is an aura about a Munster final which is special for the hurling counties in the province.

On the morning of the game, rain fell on Thurles but it wasn't going to put off the 54,000 fans who were already heading for the turnstiles. Brian 'Bull' Phelan remembers fans literally shaking the team bus as they drove through Liberty Square.

An Everton fan, the Bull would watch *Match of the Day* the night before big matches and try to sleep early. 'If you didn't get to sleep in the first three-quarters of an hour, you're fecked, you're head would be wrecked,' says Brian, who was confident about the match as Justin had told him Cork forward Garvan McCarthy wouldn't last half an hour. And how right he'd be, he would be taken off at half-time. 'Justin would have everything off to a tee player-wise, about who you are marking, saying he likes turning this way or that, he was very good that way,' says Brian.

Brian Greene, another player not asked back by Justin, was sitting at home watching the match on television, as he would watch all matches for the next five years, still thinking about the attempted coup a few months earlier. He didn't want people remembering him just as somebody who tried to get rid of Justin. 'I'd go crazy watching the match,' he says. 'Debbie would come back later with the children. You wouldn't want to be near me when a match was on. I couldn't watch it with anybody else and I couldn't go to a match because if anybody who didn't understand the situation made any sort of a judgement towards me, I'd have gone mental. Queally, Flannery and me were very heartfelt players who would throw ourselves in front of a truck for Waterford. Me having been involved had nothing to do with my father but he was definitely next in line in my eyes. I honestly think the reason why we didn't win an All-Ireland was because we didn't get rid of McCarthy.'

Waterford hadn't beaten Cork in a Munster final for forty-five years but Waterford felt confident they could revenge the previous year's defeat.

The mood in the Waterford dressing room was tense, but mixed with confidence – the lads had a marvellous season so far and were buzzing. Paul Flynn had a knee injury but he'd play through the pain. Justin made a speech, though some players would say later it wasn't a very inspirational one but, then, they didn't need inspiration at this stage. The dressing rooms below the stand were so insulated that the players could be forgiven for thinking there was no one out in the stadium. And the dressing rooms and the tunnel were so dark, you didn't know what was waiting for you – but then came the roar, the arena, the cauldron.

Cork came in from their puck around and WLR commentator Kieran O'Connor thought they were swaggering in a little. 'They are probably that way anyway.'

Cork won the toss and the players took up their positions. The Waterford full-back line could smell Brian Corcoran from a mile off, as he had a chest infection and reeked of the Deep Heat that had been rubbed all over his chest. Stephen Brenner took up his position with his back to the Killinan End terrace, in which thousands of Waterford fans were packed.

After only a few minutes, Garvan McCarthy slapped at the ball as it came up from a group of players just outside the Waterford twenty-one. The ball was slithering towards the goal. The bas of Brenner's hurley was a few inches off the ground. The ball was going to hop up, surely? But it didn't – it went flat, skidding and rolling, unbelievably, under the hurley, between his legs and into the net.

Belief was suspended before the groans, moans and shouts of, 'Wake up, ya bollix' and 'Is there a fucking hole in your hurley?' Brenner picked the ball our of the net, breathed deeply and pucked it long.

The Cork short game was working well for them and they were five points up with only eight minutes gone. If the scores had kept coming, they might have opened up for goals.

Brian Corcoran was at the top of his game for Cork. John Gardiner went out on Big Dan. A Tom Kenny shot was given as a point but it looked wide. Brenner was shouting. It was all going wrong. Then Dan made a magnificent catch up high and eluded Gardiner to put it over the bar. The first fifteen minutes were phenomenal, players felt knackered. John Mullane put a superb point over on the run.

Then with fifteen minutes gone, Eoin Kelly got the ball and, on the forty-five, hugged the sideline in front of the Old Stand. Jerry O'Connor hooked him. Kelly picked up the ball and cut inside at the Thurles Sarsfield corner and made it to the endline. He moved in at pace, getting ready to shoot. Cusack moved ever so slightly to his right to spread himself. Kelly kept running.

Kelly switched to hit the ball on his left. Only a genius could do this at such pace with O'Connor behind him and number four coming in on him. The angle was incredibly tight. He shortened his grip. Shot. Near post. Over Cusack's shoulder as he fell. Goal. A great goal. One of the greatest goals ever scored in any Munster final. Game on.

But Cork stuck to their plan with sharp, low balls into their forward line. The Cork full-forward line got the ball sixteen times, Waterford's full-forward line only six.

For the first time in his hurling career, Dave Bennett was marking Cork's Tom Kenny, who normally played wing-back but was in the centre for this game. Bennett won a lot of ball but he was amazed at the level of Kenny's fitness, he was like a machine, gliding over the ground and wasn't even out of breath when he was running back to position. He was the greatest athlete Dave had ever played against. After twenty-five minutes, he said to himself, 'How the fuck am I going to keep up with this guy for the rest of the day?'

The game had an intensity that few players will forget.

It was a physical but not dirty game. Dan and Gardiner squared up to each other, Gardiner went down. Winding up is part and parcel of the game. Dan laughed at Gardiner as they came out. They were all men possessed.

Cork were playing some of their best hurling of the season in this first twenty minutes but instead of going for goals, they were content to take points – Corcorcan got a beauty.

Waterford were five points down with twenty-six minutes gone when an Eoin Kelly shot dropped short, Dan drifted in behind Diarmuid O'Sullivan, caught and then smashed the ball in on his left at Cusack's near post from a few metres out. Then Paul Flynn in his black helmet got to a cross-field ball before O'Sullivan, looked up and it was over the bar.

Half-time. Waterford were only three points adrift, which was good as it could have been a lot more. Waterford had done enough to make sure they could stay in the game, but not enough to convince anyone that they were going to win.

Players patted Brenner on the back, telling him to keep his head up, there was more in this. Justin got them all sitting down, told them to relax, went round to all the players, told them to keep going, keep going, keep moving around, don't stay in the one spot. He felt they were not playing to their potential. McCarthy stopped. The players huddled. McGrath told them not to leave it behind them. 'We're coming back in here as Munster champions.'

For the second half, Brenner had the Cork supporters at his back and they gave him some roasting.

Story of three managers:
Gerald McCarthy (*above left*), Justin McCarthy (*above right*) and Davy Fitzgerald (*above centre*).

The back-room boys:
Roger Casey, Jim Dee and Sean Power (*above, l-r*)
and former county board chairman Pat Flynn
(*right*).

Waterford captain Fergal Hartley in 2002, raising the cup on the county's
first Munster title in thirty-nine years.

2004 All Stars –
Paul Flynn,
Dan Shanahan
and Ken McGrath

Tony Browne (*above*) and Paul Flynn (*left*) heroes of
the 2004 Munster final against Cork. Flynn was man
of the match with a 1–7 haul.

After raising the Munster cup, Waterford captain for 2007 Michael 'Brick' Walsh gives the thumbs up to jubilant fans as he celebrates with team-mates John Mullane and Aiden 'Ringo' Kearney.

Dan Shanahan salutes the crowd during the 2007 Munster final against Limerick during which he scored 3–3 to win man of the match.

Some of the Waterford players – including Dan Shanahan, Eoin McGrath, Declan Prendergast and John Mullane – after their run on Tramore strand on 4 June 2008. Hours later in the Majestic Hotel, the majority of players decide to call an end to Justin McCarthy's reign as manager.

Selector and former player Peter Queally celebrates with Eoin Kelly, who falls to his knees at the final whistle of the All-Ireland semi-final against Tipperary on 17 August 2008. Kelly scored a magnificent 1–10 out of Waterford's total of 1–20. The semi-final jinx has been broken and the team are heading to their first All-Ireland final since 1963.

Heading into a hellish battle: The players walk out to meet Kilkenny in the
2008 All-Ireland final. The starting fifteen are (r-l): captain Michael 'Brick' Walsh,
Clinton Hennessy, Eoin Murphy, Declan Prendergast, Aiden Kearney, Tony Browne,
Ken McGrath, Kevin Moran, Jamie Nagle, Dan Shanahan, Seamus Prendergast,
Stephen Molumphy, Eoin McGrath, Eoin Kelly and John Mullane.

Twelve-year-old Waterford
supporter Sean O'Sullivan,
from Ballysaggart, cries during
the last ten minutes of the 2008
All-Ireland hurling final.

© Michael Kiely

©INPHO/James Crombie

On a day during which nothing goes right for Waterford, players such as John Mullane never really get going as Kilkenny power home to victory.

A joyous Waterford panel celebrate in the dressing room at Semple Stadium in Thurles after the 2010 Munster final replay victory over Cork.

Seasoned champions: Tony Browne and John Mullane celebrate Waterford's fourth Munster championship in a decade.

Mullane rushed out, got the ball, cut across and, on his left, fired high and over for a point with only ten seconds gone. Then, just as Ken McGrath got ready to take a free out the field, Mullane was caught in an incident off the ball with Brian Murphy. They had been niggling each other but Mullane was seen by the umpires.

Umpire Seanie Arthur had a look, referee Seanie McMahon ran in, Cusack ran out and slapped his hurley off the ground. The two Seanies talked and Mullane was gone. He walked the long journey across the park. He put the hurley over his neck, holding it from behind – if it had been slightly longer, it could have been a crucifix. Waterford fans had their hands on their heads in disbelief. One of their best players had gone.

On the sideline, Justin and the Waterford selectors were concerned but Seamie Hannon saw Paul Flynn. 'He shook himself,' says Seamie, 'making some kind of visual statement that he was going to pick up the slack and he did. He had some talent but he'd try and test ya. That was one regret over the years, if we had that lad firing all the time, we'd have been a serious outfit.'

Donal O'Grady decided that O'Sullivan was going to be his 'extra man'. He was thinking, Yeah, we're playing with the breeze, fifteen against fourteen. Yeah, we'll get out of this all right. 'Sometimes when a player gets sent off, the ref starts giving decisions to the team that is a player down,' says Donal, 'and we found we weren't getting those calls.'

Cork changed their tactics, they no longer ran at Waterford and their intensity dropped suddenly. Waterford were racing everywhere, there was no pattern to the game, it was just do or die. Flynn drifted out, won another ball and floated it over from nearly halfway, this time on his right. With fifty-two minutes gone, Waterford got a free thirty metres out.

Kieran on the radio called it. He commentated on most of Flynn's matches for club and county all the big games and said, 'He might just go for it', noticing Flynn's stance.

Gerald McCarthy was in the Barr's clubhouse in Cork watching the match with his parents. The way Flynn was lining up to take the shot reminded him of the countless times in training that Flynners had practised his art of putting top spin on the ball so it would dip suddenly five yards out. He could catch them here.

Cusack in the middle, Sully on his right.

'I still think to this day we were badly organised for the goal,' says Donal O'Grady, saying Brian Murphy had his back to the free.

Flynn stood over it and looked. The television replays can show him looking and looking, not up high, but at the goal. He hit it off his normal right, not too fast but with top spin, like he'd done countless times at training under Gerald and now Justin.

Sean Óg and Dan were on the edge of square. Dan was trying to impede the view Cusack and Sully had. The ball came over them, Dan swung but didn't connect. It dipped a bit. O'Sullivan tried to bat it. But it dropped under him. The net rattled. Goal.

Cusack looked aghast but got on with game, trying to concentrate on the next play.

Ger Cunningham, a former goalie, was looking on. He knew Flynn was taking a bit of a chance but felt Donal Óg was out of position, a bit too casual, and he'd tell him as much later.

'Unbelieveable!' came the shout on WLR.

With a raised fist, Brenner turned to the Cork supporters, who were silenced.

Flynners signalled to Roger Casey that he needed his inhaler. Roger had a towel up his tracksuit and Paul's inhaler in his pocket. Asthma sufferers are advised to use it maybe three times a day; sometimes he would use it three times during a match. Roger and Paul are lifelong friends, so much so that Roger attended Paul's wedding. 'I used to have his inhaler in my pocket. He did have it in his stocking but it was uncomfortable, so I used to have it in my pocket. He would [make a signal] to me and I'd go in with the water, but it wasn't the water he wanted at all.'

Roger ran on and put his arms around him. 'Fair play to ya,' he shouted, 'and there's another one in you, too.'

'I miss-hit it,' Flynn laughed, with a twinkle in his eyes. 'I wasn't going for the goal.'

It's a story Flynners will later tell people – but Roger, and thousands more, think differently.

Flynn missed an easy free but then batted a ball down near the sideline, lifted it, turned and sent a super ball over the bar. Next Cusack was pucking out the ball short, but when the defenders hit it long, not much was happening. A long ball down the field from O'Sullivan and James Murray intercepted a pass. Cork went ahead, then Kelly got a great point from the right, some wides were hit before Flynn got them ahead. Jerry O'Connor raced through but Declan Prendergast intercepted and cleared it long. His brother got it, over the bar – two up.

But then Cusack found Tom Kenny – point. Mullane was on the sideline, every minute felt like ten, he was biting his nails.

Young players were also delivering, with Michael 'Brick' Walsh was having a marvellous, breakthrough game and Brian 'Bull' Phelan delivering exquisite moments of hurling. Tony shouted over to the Bull, 'there's nothing going past us'. Everything was going so fast. Ken McGrath was leading by example. The last minutes of the game were frenetic.

At this stage, all Donal O'Grady wanted was a replay, not a win and he moved Diarmiud O'Sullivan up front for one last push.

Dan didn't even know what the score was, he asked Seán Óg Ó hAilpín if he knew. 'You're up by a point or something,' came the reply.

Ronan Curran launched a big one, a massive one, up towards O'Sullivan. Players moved towards where it was dropping. One was Ken McGrath, the captain, the boy from Mount Sion who knew no fear, heard no sound, had one thought – to catch that ball. The sun was in his eyes; O'Sullivan was in front of him. McGrath's momentum launched him high and, as he jumped, he put his hurl in his right hand, lifted it high. His left hand came up like Excalibur from the lake. Fans held their breaths. He judged the flight of the ball perfectly. Sullivan was in front slightly to his right. Ken rose, higher, higher and caught it with his left hand just as O'Sullivan lashed back.

Majestic.

He dropped, but he wasn't going to drop the ball. He started running forwards no matter what. McCarthy rushed in and shouldered him. Foul. Ken got to his feet, a fist raised, a symbol of all that is great about hurling, about Waterford, about this man. He looked to the fans like a gladiator. It was a moment players and fans will talk about for decades. There was nothing in the world like it.

Paul Flynn ambled out to take the hit long, Cusack caught and hand passed but the final whistle was blown. Waterford 3–16, Cork 1–21.

Delirious Waterford fans rushed the field. Each player was hit by a flood of people, many of whom they didn't know but who were hugging them like long-lost brothers.

The throng. The hugs. Brenner's crucifix was ripped off and fell to the hallowed turf of Thurles. He never found it and it remains embedded there. Mullane was raised shoulder high by tearful fans. Emotion has a big part to play in hurling. He thought of his family, the supporters – and started to cry himself. Brenner noticed his mother Charlotte was crying in the stand.

John Mullane gave a television interview, crying and saying how much he loved Waterford. Behind him were friends Barry Murphy, Murt Doyle, the Quinlans and James Bannon, roaring his eyes out. Everyone was so happy, considering all the nasty stuff opposition fans had shouted at the likes of Mullane. Ken went up to get the cup. He had two sentences of Irish made out in his head, and was trying to remember them. He was more nervous at this point than he had been in the game. He lifted the cup high in his right hand. An amazing feeling. All his life, he had been waiting for this moment and he took time to think of all the great hurlers who had never been in that position.

Afterwards, the team walked down the streets of Thurles with the cup, meeting friends and people they'd never seen before in one massive outburst of joy. Dan Shanahan was particularly happy. He scored 1–3 from play and had shown the hurling world – and Justin in particular – that he could be one of the best if given the chance.

The Cork goalie Donal Óg Cusack, will say it was the worst and most sickening defeat, to lose a Munster final by a point. His team-mate Brian Corcoran felt they made very bad use of the ball and made a promise to go for more goals against Tipperary in the next match. Donal O'Grady was already planning for the qualifiers, his team were not going to make the same mistakes.

Even though there had been a lot of loose marking, fans believed they had just witnessed one of the greatest games of hurling – high scores, high tempo, high drama; fizzy, daring, romantic hurling; a game people will talk about for decades.

Back in Waterford, the celebrations continued when the team arrived back and an open-top bus took them across Rice Bridge to a reception in Ballybricken. Kieran O'Connor's voice was nearly gone by the time the evening ended. The fan's anthem, 'Dig Deep, Aim High' had already been updated with clips from the day and blared across the city. Pat and Anne McGrath were particularly overjoyed for their two sons, Ken and Eoin, and after some food in the Granville, everybody made their way to the Mount Sion centre for one of those magical nights that nobody wanted to end.

Being from Ballyduff Lower, a small rural club that rarely has a county representative, Jack Kennedy was so proud to be on the panel. He went back to his parish that evening and, just like in every other pub in Waterford, the celebrations were marvellous.

On the field of dreams in Thurles, he had met many club members, including his near neighbour and best friend Kevin and Kevin's parents, Derek and Carmel, great hurling people one and all. But the next morning, he got a call at 11 a.m. from Carmel. Kevin's father Derek has dropped dead on the farm that morning of a heart attack. It put everything in perspective.

The Waterford players watched the Leinster final on television in their homes and the players started to look forward to meeting Wexford in the All-Ireland semi. They felt as if they could beat them – and that would take them to the final.

But the Leinster final didn't work out that way – Wexford got a goal in the last minute, upset the odds and won! That evening, the Waterford players were training and were talking about what had happened, saying they couldn't believe Wexford had won, and ruing the fact that they would now have to play Kilkenny in the semi. Not only that, but they would be without John Mullane, who was suspended because of his sending off. He and the county board decided not to appeal the suspension, a decision which was greeted by many in the papers as a sign of maturity and respect for the rules. But many fans believed Waterford should have tried to overturn the suspension, believing that they needed one of their best players if they were going to win.

Another problem was the long gap between the Munster final and the Kilkenny game. To reduce the likelihood of players getting injured, senior club games were put on hold. But the effect was a degree of staleness and sameness permeated training. Kilkenny are able to get over this gap every year as they have more players hurling across the county at top level (football in Waterford is also strong so the potential pick is smaller) and Kilkenny run off some club games.

'Kilkenny is a one-game county,' says Waterford selector Nicky Cashin, who was deputy principal of St Kieran's College, the great academy of Kilkenny hurling.

So when is the GAA going to force the Kilkenny county board to promote and better develop football in the county?

Three weeks before the All-Ireland semi-final, Sean 'Powery' Power in Harvey Travel had been contacted by Justin, who thought it'd be great to fly the team up to Dublin on the morning of the match. Sean was also involved with Waterford airport, but thought it too risky a thing to do on the day of the match.

'I don't believe this is right thing to do,' he told Justin.

'No, no, no. We'll go ahead with it,' came the response, with no discussion about possible alternatives.

So the decision was made not to go up the night before, with the late Seamus Grant and others, believing it would be best for the players to sleep in their own beds the night before a big match.

A seventy-two seater Aer Arann ATR 72 was chartered but because the airport was prone to fog and low-lying cloud, Sean was worried. The plane (costing €10,000 for the day) was to come down from Dublin on the Sunday morning.

In training, Stephen Brenner was going through a hard time, as his wife Helena was sick (he documented it later in the book *Last Man Standing*) and Stephen had suffered very badly with back pain. The other players weren't aware of Helena's pneumonia, but they could see Stephen's concentration wasn't up to its normal high standards.

Meanwhile young Mount Sion goalie Ian 'Iggy' O'Regan was doing very well and was playing his way onto the team, as was eighteen-year-old Shane O'Sullivan (Sully). Shane's first touch had improved immensely under Justin.

Ken McGrath noticed all this and, the week of the match, told Sully he thought the youngster would be playing as he was doing so well at training. Shane was buoyed by this and, sure enough, the week of the game, Justin sauntered over.

'You're in,' he said quietly. That was all.

'All right. Thanks, Justin,' Shane responded.

He said the same to goalkeeper Iggy O'Regan – his first championship start would be an All-Ireland semi-final! 'I couldn't believe it!' he says now.

After training that evening, the panel went to the Holy Cross pub for food. Tom Feeney had trained very hard and thought he was going to make the team. In the back room after the meal, Justin formally announced the team; Tom's heart sank, he wasn't on it. Declan Prendergast was in at full-back.

'I didn't sleep at all that night,' he says, 'I didn't know how I was going to get through the next few days. Friday, I went into Cork with my good friend Ciarán for a bite to eat. I'd a fry the following morning and went to Ballyduff Upper to stay with my parents before going up to Croke Park on the Sunday morning.'

It may be only a game but a totally committed player has hurling in his DNA. For many, it can be the one thing they see as a success in their lives. And not being on the team is like the break-up of a relationship.

'It's a very intense relationship with a group of players, with a hurley, something you can't define,' Tom says. 'I always had a hurley in my hand. I always knew I wasn't the best hurler but knew I was capable of winning. You see the picture of Waterford winning without you and you wonder how you're going to live with this for the next fifteen years; you tend to blow it out of all proportion. That's why players find it very difficult to be on a panel but to be on a bench. You don't have to be the fastest player in the world because championship day is totally different from the sum of the training sessions to an extent. Certain people are just programmed for championship days when it's all about the positional sense, particularly in the backs.'

Iggy went home where his father Nicky, mum Ger and brothers Alan and Mark were thrilled he'd be starting. Shane O'Sullivan had got the *Irish Independent* on the Friday morning and couldn't believe the hype over him getting a starting place. 'There was a picture of me with the headline 'O'Sullivan To Make His Debut'. I caught it and put it aside so I wouldn't get involved in it. Then there were the phone calls, they never stopped. I never experienced anything like it. People were wishing me well, people who I'd really respect, but some wanted half-hour chats! I was trying to be everyone's friend. I'd learn for future times.'

When the fans heard about Iggy starting in goal ahead of Stephen Brenner, many questioned if it was right to change the goalkeeper going into an All-Ireland semi-final, but some of the players realised Justin was trying to strengthen the team. But it was a huge gamble.

'We had no option,' says then selector Nicky Cashin. 'We didn't want to lose or risk the mistake, like the ones in the Munster final, being repeated.'

The Saturday morning before the match and the weather was not looking good. Sean Power was told by colleagues at the airport that there was a big low coming in over the south-east at noon on Sunday and that the planes probably wouldn't be able to land in Waterford, never mind take off again. Without asking Justin, Sean went to see Walter Morrissey, the local manager with Iarnród Éireann, explained the situation and out of the goodness of his heart, and with a certain amount of rejigging of the trains, Walter said he could have a carriage for them in the morning if it was needed.

Sean didn't sleep a wink all night and, at 5 a.m. on the Sunday, drove out to the airport, where the air traffic controller told him the plane wouldn't be able to land. At 6.45 a.m., he rang Justin in Cork and told him about the situation.

'It's grand down here, Sean. No bother down here. It's lovely down here.'

'It's bad here and we won't be able to fly.'

'Well what alternative do you have? Is it a coach?' asked Justin.

'I have a train arranged.'

'Great.'

Sean phoned Jim Dee who started texting all the players and back-room staff redirecting them to Plunkett Station in Waterford for 10 a.m. Luckily, all the players got the message in time and filled the special carriage at the front of the train. Justin arrived, as did Roger Casey with the gear and they headed off.

But there was another problem.

They had arranged for their special pre-match food to be at the Holiday Inn at Dublin airport and it was too late to find another hotel. So a coach had to be arranged to pick them up at Connolly and take them out to the airport hotel.

Sean Power thought problems such as these should never have arisen — it was always the small things that mattered. 'It might have contributed to our performance later,' he says. 'If you are put out of your stride, like in running, you might often lose the race. This is a big day for Waterford; it mightn't be as big for Kilkenny and we had a lot of young players and the change in travelling might have unnerved some of them. I saw some of them at the train station and they were white in the face; it was such a massive occasion for them. If you have everything on an even keel, things can go well for you.'

And even though an extra carriage had been added, it didn't stop Kilkenny fans getting on at Thomastown strolling through and slagging the lads.

When they arrived in Dublin, one of the selectors Kevin 'Skin' Ryan, took Shane O'Sullivan aside and said, 'All the advice, all the things that have been said, don't worry about it. Just play your own game.' Shane was happy to hear this but felt somebody should have said it to him earlier in the week.

Because of the change to travelling arrangements, Waterford's schedule became more condensed than anyone had anticipated, and they had only seventeen minutes in the dressing room before going out on the pitch.

Some players spent the last few minutes prancing up and down; some spent time in the toilet, gathering their thoughts; John Mullane was not playing but was geeing up some of the others, especially his replacement Shane O'Sullivan. Ken McGrath was intensity personified, his face telling it all, he was so totally focused, ready for the battle.

In goal during the warm-up, Iggy wore his coveted and lucky Féile top from an under-16 Mount Sion win. Waterford then paraded on the outside, nearest the fans, and he could see and hear Mount Sion friends such as Ian Power. 'The parade was unreal,' he says. 'I know maybe you shouldn't be looking into the crowd but you could pick out the faces and hear them shouting.'

The first half was a disaster. Kilkenny, well used to big days like this, were totally zoned in. It'd take a monumental team, which made no mistakes, to beat them.

James Ryall was marking Shane O'Sullivan and three fifty–fifty balls came in which Shane couldn't quite manage to get hold of. Nothing was happening for him. Kilkenny got three goal chances and scored all three – but then didn't create any more in the game. They just knew how to win matches. Wet conditions, inexperienced goalkeeper, Henry Shefflin: four minutes … bang … near post … goal; twenty-four minutes … Eddie Brennan … rocket … save … Declan Prendergast slipped … Brennan swooped … bang … goal; just before half-time … high ball in … Iggy goes to claim it … James Murray lost his footing … Shefflin in ahead of both… goal number three. The three goals were not Iggy's fault.

Tom Feeney was sitting on the bench and he sums up the awful internal conflict which many inter-county or club players feel when they are part of a team but not on the team. 'To be honest with you, there's a part of you that nearly doesn't want them to win because it means so much to you to be part of Waterford and the idea of winning a championship medal and not being on the team is just horrendous. It's just dire. When you are outside a group, it's a horrible place to be because you are waiting for everybody's look and any chink of light that you might get a chance to get in there.'

Also on the bench was Andy Moloney, who was concerned that Waterford hadn't trained the way Kilkenny had; that Waterford were not hitting each other hard enough in training matches, 'By the time we got to the semi-finals, we had played a lot of great games with superb performances but some didn't perform as well as they could.' He was also surprised that Ken Coogan lorded it in midfield for Kilkenny that day.

At half-time, Kilkenny were leading 3–6 to Waterford's 0–11. Two minutes after sitting down in the dressing room and taking in liquid, Shane was approached by Justin who only said, 'Jack's coming in there.' Shane was obviously gutted but wanted Waterford to win now more than ever, and so he went straight over to Jack and said, 'This is your fucking day, Jack. Go for it.'

Justin said a few words to them all, announced the change and said they were still very much in the game. John Mullane spoke too about what they needed to do to win.

In the second half, Jack Kennedy played an excellent game and scored three points from play.

Waterford had tightened up considerably at the back and out-scored Kilkenny seven points to six in the half. But they needed a goal which never came. At one stage, James McGarry, Kilkenny's goalkeeper, stood his ground when Eoin Kelly blasted a shot which hit him on the shoulder, rebounded onto the crossbar and away from the net. The Kilkenny defence was stoic, even though Paul Flynn gave another performance of his life scoring thirteen points and earning the man of the match accolade. But it wasn't enough and the Cats won: 3–12 to 0–18. There was only one score in it at the end but Kilkenny's winning mentality prevailed.

Soon-to-be president of the GAA, Nickey Brennan of Kilkenny believes a lack of leadership and not enough balance in various parts of the Waterford team contributed to them not winning.

Another semi-final defeat and heartbreak yet again. The Waterford dressing room was a scene of devastation, players wiped out. Players such as Eoin Murphy and Ken McGrath came over to Shane O'Sullivan and, with few words and small actions, made him feel better. He couldn't feel any worse but he knew he'd be back. For Iggy O'Regan, the quietness and sadness in that room was something he'll never forget.

After the match, with the ATR 72 still at Dublin airport and paid for, they got the coach back out to the hotel, had a meal and boarded the plane for the twenty-minute flight to Waterford. When it worked, it was perfect.

The few drinks that evening dulled the pain of defeat.

Kilkenny got to meet Cork in the final, and the Cork team that

Waterford had beaten in the Munster final went out and won the All-Ireland. That hurt Waterford players even more than the loss to Kilkenny. In fact, in all the semi-finals in which Waterford were beaten, their victors didn't go on to win the title.

'We were all best of buddies in the dressing room,' says Stephen Brenner, 'and we'd have right craic. But we weren't like Cork in that they were having separate team meetings [to sort out issues]. We were miles behind them. We didn't have that winning mentality; Cork though would do anything to win.'

The team, the structure, the team, the plan (and sticking to it) and the team was everything to Cork. They had gone on strike in 2002 and the result was All-Ireland medals in 2004. Waterford had three All Stars in 2004 (Ken McGrath, Dan Shanahan and Paul Flynn) but no All-Ireland medal.

A team reflects its manager. Justin was stylish and enigmatic but had apparent failings and so had his team.

It made for another very long winter indeed.

10

2005–2006 – THE WANDER YEARS

Twelve days in Cape Town in January 2005 was the players' reward for the endeavours of the previous year and they had a marvellous time on the men-only holiday. Most of the trip had been organised by Sean Power who had been asked to get involved in the Finance Committee to help raise money for holidays for the players because it was felt they deserved a big holiday and the other teams were doing the same thing.

Along with Tom Murphy, Liam Cusask, Tom McCarthy, Karen Dempsey and others, they set about organising race and dog nights and a corporate night raised €73,000, money which the county board could not have come up with.

Discarding suggestions of going to Seattle, Sean advised Cape Town, as he'd been there before and knew the players would love the tours and activities, such as rafting and golf. They picked the Cullinan Hotel (the Kilkenny hurlers had been there previously) and said the trip would cost €1,200 per person. Between players, selectors and back-room staff forty-five people were on the list to go. Each player got €500 spending money before they boarded the coach to the airport. The players really appreciated it and, while they wanted to have fun, they knew they had to behaved impeccably. And they did.

In the evenings, they had good food and cold beers. Sean stayed

up with them until 4 a.m. most nights, even though he doesn't drink, he enjoyed the lads' company.

One day by the pool, Jim Dee was telling the lads about the fabulous digital camera he had. They didn't know it was in his shorts' pocket, along with his wallet and phone, when Shane O'Sullivan pushed him in.

They also didn't know he couldn't swim!

Even though the pool wasn't very deep, Jim started splashing around, shouting for help, which is when the others realised he was in trouble. Like Mitch out of *Baywatch*, Eoin McGrath jumped in and saved him, with Shane and the others helping him out. Jim's language was choice.

Lying back on the sunbed, Andy Moloney said in his Tipperary accent, 'Jaysus, them young fellas. They're terrible! How could you do that?' Shane apologised and ran to get Jim a big sandwich and a drink to make it up to him.

After trips to Robben Island and Table Mountain, one night they went to an open air resort outside of Cape Town called Le Med. There were people from more than a dozen countries there but the Waterford hurlers sang better than any of them.

On the Sunday morning, Dan was arriving back in the hotel around 7 a.m. after a great night out with the lads. Justin and Seamie Hannon were heading out to mass when they saw Dan on the other side of the lobby, heading upstairs. Thinking Dan had been out for a jog, Justin turned to Seamie and said, 'Jesus, Dan is doing well. He's focused.'

After the holiday, hard training was needed if the players were going to go one better than 2004.

Having coached Irish basketball teams, Gerry Fitzpatrick was used to dealing with pros where 'it's business' and he tried to instil a similar discipline in the Waterford set up.

'In hurling or football, why do you enter the All-Ireland?' he asks. 'To win it, not to have fun or to come second. You might enter it knowing it's difficult to win it this year, but it's a progression to winning it in four years time; to start putting the pieces in place like the fitness and accumulate that over three, four or five years until you are in a position to win it. So you enter an All-Ireland to win it either now or in the near future. And that's just business and unless you win it, you haven't got the job finished.'

Each player got a personalised worksheet at the beginning of each season, in which they were to log all their training sessions, their resting heart rate in the morning, the number of hours sleep, their diet and how hard each training session is.

Well, that was the theory.

'Some of them maybe did it religiously, some of them did it for a while, some of them probably never even used them,' says Gerry.

The 'game evaluation sheets' in particular where each player was to write down how they had played in a game and what they needed to improve on should, in theory, have been a launching pad to an even better season, but in Waterford's case they weren't.

'It depends on how much the management want to get into it,' believes Gerry. 'The big difficulty across all the inter-county teams is that they are all trying to be professional without having the time. If you are a pro, you come to work every morning and you don't go home until the work is done and that is six days a week. In the GAA, you are coming to work for an hour and a half twice a week and the rest of it has to be done by text messages and phone calls and a lot of this stuff you try to do but it can't get done at that professional level because you are not in work every day and that's a big stumbling block I think, especially for teams who are trying to catch up, catching up with Kilkenny, catching up with Tipperary.'

So up-and-coming teams like Waterford or Galway were not going to win an All-Ireland by doing less than Kilkenny or Cork. And even the same amount of work would not be enough because Kilkenny were starting from a higher plateau. But having

had the (relative) success of 2004, some Waterford players started even doing less. Progress was stalled.

In 2005 and 2006, Waterford lost too many league games, and these losses invaded the culture and psyche of the team. When they tried really hard to win the league, as they had in 2004 they had a good championship.

So what was going wrong? Why weren't Waterford making the breakthrough?

'Justin always believed in us as a bunch of players that could be great,' says Tom Feeney, 'but there was no consistency in his training. He could be ruthless one year but the next year, he could tone it down, and then following year up again. The years he was ruthless were when Waterford progressed but there were many years we slipped under his management.'

After being dropped in 2004, Tom became obsessive in his drive to reclaim his place. He did yoga, 6 a.m. weight sessions, stuck to the dietician rules of chicken, rice and broccoli and did what no other player did (though many of them should have done it), he started seeing the Olympic team sports psychologist Niamh Fitzpatrick in Dublin once a fortnight. 'A lot of what we discussed was about team dynamic. When your head is in a pile of shit, you need someone to unravel it and you say, "You know what, Feeney, you'll be okay, you're not dead, you're only thirty-one, you can come back and play for Waterford again." But nobody was telling me that. Ken McGrath has probably gone through that as well. Is it a failure of management? Look at Liam Griffin of Wexford; he had players who believed in him and he believed in them and they won in 1996.'

The former Wexford manager credits Justin with getting Munster success but says that with Waterford not having settled on a full-back, and the goalkeeper situation fluid, progress was going to be difficult.

'There are four ingredients for further success,' says Liam, 'physical fitness, technical ability, mental capacity and tactical awareness. If

Waterford didn't have all these, then individual players can become mentally frail in big games.' And when other counties were using sports psychologists, Waterford weren't.

But selector Nicky Cashin thinks Justin was fantastic.

'He was a great man for working behind the scenes and giving lads confidence. He took lads like Brick Walsh, a footballer, and made him a great hurler. He developed Dan's skills. And you have to remember the lean years we were coming from. Waterford were now competitive. Also in 2005 and 2006, teams got to know how to play against us; they tried to isolate our danger men; so we had to juggle round players and positions.'

But not enough players were making the necessary sacrifices to their private lives to show they were leaders on and off the field.

The team dynamic was constantly fluctuating. Training one day in March 2005, John Mullane got the ball and even though Tom Feeney wasn't too slow, Mullane whizzed past. 'Come on, Feeney! Try and catch me!' he shouted back.

'I completely believe in earning respect and sometimes that has to be earned by the sword,' says Tom. 'So I caught him and wore the hurley off his chest. He asked me what the fuck I had done that for and I told him not to ever say that to me again. We started hauling out of each other. John texted me that night, saying, "Fair play 2 ya."'

Another reason was that it was very hard for all the Waterford forwards to hit form on the same day.

Selector Seamie Hannon claims he saw it in training and at matches. 'Shanahan, Mullane, Kelly, Flynn – a lot are the same mould – lovely fellas but they could never get serious enough together about the game. To get everyone to go that extra mile and get them all on that frame of mind was very difficult. The hurling was there, the management was there, everything was there, but to gel it together? As Justin often said, "Family life, work life, everything has to be put on hold", but you couldn't get them all to do that at the same time.

'It was blatant when you went away on the eve of a match. It was a nightmare, so bad. We'd even try to go to places such as Antrim on the day of a match instead of the night before. It wasn't drink, we just couldn't settle them, they were all over the fucking shop. Some fellas couldn't sleep. Other lads would be snoring two rooms away and lads would say they couldn't sleep. Some others were easily sidetracked. What used kill me altogether was in Croke Park after a match and win lose or draw, it was the same – players would fucking have serious problems with bottles. They'd bang as many as they could into their pockets, coats, caps and onto the bus or train. Then trying to get that out of their system going forward again; I couldn't see any other team doing it.'

In this period, Justin and his selectors believe they devoted an inordinate amount of time to player matters off the field. In the space of a few years, players had gone from being not very well known to being gods in the eyes of some. The selectors had long meetings amongst themselves trying to unravel the complex processes at work in the minds of some players. At one such meeting, a high-profile player rang, telling Justin he hadn't been able to sleep. Justin advised him to keep the window open and mentioned other ways of relaxing and, a few days later, the player had settled.

A special 'leadership programme' was introduced for the players about how to manage success, what makes a good leader, etc. But it didn't get through to them all.

Selectors were also trying to stop stories getting to the papers, particularly the tabloids, as well trying to manage financial demands – some players were being offered up to €700 for newspaper interviews through endorsements and deals with sponsorship companies. Trying to control and manage all that with a small panel of players involved Justin and his selectors putting a huge amount of time into the job.

A number of times Justin, talking about the players, has said to confidantes around the squad, 'It's not what I do here, it's what I have to endure.'

Seamie believes Justin had the players' interests at heart, but that they didn't see it that way.

'He got jobs and cars for them and when Mullane got into trouble, he spent a day in a hotel waiting to be called as a character witness. He was never called but he did an awful lot for them,' says Seamie, adding that it galled him that, in his view, the players didn't see how much Justin tried to help them.

John Mullane had been in trouble when he was alleged to have assaulted a man in a pub in Waterford on St Stephen's Day in 2002. The man subsequently withdrew the complaint but the case was mentioned in court a number of times before being eventually dropped. In a newspaper article in April 2010, Mullane spoke generally about his life in the past saying the birth of his daughter in 2006 was an important milestone. 'That probably was the turning point in my career. You're not only thinking of yourself. You've got someone else to look after and that affects everything you want to do. I've had to grow up fast through the course of my career,' he said in an interview with the *Irish Mail on Sunday*.

The attitude of some players being 'as mad as march hares' that needed taming fed into Justin seeing himself as a father figure, a benevolent despot. He used to say that Waterford had more of a problem getting over winning than losing. His favourite phrase if players were going out drinking was for them to 'keep it tidy'.

'Some hope with our lads,' says one of the players.

As a non-drinker himself and a Pioneer, people might have thought that Justin would ensure that he knew what the players were doing but that wasn't the case. 'No,' says one player. 'He didn't even set up a system of spies. He didn't even realise some lads would be drinking when they shouldn't have been.'

The pressure that high profile inter-county stars face cannot be overstated. Big Dan said he experienced a lot of awful comments from so-called fans in Dungarvan and west Waterford.

Eoin Kelly says he went from the age of sixteen to twenty-four flat out playing hurling, with literally no break and feels in a way he missed out on his teenage years. Burn out was always a possibility. 'I felt I had enough of the game; that life had passed me by. I was literally packing the thing in; I hadn't had a break and I had had enough of it. You couldn't go down to the local pub for a pint because everyone was talking about you. It was gone fucking ridiculous. You play hurling, you play hurling; but my time is my time. I never did anything wrong.'

Having missed friends' twenty-first birthday parties because of his commitment to hurling, he needed to look again at what life was all about. And he says the same happened to players from every other county who feel they've missed their teenage years. 'The way it's gone is you have to be single, not drink, not like socialising, to be like a robot,' he says.

Kelly had a highly publicised break-up with his Mount Sion club and he joined Passage, where he was living with his girlfriend, Sharon. He'd given his life to Mount Sion and played in six under-21 finals (he was so good he got on the panel at the age of fifteen) and now he was moving to a new life and new start in Crooke. He and Mullane became the GPA reps on the Waterford panel for 2005 and 2006.

The relationship between alcohol and the GAA (and most sports) is a difficult one, and the use of players to promote beer is one of the best advertising methods for drinks companies. The inducements can be very tempting, with one drinks company offering certain players more than €6,000 for a one-day photo-shoot. And then there was the problem of some players drinking while the championship season was on.

'I confronted players about it several times,' says Seamie. 'I don't drink, maybe take an odd one but that's nothing to do with it. You'd wonder the mentality of some lads, if they gave it a real belt what they could have won, but they were so easily side-tracked, and Justin sussed that out from the start, he wouldn't allow them to talk to the press or radio. Maybe he sheltered them too much but we couldn't ever slip up because we had no reserve to fall back on, we were paper thin.'

Roger Casey says he could see a division between some players and management, 'Justin mollycoddled some players and a lot of them got away with murder.'

To be at the top physically and psychologically, some players have to not drink for nine months of the year. The drinking problem can be, and has been, overstated but it was a symptom of the squad–management dynamic that patently wasn't working as well as it could have. Management felt some players were not as fit as they should have been and even got a private physical trainer to call at the house of one player who wasn't drinking and take him for personalised sessions. 'He did it for a while but then stopped,' says one of the back-room staff.

Dr Tom Higgins, though, says he wouldn't be too strong on the drink aspect. 'The rugby lads go and have a drink and in GAA circles, alcohol is part and parcel of life. Life is all about choices, if you say no alcohol, you have to stick to it. Declan Kidney doesn't tell his players not to drink and they are all mature successful individuals, lots of whom have gone to college and have degrees. Maybe rugby is a different scenario from GAA, a lot of rugby guys are very successful in their own lives anyway, so maybe they have a certain amount of in-built discipline; there's possibly a different milieu in the GAA. There's nothing wrong with having a few pints after killing yourself in a match. If you make a monk out of a guy for six or nine months – that's not good for them mentally because what happens is they break the curfew and they go mad when they break it.'

Gerry Fitzpatrick remarks about how discipline is handled in professional situations, such as basketball where a player can be given a $5,000 fine if his shirt isn't inside his shorts at training.

'If your body fat goes above 12 per cent it's a $10,000 fine; that's how it works at the professional level,' says Gerry. 'You can't do that in the GAA, so you have no sanction other than if a great player goes on the beer and you want to embarrass him publicly by dropping him and then it's in the media and affecting his family, you could do that but what manager wants to do that? So your alternative is say, "Oh, he's pulled a hamstring", and not play him but now you are hurting a team because they don't have one of the best players.

'Sure there were guys in Waterford who went on the beer when they shouldn't have, but I think the same thing happens in every single GAA team in the country because you have no sanction in an amateur sport.' Everyone was supposed to be on Gerry Fitzpatrick's 'programmes' but some players weren't and were still being selected.

'If a player doesn't do them and still gets selected, then why should he do them?' asks Gerry. 'In 2005 and 2006, there were guys that didn't train as hard as they should have, but still got to play. And others who trained ultra hard, like the Denis Coffeys of the world, who didn't get to play or get enough of an opportunity to play. I suppose one of my overriding things about this particular team and the reason that I stayed with them for six years was that they were actually a team that wanted to train harder than they were very often being encouraged or allowed to.'

'In a way, we didn't have a big enough squad,' says Iggy O'Regan, citing the problem facing many counties with limited talent – a big gap between the 'stars' and how they are treated and the 'soldiers'. And stars are stars because they are very good players; but have they everything that's needed to lead the others to an All-Ireland?'

In these two years, Tom Feeney says that in training for key matches, some players did not keep it simple. 'To just go to training, train, shut the fuck up, and come back the next night. Some were maybe too mollycoddled and there's no doubt there were some egos. A lot of these guys are nice guys and I have a lot of respect for them but in key matches, key mistakes were made.

And beer was an issue for some players where maybe Sunday, Monday or Tuesday, codes were broken. We knew about it. You really miss a few bottles, you crave it, you can convince yourself, "Jesus I'm training hard, I'll be grand", and you can always find places that nobody knows.'

At the time, the Cork players were living the life needed to get to the top. They had won the All-Ireland in 2004 and 2005 and, in November 2005 (the day George Best was buried), Donal O'Grady gave a talk to hurling coaches at a conference in Dublin City University. He started by asking who in the audience was from which county and when Waterford was mentioned and nobody put up their hand, he said, 'O, ye know it all down there!'

The comment was slightly in jest but it had a ring of truth as he went on to talk about the importance of tactics for Cork in their victories: retaining possession, running at the defence, hitting diagonal balls like bullets chest height to team-mates – in effect having what he defined as the MPO – a maximum positional opportunity. He also spoke about 'adrenaline enhancing and not drowning the thought processes', such as those crucial moments near the end of tight games and the months and months of hard work needed to allow such moments to occur. This was a revolution in hurling thought.

Back in Waterford, Pat Flynn (no relation to Paul Flynn) the new county chairman, could see that Justin had his own ways and methods of doing things. 'He did his own thing,' says Pat. 'He didn't look for advice, not that I'm aware of, nor was he open to taking advice. He preferred to do it himself.'

But Justin knew the squad needed freshening up. He often held trials, and Seamie says, if anything, he gave a country lad 'a better hearing than a lad from the city'. This was because the lad from the country would be more raw, Justin would 'put him down as a better prospect, he'd dig for you and graft, more honest – and that's what Justin kept saying he wanted, an honest effort'.

With this in mind, many of the January and February training sessions in 2005 and 2006 were organised for Aglish in deepest west Waterford. With driving wind and howling rain, the players would be told honesty was the cornerstone of success.

But other issues were coming up. Some players on the periphery didn't feel that Justin was involving them enough or connecting with the players. Wayne Hutchinson remembers one particular team talk in the summer of 2005 as typical. 'Justin was going on about the buzz around the town with the Tall Ships and we said we weren't interested in that. Next thing he said, "I've worked on ships. I love ships. I'd love to be here for the weekend to watch the ships coming in, but we have a mission to go up to Thurles and win a Munster championship game." It was just the way he came out with it, it didn't really work.' Though Wayne says he found Justin's drills excellent in their execution.

Some of the younger players on the periphery felt Justin preferred players to go and talk to him but that they felt somewhat intimidated and disinclined to do this. As well as some of the players, Sean Power of the back-room team wasn't getting on with Justin as well as Justin thought. 'His communication skills were shite,' he says. 'I believe you need to have different skills for each player and management is a job which involves huge interpersonal skills. They are amateur players, they are playing for a medal, for club, for county, for their families. Every now and then they need a pat on shoulder.'

One of the things that Justin did around this time was bring in guest speakers to try to inspire the team. On 12 November 2005, after a challenge match against Tipperary in Dungarvan, he got all the players into the Park Hotel where former cycling great Sean Kelly told them that 'one bad cup of coffee in January can take it's toll on you on Alp d'Huez in July'. It was an exaggeration but the players knew he meant that they – stars and subs – needed to be totally professional in their approach if victory was to be theirs. He also spoke about the parade in Croke Park or Thurles before a game, 'Looking at your opposite number such as Seán Óg Ó hAilpín and knowing deep down with honesty that you've done more over the past nine months than him; that you've made more sacrifices; that you'll have that small but ever so significant psychological advantage going into the last five minutes.'

Another guest speaker during the season was Waterford man Neil Gough who had won eight national senior boxing titles. He spoke to the players about routine and not drastically changing your routine the night before a big match. He also showed them a loser's and a winner's medal, saying the loser's one is one you focus on more sometimes because it encourages you to win next time. He also said that he would always have a freezing cold shower the morning of a fight to know it's time.

Liam Griffin told the players the lack of discipline off the pitch would have an effect on it. Whereas John Treacy, speaking in 2006, talked simply about his efforts in the 1984 Olympics; where in the marathon he was thinking about how he didn't want to be defeated as he had been in the 10,000 metres; he refused to give in and ended up winning a marvellous silver medal.

Another problem was that while Cork players were organising player meetings, Waterford weren't – and they needed to be. When Paul Flynn was captain, he organised a few talks amongst players but the Donal Óg/Brian Corcoran/Sean Óg way in Cork of teasing things out so that there would be total unity wasn't being replicated in Waterford.

Players recall that everybody wasn't on the same wavelength, something vital for victory in any situation.

'There were funny situations where at a championship match, lads would be togging out, getting geed up and Justin would be there and he'd be rasping away at the hurleys in the corner. He'd have the rasp in the bag. It was a strange thing to be doing an hour before a championship match. He had funny ways. He was a great hurling coach but not a manager. In training, Justin would take us for some time and was supposed to get us back to Gerry for his workout, but he wouldn't leave us back and then Gerry's programme was scuttled,' says one senior player.

Shane O'Sullivan said Justin's drill work was very good but his man management was very poor. 'It was crap, absolutely dire. If you were playing, Justin would talk to you; if not, he wouldn't. Especially players on the fringes, didn't even say hello to them sometimes.'

Added to the simmering discontent among the players, Gerry Fitzpatrick wasn't being used properly. Here was a man who spoke psychology in layman's terms, who could change mindsets without players even knowing it. He would meet players for a coffee on a Monday morning and have a chat, knowing full well that they had many issues to deal with, from family matters to losing jobs. 'At one stage, Eoin Murphy kind of got burned in a game and we spoke about how we were going to get him quicker,' says Gerry. 'With little time, speed training wouldn't work so we looked at his body fat to knock a few pounds off him. He went on a very strict diet for six weeks.'

As a sales rep, Eoin Murphy did a lot of driving and there were days he'd pull up to a hotel but all they had was creamed potatoes and steak with gravy and stuff. He'd have to get back into the car and drive to another town where he could get a salad. That's some dedication for an amateur.

Doc Higgins, who had seen many managers pass through the gates, says of Justin. 'He mightn't be the most diplomatic, mightn't remember some of the reserves' names, might be self-obsessed, but he's a decent fella.'

Seamie Hannon defends Justin as being a very private man whose number one aim was to put the best Waterford team every time. Nicky Cashin said they were trying to develop a very tight ship and obviously some players weren't going to be happy with that, 'Over the years, I think we slightly overachieved with the players we had considering where we had come from.'

One of the key players whom Justin and Seamie brought onto the panel was Stephen Molumphy from Ballyduff Upper. A captain in the army based in Stephen's Barracks in Kilkenny, Stephen regularly trained up to thirty recruits for sixteen-week periods. He and his four older brothers all played for the club and he doesn't accept the level of criticism directed at Justin.

As for his style of management, Justin feels he's always been very open and he can't see why some players feel differently. He liked helping them get their hurls right, even an hour before a match, but some players got annoyed with this and hid their hurleys from him.

He feels he didn't have favourites in the panel and while him and Seamie Hannon had very few players who were pencilled in on a team sheet automatically, he couldn't afford to drop some key players. 'It was souring some of the older players a bit because we couldn't afford to leave them out for league games,' says Seamie Hannon. 'They were looking for a break from it but Justin was fierce competitive and he wanted to put out best team all the time. We weren't in the privileged position of being able to put out weak teams and concede big defeats in the league.'

Seamie also says he and Justin always worked on tactics, on the puckout, but both had the view a lot of that could be overplayed in that a player still had to win his own ball, get possession first and then options become available. But for many of the players many of the team 'tactics' seemed to be no more than 'hit it long to Big Dan'.

'He had the big hand but then after a while it wasn't happening for him,' recalls Seamie. Maybe that wasn't his fault but there was never a time when everyone clicked at the same time. Maybe if you're expected to play at your top every day, it just doesn't happen.'

But Jack Kennedy disagrees. 'Justin was stubborn, a brilliant coach, but tactically he wasn't good and it was hard to keep going back listening to same thing. Thursday nights before matches, you could be in there for an hour and a half, he'd go through the team, your team, give you a rundown on his ex-hurling days, everything and anything. It wasn't a whole lot of benefit looking back on it. For some team talks, he'd tell Ken McGrath to play Ken McGrath hurling, same with the others, whatever that was supposed to mean. They always talk about Dan drifting in off the wing but it was his own doing, he just wanted to get in there. There were no tactics, it was pretty straight forward – get it and hit it.'

'Justin could be praising some players,' says Feeney, 'but he would have a cut off the rest of us, take slices off us, and when it came to some others, he'd let them off.'

With all this going on, the players developed a cocoon of humour and wit around their endeavours.

One Sunday, when the squad was coming back from a match in Ennis, they stopped in Tipperary town at a shop, each one of them hungry. Many went for Lucozade and crisps. 'It was like coming back from an under-12 match,' recalls one of the players. Richie Foley came out licking a big Magnum while Brian 'Bull' Phelan was eating jelly snakes. Bull remembers the day well as Eoin McGrath had been sent off in the match and Justin wasn't on the bus. The following Tuesday in training, they had a meeting about food and diet and Seamie Hannon brought up the previous Sunday's happenings. The players knew it was coming. Seamie spoke about Cork players after matches drinking milk and eating steaks and potatoes and how 'our lads are eating jelly snakes and ice cream'.

Everyone looked over at Bull Phelan and the jelly snake story was born!

As a player, Brian Phelan had always been dedicated to the Waterford cause but had a phrase he said regularly, 'My head is wrecked' – even when there was nothing wrong with him.

One week before a championship game, he was flying in training. 'How are you feeling?' Justin asked.

'Ah my head is wrecked,' responded Bull.

It was later said to Bull that the phrase was one of the reasons Justin didn't play him more in his time at Waterford.

Also at this time, hurlers and officials all over the country were having a row about balls.

There are two types of sliotars in use by inter-county teams: those made by Cummins and those made by O'Neills, which are slightly heavier and whose rims get a bit thicker if it's wet. The issue was raised at Croke Park headquarters and at county board meetings across the country; nobody could decide which was best.

In the league campaign of 2006, Waterford were due to play Cork in Páirc Uí Rinn.

Donal Óg Cusask and Cork mainly used Cummins balls while Waterford have been training with O'Neills. Justin sent Roger Casey down to the goal with a bag of the O'Neills balls for the umpires to give to Cusack when he's pucking out the ball. But they wouldn't take them and they called the ref who moved Roger away.

'Sure what would ye know about good balls in Waterford?' said Cusack, as Roger was walking away. Roger told him 'politely' to mind his own business!

Seamus Prendergast got sent off but Waterford upped their game and with five minutes to go, Paul Flynn buried a goal past Cusack. Waterford won and, after the game, Flynn winked at Roger, who had an O'Neills ball in his hand.

'Here, Cusack,' he shouted over at Donal Óg, showing him the ball. 'You'd want to practise a bit with this!'

Donal Óg looked at him and walked away dejected.

Roger liked to mix up the Cummins and O'Neills balls, especially when they were playing Cork or Clare.

In the summer of 2005, Waterford played their Munster semi-final against Cork and Justin tried Eoin Kelly in midfield. He scored six great points from midfield but with Brian Corcoran scoring a goal in the second half and Niall McCarthy scoring some good points for the Rebels, Cork went on to win by two points:

Cork 2–17, Waterford 2–15.

After dancing through the back-door games, Waterford again met Cork, this time in the All-Ireland quarter-final, but another excellent goal from Corcoran ended their hopes with Cork winning 1–18 to Waterford's 1–13.

'The games are some experience to play in,' Waterford's James Murray will later tell Kieran Shannon, 'because the atmosphere is always brilliant. I can't ever remember it getting really niggly. It's all about the ball and that's when you get the best of the games. I've never seen any negative elements to it off the pitch either.'

Manager of that 2005 Cork team that went on to win the All-Ireland was John Allen. 'I think that Waterford's target was winning Munster and they weren't focused enough on the All-Ireland. History and tradition were a huge burden for them, but we never thought we were going to lose. I got on great with the Waterford lads when we went to Singapore for the 2005 All Star trip (he made John Mullane captain of his team) but I could not believe they were still looking for basic stuff from the county board, such as enough proper sliotars and the like. I suppose our players had benefited from the strike a few years earlier.'

In January 2006, Justin brought an eighteen-year-old Manchester Utd fan onto the panel. Kevin Moran had played his soccer with Bohemians in Waterford city and has such a good left peg on him that he got trials with Newcastle (seven times), Celtic, Middlesbrough and Blackburn. Aged sixteen, he got a six-week stint at Newcastle and was offered a three-year contract. But he would have had to leave school and, in the end, didn't take it. Hurling and the Harty Cup with De La Salle took over and the boy who could have been playing professional football in England was on the Waterford panel. His experience with the soccer clubs, though, meant he didn't get fazed by big-match occasions.

One of the players who was coming on massively was Michael 'Brick' Walsh, who was captain of the WIT team (and would very soon be captain of Waterford). The players respected his intelligence and his ability to handle things well. He also had a sixth sense and knew when lads were pissed off – he also understood Justin to a tee. The younger players in particular saw him as being top class with everything, and his discipline and hard work were something they strove to match.

In March 2006, the players were taken on a weekend trip to the Curragh army camp, when they went commando training under the auspices of the ruthless Rangers.

'It was horrendous,' says Tom Feeney. 'Just when you thought you were dead you had to get up and go again. On the Saturday, we went from 6 a.m. till 11 p.m., it was crazy army stuff, with players thinking, What the fuck is this shite about? There was lots of orienteering, up into hills, fields, running through water up to your chest. There was pain everywhere. I was sharing with a player and at 6.00 a.m. the next morning, he just didn't want to get up.'

Stephen Molumphy also remembers the incident. 'We were all lined up outside and could see someone peering out from behind the curtains. The soldier went in and got him and pulled him out.'

The torture continued. The same weekend, former Irish Olympic boxer Michael Carruth met them and gave them what Justin hoped would be an inspirational talk.

After all the extra preparation though, the 2006 season didn't go much better for Waterford. They were badly beaten by Tipperary in the Munster championship and had to go the back-door route. However, they knuckled down and beat Galway in a thriller and then beat Tipperary and were back in the All-Ireland quarter-final against Cork.

One of the things that had really impressed twenty-two-year-old Stephen Molumphy, the new kid on the block, was that on the bus journeys to some of the matches, Justin walked down the bus and gave out hand written 'cue' cards to each player, with individual instructions or points. Each had reminders or directions to the players, such as 'Follow up on goal', 'Breaking balls',

'Make run on goal whenever you can' and 'Support your wing-
forward'.

Stephen was settling quickly into the team and was good friends
with Aiden 'Ringo' Kearney, who all agree is a great singer,
especially of Westlife songs and a really nice, genuine guy. Ringo's
nickname comes from side locks he had in his school-going days
when someone thought he looked like Ringo Starr. He found
everyone on the panel brilliant to be with and thought they all had
great personalities.

Cork organised a meeting of their players before the game as
Donal Óg was concerned they wouldn't beat Waterford. They
showed the players the last five minutes of the 2004 final, to stir the
fire within, as they knew Waterford were one of only two teams in
the country who really believed they were better than Cork.

Brian Corcoran told the others it sickened him to relive that
again. He told his team-mates about 'deserving victory' in that
Waterford felt they deserved to win because they hadn't won an
All-Ireland, or that they were better than Cork. 'The reality is,
they have had plenty of chances and haven't taken them,' he said in
his autobiography.

He reminded them of the quarter-final in 2005 with ten minutes
to go, when Tony Browne won a free and jumped up and clenched
his fist, turned and roared at Corcoran, 'You can fuck off back to
Cork, Corcoran. We have ye today.' But Corcoran scored a goal
a few minutes later and, as he was running out, Tony was bent
over with head in hands. 'I want to see him like that again on
Sunday week.'

The week of the match, all the Cork subs were as focused as the
first fifteen and Cork saw themselves as being more of a team than
Waterford, who they felt were more a grouping of individuals.
John Carey, 'performance coach' for the team, had put up photos
and slogans in the dressing room, one of Justin McCarthy
embracing Tony Browne after the win against Tipperary, with the
newspaper headline: 'Bring On Da Rebels!'

He also put up two lists.

'Our World: Winning, Discipline, Professionalism, Team spirit, Unity, Positivity, Performance, Taking responsibility, Setting standards.'

'Their World: Losing, Fighting, Blaming others, Playing for oneself not the team, Relying on luck, Bringing down others to their level.'

Brian Corcoran asked, 'Which world do you want to live in? Now is the time to fight for it.'

Waterford were training hard but the little things still popped up every now and then. Even though club rivalry was now nearly always left outside the gate, one evening a Mount Sion player said something to a Ballygunner player, forcing Dan Shanahan to turn around and say, 'Leave that shit at home.'

Waterford had gone to the Clontarf Castle Hotel for their pre-match puck around and the big statue of Brian Ború looked out on them as they prepared for this massive game. On the morning of the match before they left for Croke Park, Tony Browne's neck muscles went into spasm and seized up. Selector Kevin Ryan phoned John Dineen, who over the years had treated a lot of the players at his chiropractic clinic in Waterford. John was in his parent's house in Macroom when Kevin rang at 11.00 a.m. Tony needed an adjustment to his neck or he mightn't be able to play. There was nobody there who knew how to treat him. It was agreed John would fly up. He drove to Cork airport for a noon flight but couldn't get one and had no option but to drive. Would his recently purchased vintage 1978 Merc 350 make it? It did, and two garda motorcyclists met him at the Brown Barn on the Naas Road. With sirens blaring, they screeched into Croke Park at 3.15 p.m. just before the lads went out. Tony hadn't known John would make it. 'Sorry for doing this to you, for getting you to come up,' said Tony, as John clicked his neck back into place, giving instant pain relief. Tony would later say his getting an All Star Award that year would not have happened if the old Merc hadn't made it.

As Hill 16 filled up, die-hard Waterford supporter Jamie Fenton had brought an Italian friend of his and a Sunderland supporter to the game. Two Canadians asked him what exactly was going on (they had seen the crowds and decided to have a look to see what all the fuss was about). Jamie told them, 'Rule 1 – above the bar – one point; rule 2 – below the bar, goal, which is three points; and rule 3 – We Hate Cork.' The Deise fans around cheered mightily.

The following year, the same Jamie will do serious damage to his ankle when he fell after jumping on the terrace, celebrating a goal by Big Dan against Cork. This forced him to be stretchered off to rounds of applause from his county comrades, with shouts of, 'Fair play, boy, you took one for the team.' Then, as he left Nenagh hospital, his leg in plaster and sat in a wheelchair with his jersey on him, he is told by an auld fella from Tipp, 'Oh Jaysus, boy, you played a great game out there today, boy.'

The pitch was wet and slippy. Donal Óg made sure the lad behind the goals only gave him the Cummins sliotars. He also got the young lad to go up and get the Cummins sliotars after half-time for the other end – and he gave him his jersey afterwards.

It was 0-8 apiece at half-time. Cork knew they had a battle on their hands but had scored seven points from play to Waterford's three.

In the second half, Waterford went four points up but couldn't get away from Cork, whose Timmy McCarthy beat three defenders and found the net. Then, they brought on Cathal Naughton and he got a point and then a goal. Shortly after Ken McGrath slid into Joe Deane who put the resulting free over the bar. Waterford were a point down. Tony Browne was fouled and there was a free to Ken McGrath ninety yards out.

'I remember thinking it was a bit far out,' says Ken, 'and I was trying to get an extra metre or two. It was raining at the time and it was the last puck in the game. The noise was unbelievable before I hit it, and I hit it as hard as I could. I caught it right in the middle … It was a fair bit out, behind the other sixty-five.'

Dave Bennett, who was not playing because of an injury, was standing behind the goal. He saw the ball coming in and was sure it was going over – and it was, by around two feet.

Ken looked at it and he was sure it's going over.

But, unbelievably, Donal Óg jumped high and extended his hurley the full length but still held on to it with both hands to maintain strength. He knew what he had to do. He somehow got to the sliotar and amazingly hit it at the same time with such force that it went out to the side and away from the crowd of players. Brian Corcoran got it and held on to it and then the final whistle was blown. John Mullane was on his knees, staring at the ground.

Cork had won by inches. The margin between winning and losing is so tight those 'inches' many believe are gained by what is done off the pitch as much as on. Brian Corcoran praised Ken McGrath as someone who always gave his all, saying that all the games had been battles, epics, with hardly any messing, 'The odd time they win, most of the time, we win.'

'The greatness of Cusack beat us that day,' says Dave Bennett. 'He never got the credit he deserved for it, it was an incredible save. It just shows you the confidence he has, not alone did he save it, he got it away from the danger area; to get a greasy ball that far away was amazing.'

Ken McGrath admits it was a very brave thing that Donal Óg did, 'It could have gone over but he had brilliant skill to stop it; he was very brave. Sure what can you do? I couldn't have hit it any better but that was another big chance gone again. Jesus we couldn't talk for a week after it.'

The 'celebrity' status of the team really developed in 2005 and 2006, but the years ended with no silverware, no progress, some joy but no satisfaction. Justin knew questions were being asked and he would launch into the next season with renewed vigour.

11

2007

The roars from the dressing room were like something out of *Braveheart*. Lads were screaming for mercy but none was being shown.

It was January 2007 and the dreaded ice-bath time!

Roger Casey was dispatched to Dunmore East before training started in Walsh Park to collect several large bags of ice from the fisherman's ice supply on the pier. This type of ice lasts longer because the salt in it has a lower freezing point than water and that makes it colder than ordinary ice. Back in the dressing room, he poured it into the two large plasterer's cement tubs they'd been given. It was to be some players' purgatory.

The dressing rooms were cold and when training was finished, water was added to the baths and physio Peter Kirwan called out which pair was going first – three and a half minutes in the tub, out for a quick hot shower and back in the bath for another three minutes before showering and changing. The formula was to stop the build up of lactic acid in the muscles, which can lead to injuries.

Some players loved the pain and the shock of the ice, with Tony Browne, Eoin Murphy and Tom Feeney jumping in straight away when they were called, revelling in it. It took Peter a while then to find Paul Flynn and Dave Bennett who were trying to hide.

When they dipped their toes in the water, they shuddered and called out to God.

Going to and from training or being in a happy dressing room becomes a home from home for many players in all sports. It's a sanctuary, where slagging is an antidote to depression.

For years, Ken and Eoin McGrath and Tony Browne had been travelling together if training was in west Waterford. Eoin normally drove with Tony in the back.

'It's the best craic you'll ever have after a hard day's work or whatever,' says Ken McGrath, who doesn't have any superstitions. 'As long as I remember to take me teeth out!' he laughs. 'I forget that sometimes and Dan would be the same and we'd be roaring laughing. The craic in the dressing room is what it's all about. You train hard and then the craic starts again. When you miss a lot of training with injuries, you feel there's something missing.'

The craic also extended to the team holidays, such as the time they went on a short break in New York. The Waterford Association in New York regularly holds $75-a-plate dinners with 300 guests to raise money and show the loyalty Waterford supporters around the world have for their native county.

In the hotel, Justin's bedroom was beside one to which, one night, six players retired in their T-shirts and shorts at 3 a.m. after a good night out. As they downed some more beer, they turned on one of the exclusive pay-per-view channels and one of the jokers started to do a Micheal Ó Muircheartaigh commentary on what was happening in the movie.

'Quiet, lads. Justin is next door!' shushed one of the lads.

'Dustin? Dustin's next door?! Fuck Dustin!' shouted another, in reference to Dustin the Turkey.

Next thing, there was a knock on the door and Justin was standing there. He walked in and saw what was on the television. The lads couldn't help themselves and started to laugh uncontrollably. One of them even fell off the bed, he was laughing so much.

'I'm very disappointed in ye, lads,' Justin said, through the howls of laughter. And pointing at the player on the floor who could hardly breathe, he said, 'And especially you. Fierce disappointed.'

Another night, they all went to a nightclub and New York-based businessman and avid Waterford supporter Philly Hennebry (originally from Portlaw) gave Sean Power a $1,000 and told him to take the lads out for a drink. Justin was invited, but Sean had received instructions to take him home early.

Justin said to Sean that evening, 'What are you doing?'

'I'm buying a few drinks for the lads.'

'There's no need for that,' said Justin.

'Sure they have no match next Sunday,' Sean replied.

Sean and Justin were born the same year, 1945, but Sean thought Justin didn't seem to understand the purpose of the few days away.

Back at training in Waterford that January, the moments of light relief continued. One evening after a hard session in Carraigbeg near Carrick-on-Suir, Brian 'Bull' Phelan was wicked thirsty. On the couch, Tony Browne was getting a rub from Peter Kirwan and his colleague Emmet, who had forgotten his container and had put the almond oil temporarily into one of the drinks containers. Bull came flying into the room, grabbed the container and before the boys could tell him to stop, he took a big mouthful. The disgusting oil was sprayed against the wall as the cursing and laughing began.

From the time they could walk and hold hurleys, Dave Bennett and Dan Shanahan had been great friends. They learned their trade in 'Dick's Leagues' in school. Even as a young lad, Dan's strength had been his hand, a great finisher, a great target man. And in the dressing room, close bonds of friendship were formed between him and Paul Flynn, Dave Bennett, Tom Feeney, Tony Browne, Eoin Kelly and John Mullane.

As the new physio for the team, the commitment Peter Kirwan had to give was unforgiving. He had to be at training an hour before the official start time to give lads rubs and, most evenings, was there an hour afterwards. His wife Freda and young children Ciaran, Roisin and Niamh wouldn't see much of him that year.

Having worked with the Irish Compromise Rules team and many others, Peter knew how much players sacrificed for the love of the game. And what commitment was required from their families, wives and girlfriends. He was very impressed with the work Big Dan was doing. Not only was he a pleasure to work with, but Dan was doing heaps of gym work outside of the normal training. And it was improving his speed and turning in practice matches enormously. And the fans loved him. Other players who were new to the panel, such as Aiden 'Ringo' Kearney and Stephen Molumphy, were also progressing nicely.

Former Waterford women's football team manager Michael Ryan had come on board as a selector. Most training sessions in early 2007 were in Aglish, where, in January, new boots were arranged for each player (the biggest, size twelve, being for Big Dan).

Waterford made a real go at winning the league and beat Tipperary in the quarter-final by just one point, it was the first time Stephen Molumphy got a run. In the semi-final against Cork, he got fifty-five minutes. Before the match, the team did their normal Thurles routine, having tea and sandwiches in St Patrick's College on Cathedral Street in the town (at a cost of €175) and a puck around. Running a county team is expensive business, with each training night costing an average of €2,000 when mileage, food, sundries, everything is included. For example, sometimes food for forty in the Ramada would come to €800.

Waterford beat Cork and, next, were playing in the National League final against Kilkenny in Thurles.

In the dressing room, a player who only spoke on those rare occasions when it was necessary, decided this was one of those times.

Eoin Murphy spoke loud, and true for them all, when said he'd been playing Kilkenny for years and was fed up losing to them. He implored every player to fight for every single ball. The players had a belief in themselves that they hadn't had since 2004. And

Justin had broken with tradition and given the captaincy to a player
not from the county champions – his trusted lieutenant Michael
'Brick' Walsh. Players also got analysis of their own game on
DVDs. Justin's central message remained the same: 'Work, work,
work and keep it handy, keep it tidy.'

Ken McGrath was feeling confident even if Kilkenny were the
benchmark team. Ken knew and respected the Kilkenny players
and when he looked across the Suir at the Black and Amber
county, he thought of how hurling was everything for them over
there. And they had the ability to win the big games, something
Waterford couldn't do. He looked on Kilkenny as the Manchester
Utd of hurling – they had medals hanging out of their pockets, but
you couldn't give up trying to beat them. He knew hurling and
winning had been bred into the Kilkenny psyche for the past
seventy years.

In a pulsating match, Waterford played brilliantly. The 'diamond
formation' worked for them and all their big players had a big
game. Eoin Kelly was deployed at centre-forward – he was a
'happening player' and this time was no different, he made things
happen with aplomb. Ken McGrath at half-back and Brick Walsh
in midfield also hurled magnificently, Kilkenny were harried and
hassled all through.

Henry Shefflin got a chance to equalise from a free near to the
end of the match but missed, and later said the ball – a Cummins
one – had something to do with it.

In the end, the Waterford players kept their heads and didn't
fold. They'd won. Beaten Kilkenny and won the National League
title for the first time since 1963. Kilkenny – the All-Ireland
champions – had been defeated!

The fans poured onto the pitch. Players got ferocious slaps on the
back. Stephen Molumphy, who'd played the full match, looked up
to the stand and saw supporters dancing. His entire family was
there, his mother was crying with joy and his brothers were thrilled.

After the match, when they were celebrating, Eoin Murphy

went to Molumphy and Ringo. 'Fair play to ye, lads. Ye were brilliant,' he said. 'Ye are only on the panel a couple of months and ye've adapted and fitted in brilliantly, ye're flying it. And now ye have a league title! What are ye thinking when ye're going out to play because it seems to be working for ye?'

The lads felt honoured and delighted with the comment; they hadn't been doing anything special but had tuned in to what was required, both on and off the field. As Kieran Shannon pointed out in his column for the *Sunday Tribune*:

> '*Waterford are hitting the win rate of champions. For only the second time under McCarthy, they managed to go three league games unbeaten against the top nine. The last time they put a sequence like that together was in 2004, a streak that created the confidence and momentum for winning possibly the greatest Munster championship ever. Now, after winning one of the best leagues ever, Waterford are again eyeing more.*'

On 14 May, the panel and back-room staff went on a training camp to Villa Mora in Portugal. They were all in great form after the league win and had fifty-five team training sessions and matches under their belt by this stage. For various reasons, selector Seamie Hannon wasn't able to travel.

Training was hard over the week in the heat but spirits were high. Each day, they did a session in the gym, two training sessions outside and the meals were specifically made for athletes. Recovery work was done in the pool and some Pilates and yoga classes were held to improve flexibility. Each day was broken up nicely so the players had four hours spare time in the afternoons to relax, play golf, go into town or sit by the marina.

Gerry Fitzpatrick loved the training camps believing it gave the players a tremendous sense of preparing like professionals. The Birmingham City team had been there three weeks before them and the Australian rugby team were due after them.

The facilities at the complex are second-to-none and, behind the scenes, Sean Power had done a marvellous job in making sure everything was organised impeccably. Even the ice baths were brought out onto the pitch, hooked up with cables and kept at the correct temperature, even as the temperature on the pitch rose to 30 degrees Celsius.

They went out every night and not one player drank until the last night when they were allowed pints.

Justin brought everyone in for one-to-one talks, telling each player where he thought they were at and what they could do to improve. Stephen Molumphy was worried he wasn't scoring, but Justin told him he was happy with his performance, 'doing the donkey work, setting up other guys'. Stephen was happy with this and it helped take pressure off him for the rest of the season. With the pressure off, he started scoring!

Tom Feeney wanted to explain his case, feeling he should be back on the team and spoke with Justin and Nicky Cashin. 'They said I had a choice, I could either stay on the panel or go; I knew then I was wasting my time because he had picture in his mind of Declan Prendergast at full-back. In all of 2007, he encouraged me just once when he tapped me on the chest and said, "Keep working." Another session he told me, "Tom, go up there and mark one of them", and it turned out to be the water boy. I believe Justin tended to idolise five or six players; surely there's a better mechanism of inclusion than ignorance.'

On the plane back, most players were feeling great and were thinking this could be their year when only something freaky could stop them at least getting to the All-Ireland final.

In the Munster semi-final, they were supremely confident and beat Cork in a marvellously exciting game, 5–15 to 3–18. Cork were without some key players (who were suspended) and went for Waterford full throttle, the woodwork denying them a draw at the death.

The following day, some of the Molumphys were in neigh-bouring Fermoy, and some Cork fans told them they hadn't had their team out and that they'll 'get them again later in summer'.

But that's for later – next for Waterford, it was the Munster final against Limerick.

In beautiful May evening sunshine, players loved the expectation of another Munster final. But the ground was rock hard at training and Ken McGrath's right knee was still sore. He'd been having problems with it over the years and in a practice match in Walsh Park, the cartilage had been at him again. He had tried to get over the years of wear and tear with operations, but the pain he was now feeling was not good, even having done hour upon hour of flexibility training twice a week throughout the winter.

But he didn't want to give up, didn't want to stop, didn't want a tiny little cartilage problem to end what could be a marvellous summer. So he said nothing and didn't tell the medical boys. It was the only season he'd been officially injury free and he took Diaphene to stop the pain. He'd taken the tablets many times over the years and they'd never caused a problem. But the pain was now so bad he had to take more of them, and they were killing his stomach. Yet he wouldn't give in, wouldn't admit defeat. He loved playing so much – and loved Waterford so much – he'd do anything to keep going.

At training on the Thursday night before the match, they had a fifteen-minute match amongst themselves.

Most players have what they call their 'number one hurley' – the one they feel most comfortable with and keep for special occasions. Stephen Molumphy grabbed his to get used to it in a live combat situation; he'd had it for a month; it'd got him through the game against Cork and he'd been minding it carefully; but now that Justin had just told the players who was starting on Sunday, he was going to use it in the Munster final. As the practice match ended, he was striking the ball when Declan Prendergast hooked him brilliantly. Stephen's number one hurley broke down by the bass, an awkward spot, but it had happened before and had been fixed before.

He couldn't believe it, and was devastated. He was thick with anger as he walked into the dressing room.

'Is that your hurley?' asked Justin.

'Yeah.'

'I'll fix that.'

'But I need it for Sunday.'

'No problem. Come down on Saturday and I'll have it ready.'

On Saturday, Stephen drove down with Niamh, his girlfriend, to Passage West where Justin lived with his wife Pat. They have tea and sandwiches and chat away for ages. Justin took Stephen out the back and gave him the mended hurley. They have a puck around to test it. It was perfect, the weight and balance were just right. Stephen couldn't believe the job Justin had done with it. He liked Justin, and saw him as a totally down-to-earth person.

Thurles was heaving on Munster final day and it was Kevin Moran's first championship start. Flynners and Dave Bennett had told him not to take any notice of the Limerick crowd, particularly the nasty ones, and with the intensity of the game told him that if he couldn't hear a team-mate ten yards away calling him, not to worry about it.

All morning, Kevin had been getting best-of-luck text messages. He's loved the build-up and hadn't been fazed by any of it. It was all about going out and performing and beating your man, and if you could do that you could do it; and if you couldn't – you would the next day. 'I'd be kind of relaxed about it to be honest,' he says, 'and I think it's the right way to go about it.'

On the field, Moran couldn't believe the tempo of the game and the strength of the hits. He was able to get on the ball but was surprised at how quickly players closed him down. 'There were lads just hanging out of ya and so strong. I was never used to lads stronger than me, I used to always be a big lad. I remember I was blocked down a two or three times and that was the only poor part of my game. I was winning the ball and I was catching balls but when I got on the ball it was just so hard to get rid of. The roar when the ball went up the field is something I'll never forget.'

The game was tight and Limerick were hard to beat. Ken McGrath tried to ignore the searing pain in his ankle and Big Dan was playing the best hurling of his life. He drifted into space at the right times and came up with two late goals. Now, as in most of Waterford's goals over the years, they didn't come from intricate teamwork but rather a gut instinct from players such as Dan.

Waterford won.

After all the pressure and the preparation, they won. It was their third Munster title in five years, an amazing achievement considering that they had gone thirty-nine years up to that with just one win. Michael Walsh raised the cup, as proud a Stradbally man as you'd ever find that day.

The players celebrated that night, but not like before. All eyes were now on the bigger goal, an achievable goal, the Liam McCarthy.

Tom Feeney had been dropped again. 'Justin was probably right to drop me to an extent, because I made some mistakes but I think great managers would have realised that we still had a problem there, and he would have said, "I believe in this guy." He did tell me to go back to the ball alley because I spent many sessions there … if Justin is on your side, he'd go to the end of the earth to help you become a better player but if you are not on his side, it's a fucking horrible place to be. I don't think he ever explained why players were dropped.'

The draw for their quarter-final was made and Waterford got Cork. They'd beaten Cork earlier in the year but some of the players were already dreading playing the Rebels again, fearing a backlash. Training in Abbeyside on the Saturday morning after the draw had been made, Justin told the lads he was delighted they had Cork, 'That's exactly who we wanted,' he said.

The game would be another classic between the two sides, who in this decade met nine times over six years.

Having been freed from the pressure of feeling he had to score, Molumphy played a great game. The shackles were off and he roamed like a hungry tiger. Things had started happening for him, but Waterford were four points down. His mother was in the stand but she had her head in her hands, fearing the worst, and didn't see the moment later on when her son stole in for a crucial goal.

At half-time as they are gulping down liquid and eating Jaffa cakes, Stephen took his mobile out of his bag and saw his brother Ed had texted. Stephen thought Ed was one of the best people in the country to read a game and he sometimes texted at half-time, with messages such as 'they're bringing two guys this way' or 'they're pulling yer man that way'.

As the game neared the end, it looked as if Waterford were beaten, but they managed to stage a miraculous recovery and grabbed a draw. Cusack had made a marvellous save from Eoin McGrath but was penalised by Brian Gavin for 'lying on the ball', and didn't take the decision well. Eoin Kelly pointed the free. The replay was fixed for the following Sunday.

The players went for a run on Clonea strand on the Monday night, trained in Fraher Field on the Tuesday night and at Walsh Park on the Thursday.

Sean Power was asked to organise the travel arrangements. Roger Casey was due to drive the team van with the jerseys and hurleys while the players and others were on the train. Roger asked Sean if there was any room on the train and was told there was, but Justin wanted Roger to travel up with the van and told him, 'Sean Power doesn't run this team, I run this team.'

Sean heard back about this and rang Justin at 8 a.m. on the Sunday, saying he was very annoyed because he hadn't in any way been trying to undermine him. Justin was worried about delays, etc., but he backed down and Sean had a van waiting for them at Amiens Street to take the jerseys, hurleys and other equipment.

'Justin was a very proud individual,' says Sean. 'I think he saw nobody else but himself, even though all of us have some part to play in a gathering of fifty people. It's a family affair. He wouldn't listen.'

In the replay, Waterford hurled magnificently and won. Big Dan scored two to add to the three he had already scored against Cork already that year. His ability this year to move into the right positions, catch cleanly and fire home was second-to-none. 'Justin wasn't really into tactics,' says Bull Phelan, 'just hit it in towards the square where most of the damage was done.'

Dan's opportunism and Diarmuid O'Sullivan's inability to deal with the Lismore man would earn Dan GAA Hurler of the Year and all the adulation that would bring, particularly in a county which never had one of their own attain this goal.

Waterford 2–17 to 0–20.

Another classic, a humdinger, but one in which Waterford's passion, desire and hunger won the day. When Waterford were good, they were very, very good. The extra, renewed vigour which Justin had brought to the start of the year had stood them well; and the players knew they had thrown away 2005 and 2006, they badly needed to prove to themselves and the GAA world they hadn't gone away.

They had beaten their arch rivals – who couldn't come back to haunt or taunt them! In the years 2002 to 2007 inclusive, Waterford played Cork nine times, winning four, losing four and drawing one; scoring a total of 198 points, with Cork scoring a total of 202 points. They had been great, legendary games. But the crucial thing was in those years, Cork had gone on to win two All-Irelands, Waterford hadn't.

After the match, the lads were physically and mentally tired but only had one week before they played Limerick in the All-Ireland semi-final, which would, again, be in Croke Park.

The former Waterford manager Tony Mansfield was one of the many fans listening to RTÉ Radio 1 on the way home when he heard Justin being interviewed, when he told the nation it had been a marvellous performance and that they were ready for the next battle. But Tony said to his son in the car, 'What he should be saying is that we shouldn't be playing next week. Three weeks in a row is too much.'

Three massive games in three weeks was a lot to ask of amateur players. Some of the players felt the county board should have looked for a postponement; should have just told GAA HQ that they weren't playing and that that was that. If Cork had been in the same situation, that was what they would have done.

'We shouldn't have played three weeks in a row,' says selector Nicky Cashin. 'We talked about it on the train back and took soundings from the county board but got the impression we weren't going to get it moved back a week. Maybe the inexperience of the county board had something to do with it.'

The players were tired but it was hard to think anything but that this was going to be their year. This was their best chance of getting the county to its first All-Ireland final in more than four decades. Apart from the fatigue, there was a small bit of complacency, because they had beaten Cork and next it was Limerick, whom they all felt they could beat.

It must be destiny: league champions, Munster champions, a great training camp in Portugal, Cork beaten, just Limerick to beat and then they were in the final.

But fatigue mixed with letting their down the guard even a little played a crucial part in the Limerick match.

Only a few fans went mad after the Cork match, as they didn't have the money – they'd spent hundreds travelling on two consecutive Sundays to Croke Park and would now have to budget for a third day out!

County chairman Pat Flynn said there was no possibility whatsoever in getting the game postponed for a week. 'I think there was a general acceptance the match was going ahead the following Sunday regardless and we felt comfortable enough that we were going to win it. No one said anything to me about calling off the match because I would have been on to the Central Council of the GAA straightaway; I just don't remember.'

A spokesperson for Croke Park says the minutes of meetings taken that week 'have no record of any correspondence on the issue' between them and Waterford about cancelling the game.

The issue was raised in Waterford, with fans phoning the local radio suggesting it should be done.

Dan Shanahan says, 'In hindsight you'd think we should have looked for it to be put back a week but I don't think it would have been granted. We were on a roll, we were after playing well. We had won the league, we were after winning Munster, we were on a high we were after beating Cork in a replay and I think, as it goes, you are set up for a fall and maybe the focus was on our first All-Ireland and that's where the problem was instead of being focused on the game and the job in hand.'

This is confirmed by midfielder Jack Kennedy, 'We weren't up for the game. I don't think we were tired but maybe we had one eye on the final. Getting over Cork had been a huge thing and maybe we underestimated Limerick. But we thought Justin was the man to take us there. The team was well prepared and players have to take responsibility.'

The feeling in the camp that week was one of destiny – 'this is our year' but destiny doesn't hold a hurley. Instead of emphasising that they were in for a massive battle against Limerick and putting the fear of losing in them, at training on the Tuesday night Justin said, 'Well done last Sunday, people are talking about it.'

Earlier in the year, Bull Phelan had broken his big toe when a box of tiles fell on his foot but he'd fought back, came on against Cork for the last twenty minutes and played great but wasn't now starting against Limerick. Tuesday night at training, he'd been up since 6 a.m. working and the practice match didn't go well. After the team was announced on the Thursday, 'I lost the rag and got very angry. I didn't talk to anybody for about a month but just kept training and training.'

'Our heads weren't right,' says Tom Feeney. 'Justin didn't bring in any sports psychologist and that's what we were lacking to an extent; there are some players on our team that do need minding and working on.'

Meanwhile Limerick were coming for Waterford after their Munster final loss and they were going to target Waterford's full-back line.

'We worked very hard at stopping Tony Browne and Ken McGrath getting ball into Dan,' says then Limerick manager Richie Bennis. 'And we were going to put long ball – not high ball – into our full-forward line. We thought Waterford's full-back line was a weakness.'

The semi-final against Limerick was a major disappointment for Waterford – for the players, the back-room team and for the tens of thousands of fans who travelled for the third week in a row. In preparation, Waterford had done seventy-two team training sessions and played twenty-four matches – more than previous years.

But now on the train up to Dublin, selector Michael Ryan saw some of the players sleeping, something which hadn't happened the previous two weeks when they were going up to play Cork. He sensed this was bad, playing three weeks in a row could be just too much. 'And maybe we shouldn't have gone for that light workout on the Monday after the Cork win,' he'd later say, 'because sometimes just going to training is as much of an effort as training itself.'

Kevin Moran had now established himself on the team and was one of the quiet lads in the dressing room. He was relaxed, just wanting to get out on the pitch and get on with it. He saw how fired up other players got, players such as John Mullane. John's legs were sometimes pink because he'd been slapping himself so much with the hurley before he went out on the field. Kevin tried it one time to see if it would work for him, but the pain was too much and he decided against it as a preparation tactic. In the parade, Eoin

Kelly picked out his mother in the crowd, the first time that had ever happened.

The ball was thrown in, Jack Kennedy and Brick Walsh were in midfield for Waterford. Mike O'Brien for Limerick gave Jack a bang to his shoulder with the butt of his hurley and the stall was set for a battle. Limerick were going to harry and hassle Waterford for every ball, to get in their faces and try to catch them cold. And Waterford fell flat, while Limerick played exceptionally well.

Mike O'Brien blocked Tony Browne (the plan for them was working) and got the ball into O'Shaughnessey who rifled it home. Seanie O'Connor also did a great job stopping Tony that day, who still managed to score a point and set up a goal. At one stage, Limerick were ten points up, but Waterford brought it back to four at half-time.

Jack Kennedy was taken off at half-time – 'I always felt I was the first fella to go if things weren't going well, but he wanted to bring Eoin McGrath off the bench' – but anything Waterford tried didn't work.

A penalty for Limerick which they went for and another goal. Limerick got a total of five goals, with the Waterford full-back line peppered all day with good ball in. Final score: Limerick 5–11, Waterford 2–15.

In the dressing room after the game, players were shell-shocked. They couldn't believe their season was over, after the expectations they'd had and after their great results to date. Waterford had had more than twenty wides, Limerick had scored five goals, and Donie Ryan's eyes were closed for at least one of them! And still they only lost by five points.

'I went into the Waterford dressing room,' says Richie Bennis, 'and told them it gave me no joy to beat them as I'd far prefer to be beating Cork or Tipp or Kilkenny. I believe a general lack of tactics is the reason Waterford didn't win an All-Ireland in all those years.'

'The Limerick defeat was the worst ever,' says Bull Phelan, 'we were just in shock. And then in the final, Kilkenny weren't going to have Shefflin and Noel Hickey would go off injured; it would have been some chance for us.'

Tom Feeney couldn't believe the goals which had gone in and thought it would have been different if he had been there. The goals were not one player's fault; it was just one of those days. But out of five semi-finals Feeney played in (1998, 2002 and 2006) only one goal was conceded in each match; when he wasn't playing, there were three goals conceded in 2004 and now five goals in 2007.

Tony Browne would later say that playing three games in fifteen days had definitely taken its toll, that Waterford were flat on the Monday after beating Cork in the replay and to have to pick up and go again in hindsight was too difficult. 'But that year I felt we had a lot right,' he says.

Jack Kennedy told team-mate Jamie Nagle, 'We'll never win an All-Ireland.' He felt Justin had got the best out of the team, or very close to the best out of them, that he'd done a hell of a lot for them and wasn't overly critical of him.

Looking at the games, 1959 winner Martin Óg Morrissey says Waterford were not good at picking up loose/breaking ball and that 'while Justin was sometimes good at picking teams, but should have been locked in the dressing room then' because he didn't make the right substitutions. Former All Star Jim Greene believes Justin didn't get enough from players who were 'difficult to manage but I would have known the right buttons to press'. He also thought that 'some players slept with the light on but could be brave on the field sometimes' while they needed to be brave all the time. And 1959 captain Frankie Walsh says he'd heard that Justin was hard to get but twice as hard to get rid of.

And 'getting rid of Justin' was now being mooted again – but more widespread than before.

On the train home, the players were at one end of their carriage, drinking and chatting. As the train passed Carlow, some of the ones who had been the most vociferous in their criticisms walked up to where Justin was sitting and told him they wanted him to stay on as manager. Justin and Seamie talked about what had happened earlier and admitted a lot of things had gone wrong that day, but Seamie believed that even though tiredness had a part to play, some of the players were now blaming everyone except themselves for the defeat.

Jim Dee thought Justin was going to resign but when he heard the players saying there was no way he could leave, he thought otherwise.

The next day, Tom Cheasty, a Waterford legend and true gentleman, was being laid to rest in the Ballyduff cemetery, with Micheál Ó Muircheartaigh giving the graveside oration to a huge attendance of Gaels from Waterford and afar. Senator Paudie Coffey, himself a hurler from Portlaw, met Ken McGrath and Tony Browne in the large crowd and thought they both look dishevelled and pale. 'And I know they would have preferred to be anywhere else in the world except facing the Deise hurling public that morning. They were there though, offering their respects to another hurling great of another era, facing hurling people that they felt they had let down, but they faced them with bravery, honesty and courage in the name of Cheasty.'

That month, Seamie Hannon's mother Bridie also died aged eighty-one after an illness. Only one player, Dave Bennett, from outside the Ballyduff area rang him to offer their condolences. He says, 'When Bridie died, Stephen got in touch and then Dave, but it set a doubt in my mind, "Are we dealing with a fucking bunch of ungrateful bastards?" I didn't mind them not being able to come to the funeral, they probably had a match or something. But here I was thinking to myself, bursting me bollocks for them getting out for training and matches over the years; I lost a lot of money on the farm because of it, taking short-cuts and that kind of stuff and they didn't even phone. You don't need a third-level education to know manners. Justin came to her funeral.'

There was a long winter ahead and the players returned to their clubs and their thoughts.

Disappointment invariably leads to other things – many of which reared their ugly heads in the crucial year of 2008.

12

LAST DAYS OF JUSTIN

James Murray is one of the longest serving members of the Waterford panel; he is intelligent, mannerly, well respected and liked. In October 2007, he rang Jim Dee, the team secretary, to say he was going to Africa for a leisure break, mixing in a little bit of charity work in Zambia for the winter months and wouldn't be back until January. At the start of January, some of the panel went for a week relaxing to Orlando; a few went elsewhere instead.

When James Murray returned to Ireland, he rang Justin to let him know he was back but Justin told him he was 'surplus to requirements'. Jim Dee believes that was the start of unrest in the camp.

Sean Power, who never interfered with team selections, was somebody players would go to if they had a problem. Sean had learned to analyse what was said and pass it on in such a way that a solution could be found with Justin. On hearing what had happened with James Murray, whom he knew was one of the smartest chaps on the panel, someone who didn't speak without thinking, he contacted him.

Sean knew from the phone conversation that James had been very hurt. Sean told him he totally disagreed with how he was being treated. Sean believes that one of the crucial differences between the amateur and professional teams he'd been involved with was that with amateurs, if one player is hurt, everyone hurts. Players were doing it for medals, not money, which brings a different type of solidarity.

As a member of the finance committee, Sean also knew that questions were being asked behind the scenes about a replacement for Justin.

Training continued and the other players got on as best they could without James, but some were surprised at what had happened. At the same time, Seamie Hannon wasn't able to make as many training sessions as he would have liked for personal reasons, a fact noted by some of the players. (He missed sixteen of the forty or so team sessions from January to 11 May when Waterford went to Portugal for the training camp.)

Justin's perceived inability to work with the fringe players continued. One evening whilst training in Walsh Park, they were working in groups of three. Wayne Hutchinson had only been back for a few weeks after a chest infection.

'I was mad to get back training because I was after getting the all clear from the doctors and Justin was kind of keeping an eye on me. I was in the middle in between the two lads doing first touch work when Bull Phelan came out for training. "Justin where will I go?" shouted Bull.

Justin looked up the field and shouted to me, "Will you come over here?"

"What's up with you, Justin?" I asked.

"Leave Brian in there," he said.

"What about me? Where will I go?"

"Ah, you will have your day soon, and if you don't like it, you can go on."'

For Wayne, it was a big setback, 'That's what I didn't like about him. If you weren't in the first fifteen or top eighteen you were nobody on that panel.'

This was something the management team disagrees with. Selector Michael Ryan (who had managed the Waterford senior women's team in the 1990s) says, 'Justin was a larger than life figure. Overall, he knew all the players and it's just not true that he didn't listen. He was very open to listening. He even got jobs for several of the players.'

The 2008 league campaign was low-key and the panel was just chugging along, unsure if they could go one better than the previous year but there was nothing to suggest they could. The old confidence issues were back. Jim Dee could also sense the temperature rising.

'From the end of March and into April, I'd hear things others wouldn't,' he says. 'The Thursday we played Tipperary in the knockout stage of the league, I heard players talking. Seamie Hannon had missed a few training sessions (another great friend of mine), he found it very hard to come to training that time of the year with cows calving and milking cows. But fellas were giving out, saying if he [Seamie] opens his so and so mouth tonight, there would be murder. I asked Justin was he going to have a meeting after training, he said he was and I said for him not to let Seamie say anything at the meeting. "Why?" asked Justin.

"I'm just telling you now don't leave him say anything," I said.

"What's your problem with it?" I said nothing, so Justin said, "You're worrying about things that shouldn't concern you at all."'

Jim walked away. Seamie didn't say anything at the meeting but Jim could feel the stirrings of discontent.

Waterford were beaten by Tipperary and, with a lack of focus, old habits crept back in. That spring, some people rang Justin to say some of the players hadn't been sticking to his idea of what had to be done regarding their social lives.

Justin arranged another training camp in Portugal – a trip which would turn out to be a defining moment in his reign as Waterford manager.

Before flying out the team played a challenge match against Cork in Mallow at the opening of a new pitch. After the match, they got on the bus to go to Cork airport. Eoin Kelly made it to

Mallow but told Justin he couldn't go to Portugal as he'd forgotten his passport. He wasn't in the best of form.

They went on without him.

Seamie Hannon had told Justin he wouldn't be able to go as it just didn't suit him with work and other matters.

On the plane, Justin thought about Kelly, one of his best players. He rang him from Portugal to see how he was and for a chat.

When the players got to the resort in Villa Mora, some weren't in the mood for a week of training under Justin. Many of them had played club matches at the weekend, hurling and football. The training complex was the same as the previous year, which had gone so well, but things are never as good the second time around. The players knew the hardship that awaited them.

Paul Flynn was thinking the week in the heat might do him some good as he'd been suffering from an injury. 'We needed the week in Portugal as everything was going badly,' he says. 'The year before was great because Gerry Fitzpatrick got his way and everyone was pulling their weight. But this time was only two weeks before the championship, so there wasn't much you could do.'

The players had no problem with hard training – they'd put in literally thousands of hours under Justin. But here there was something wrong, something at the back of their minds which wasn't right. Their spirits were low.

Gerry Fitzpatrick could see the sessions were not being approached with the same degree of intensity as the previous year and they were there two days fewer which meant the training seemed rushed and crammed.

'I think in 2008 Justin's own standards hit a dip,' says Tom Feeney, 'which is amazing how this happens to experienced managers. Do they not just have the cop on to know there is something wrong?'

Physio Peter Kirwan could also see there was something wrong. The lads were called at 7 a.m. each morning and they had a hard hour-and-a-half session in the gym before breakfast. Then it was outside in the searing heat for another hour and a half of physical training. After that, there was lunch, rest and, at 4 o'clock, an hour and a half of hurling drills.

Peter could also see the tiredness and lethargy on the players' faces. In the evening, the players were restless, talking amongst themselves. Some of them gave out to Peter and Gerry Fitzpatrick about the setup. None of them went to Justin.

Gerry tried to make things more enjoyable for the players, and asked Justin if the lads could have a game of soccer the next day to break up the routines. Justin said no.

Dan Shanahan couldn't train because of a knee injury – he got pissed off when people, or reports in the papers, said he was injured all the time, which just wasn't the case. But he knew the training camp was going very poorly for everybody.

After training on Wednesday morning, a crucial point was reached. The players had enough, they wanted changes.

Ken McGrath and Michael 'Brick' Walsh went to Justin and told him there was discontent. Justin told them to have a players' meeting, to make up a list of their grievances ('five things that'd be good for this team') and he'd be back in two hours to hear what they had to say.

Thirty players and some of the back-room staff gathered in a changing room beside the swimming pool straight away to have a meeting. Pen and paper was produced to record the discussion.

At the centre of their grievance was their perception that some people weren't able to change when change was needed – and that Justin was one of those men. They wanted better and harder training with Gerry Fitz and more communication and things such as proper hydration tests throughout the year which other teams were doing. Also on the list was the belief that tactics for matches were non-existent – that when tactics are needed, all Justin will say is, 'Get the ball in.' And that if a player has a problem, Justin will do nothing about strategy, he will say it all comes down to the hurling not being fast or good enough. They also bring up the matter of Eoin Kelly's not being with them in Portugal and they also believe Seamie Hannon, whom they really like, is losing interest, citing the fact he's not been at many training sessions, some even said he should be replaced.

They whittle the list down to around ten points which Ken and Brick took with them to a meeting with Justin. As well as the training matters, not listening to players and lack of communication from management, they state that all the players were not pulling their weight.

Justin looked down at point number four – Seamie Hannon. Justin never cursed much [he is a religious man] but he couldn't believe what he was seeing. They boys explained that because Seamie was not attending all the training sessions, they were doubting his ability to be fully involved as a selector.

'For fuck's sake,' Justin said, standing up. 'Is that what I'm reading? The man can't be here, his brother is sick and he's working.'

Justin's temper was boiling. He told the players he'd deal with the issues they'd raised before the end of the training camp. The meeting ended. Justin went upstairs, got his mobile and rang Seamie to tell him what had happened.

'I'll go, Justin, if that's what it takes to make them happy,' Seamie said in response.

'No, I'm the manager. I don't consider it a problem at all,' Justin reassured him.

After he had hung up, Justin looked out over the balcony, thinking of the list the players had presented. Doc Higgins came to talk to him. Justin was ashen faced as he told the doc that he couldn't believe there was 'a bit of a coup on'.

The doc told him to relax, to make a few minor changes and let things settle down when they got back. Justin then told the players he'd look at the issues when they got back to Ireland.

The players trained for the next few days and then flew back into Cork on the Friday. They knew the training camp hadn't been as good as the previous year; that it had been a wasted opportunity and wouldn't help Waterford go farther than they had in 2007. As the issues raised by the players still hadn't been dealt with, some decided to ask Justin what he intended to do. He replied that they'd have a meeting about the points raised at the next training night.

Most of the players weren't happy with that.

One of the players was told by a back-room member that he thought Justin was on the verge of resigning.

After they landed and got their gear, they boarded a coach to bring them to Waterford. A few Cork chaps saw John Mullane and wanted to get his autograph, but Justin got on the bus and told the back-room staff to get off again, he wanted to address the team. The six back-room staff had to get off the coach and stand at the side of the road as the door closed. The players didn't appreciate this either. Sean Power felt like a schoolchild; Roger Casey thought Justin didn't trust them. Justin asked the driver to carry on up the road for about 100 yards, which he did. The bus stopped again and Justin told the players that they were all in it together, that he'd see them on Sunday morning and that 'they'd drive on'.

Meanwhile, the back-room boys had been seen by some Waterford families who asked them what they were doing standing by the side of the road.

After Justin said his few words, he got off and went to his car, and the back-room men got back on the bus before they all carried on back to Waterford. Paul Flynn couldn't really believe that Justin didn't address the issues that they had raised. 'In all his years of experience, you think he would have seen there was something wrong, even though there had been no call at that meeting in Portugal to have him sacked.'

Jack Kennedy remembers that confusion may have arisen on the Portugal trip. 'I think probably Justin wanted us to think of things where we could improve, so maybe there was a little misunderstanding. But there was a lot of frustration. And there was very little on the list that did change, so [it was] a kind of pointless exercise.'

County chairman Pat Flynn heard about what happened in Portugal. 'When Justin told them to have a team meeting that was a stupid thing to do,' he says, 'if Justin didn't take on board what was said and instigate change.'

'I think Justin got incredibly self-obsessed in the last two years of his reign,' says Tom Feeney.

In Walsh Park the following Sunday, Waterford took on and beat Kilkenny in a one-off tournament game dedicated to Tom Cheasty. It was a great result which gave some of the lads a timely boost.

The first recorded players' meeting in 2008 with management wasn't held until Wednesday, 21 May in the Ramada Hotel – the first time on a non-training evening that two hours (with flip-charts and projectors) was given over to talking about tactics.

Eight days later, on the Thursday night before the game against Clare, Pat Flynn heard some of the players weren't at all happy with the preparations for the forthcoming match. 'They were saying things during training; you could sense the body language and the way the lads were talking that they weren't happy.'

Over the next few days, some of players most loyal to Justin were upset because things carried on as normal and none of the grievances raised in Portugal were being addressed in a meaningful way. The players say they could see that Brick Walsh was annoyed with Justin for not dealing with the issues.

With the game against Clare looming, Justin spoke with the players in the dressing room of Walsh Park. In the midst of all the tension, there still was time for some humour. 'I'll do anything for ye lads,' he told them. 'I'll come down and train ye seven days a week if ye want. I'll drive a hundred thousand miles for ye. I'll come down and train ye seven days a week.'

One of the lads put up his hand and said, 'But, Justin, what's your wife going to think? She might think you're having an affair.'

As laughter broke out, Justin said, 'She's my wife, I love her and she loves me. I'll come down and train you seven nights a week if ye want.'

Justin also said he would bring some inspirational music for the bus journey on Sunday.

The same evening, Justin told Paul Flynn that he was not on the panel for the Clare match, adding that he was not even to tog out and wouldn't be travelling on the bus to the match.

'I knew what he was at,' says Paul. 'He didn't want me around in case I might undermine him or because of what had happened in Portugal and he knew some of the older lads would be spotting for things. He was on tenterhooks maybe.'

But, as it happened, it suited Paul not to travel because the captain's prize was on at Faithlegg Golf Club that morning, so he felt like he should show his face at that because he was on the committee. So he went there and then got into his car with his wife Ruth and drove to the game. On the way, he stopped outside Tipperary town and picked up Mikey Barrett, a good friend of his from Cork.

The match against Clare took place on 1 June at the neutral venue of the Gaelic Grounds in Limerick. The players, management and back-room staff all travelled up on the coach. As usual, Justin was sitting up the front beside Seamie Hannon. The players didn't know it, but Justin and Seamie had decided it wouldn't be the worst thing in the world to go 'the scenic route' because of the injuries to the team. This would mean they weren't that pushed in beating Clare. If they lost, they'd have time to regroup before playing Antrim next. If they won, so be it.

They went through Limerick to the Radisson Hotel on the Clare side of the city where they had soup and sandwiches. They went for a puck around on the car park in front of the hotel to loosen up. Justin told them to go out on the grass, but the grass was very long – some reckoned eight inches high – and it was very, very hot. Justin shouted, 'Work on your first touch, work your first touch.'

'It seemed like thirty degrees heat,' remembers Kevin Moran. 'We were sweating like lunatics. The grass was really long and there were holes in the ground. I was actually injured and I shouldn't have been playing that day but I was so mad to.'

The grass was so long sliotars start to go missing.

'I remember Pa Kearney,' says Wayne Hutchinson, 'the poor young fella who had the crash. Pa missed the ball and Justin turned around and aid, "Pa, that's not good enough. That won't do me." And the tracksuit and T-shirt were stuck to Pa.'

The tipping around only went on for ten minutes but the sweat was rolling off the boys when they got back on the bus.

The coach set off back in towards Limerick when the garda motorbike in front escorting them to the venue chugged to a halt. It had broken down. In a way it was symbolic. Two of the back-room staff got out and helped the garda push the bike to the side of the road.

The players started to wonder how much worse things could get. Then Justin stood up, hoping to inspire the players. 'I've a song for ye,' he said.

Would an inspirational song motivate them?

He gave the driver the CD and the crooning, slow voice of Tommy Fleming singing, 'Don't Give Up Till It's Over' started.

The players looked at each other and started laughing. Some of them couldn't believe this was happening.

Meanwhile, Paul Flynn had made good time and arrived in Limerick before the team bus. He walked in the players' entrance and was in the dressing room on his own when the entire team and management came in. Justin looked at him but said nothing.

'His chin nearly hit the ground,' says Paul, remarking on Justin's surprise at seeing him there. 'He was blank.'

The teams warmed up and in Justin's talk before the game, he mentioned the effort he had put in, having driven hundreds and hundreds and thousands of miles for Waterford hurling, and that the players were not to let him down. Some of the players felt it strange for Justin to mention the effort he'd put in, because they'd been busting their balls for Waterford hurling too.

'Justin never really gave inspiration speeches,' says Wayne Hutchinson. 'It was always the main players of the team like Ken, Dan and Tony. They were always the people I remember giving inspirational speeches.'

Paul Flynn was in the stand watching the match. 'The match itself was a disaster from start to finish,' he says. 'The fitness was the first thing – [Justin] hadn't allowed Gerry Fitzpatrick to do what he had been doing in previous years. I think the perceived success of 2006 and 2007 gave Justin the belief that he was untouchable for another few years. I think the man himself was actually tired of the Waterford job, of travelling up and down the road, of dealing with the likes of some of us, the media, etc.'

It was like the girlfriend you didn't want to be with and yet didn't want anybody else to have either.

'Maybe he was afraid if he walked, someone would come in and they'd win an All-Ireland and what happened to Gerald would happen to him – which I don't think would have happened.'

Waterford without Ken McGrath and Eoin Kelly, and with all the problems coming together, were going down. Clare were well up for the game and piled on the scores. Waterford's half-back line was not used to playing in their allotted positions, with Brian Phelan at centre-back and Jack Kennedy wing-back, which caused problems. And Kevin Moran was playing full-back and was not fully fit. John Mullane was the only player doing well while the rest of the players were literally all over the place.

If ever proof was needed that a team that had been playing bad all year couldn't just turn it on for one game, this was it.

At half-time, Justin and Seamie wanted to take Dan off but Nicky Cashin, the other selector, disagreed and so Dan was left on. But during the second half, the selectors decided he should come off. Dan knew he'd played poorly. He still held the Player of the Year title from the previous year and here he was with nothing going right. He was pissed off with his performance, annoyed that they were being beaten out of the gate by a team he felt they should be hammering. He really thought Clare were there for the taking to get Waterford to a lucrative Munster final.

Dan saw a substitution was going to be made and thought it could be him. It was.

He walked off the pitch towards the dugout, where Justin was standing. Justin went to pat him on the back and, instinctively, Dan moved away. Leaving Justin's hand to whoosh through the balmy air, connecting with nothing.

Dan felt he didn't deserve the clap on the back rather than being upset with Justin for taking him off.

It was a moment that shouldn't have meant anything, and yet it was a moment that would become etched in the folklore of Waterford hurling for ever – and a moment that still haunts Dan. 'I didn't deliberately shrug my shoulders not to get the clap on the back and it's the biggest mistake I have made in my life, that I didn't shake his hand.'

Instead of going into the dugout, Dan went straight to the dressing room, showered and put on his clothes.

Paul Flynn saw what happened, and thought that there was no way Dan meant things to happen that way. 'Justin never put his hand out to anyone, but he must have known he was in trouble and probably by putting out his hand to Dan, he'd get people to think, Dan is a star player and things are okay,' says Paul.

Clare beat Waterford by ten points. Humiliation.

Seamie Hannon couldn't believe what had happened with the squad. 'Dan snubbed Justin coming off,' he says.

In the dressing room, there was disappointment on every player's face. They wanted to get out of there.

Justin thought he'd give the lads a break and told them they'd be back training on Friday night. But the players wanted to train on the Wednesday, thinking a five-day break was too long. Ken McGrath told Justin they wanted to train on Wednesday, but he was not for shifting.

As events would transpire, if he had agreed to training on the

Wednesday, there might have been a clearing of the air and the season could have continued. But what Justin did was leave the players too much time to think about their problems and their options.

The players got on the bus and went back out the Ennis road to the Radisson for a prearranged meal. It was the last direction they wanted to be heading. The traffic was heavy and they were heading away from home with flag-waving Clare fans whistling and jeering at them.

They went into the hotel, had some food ('half the lads didn't even eat it' remembers one player) and had a few pints. They'd been there about half an hour but Justin wanted to get back and was already on the bus with some of the back-room staff. He sent selector Michael Ryan in to get the players, but they told him they didn't want to go and a stand-off developed. Bus driver Billy Costine remembers one of the back-room staff coming back after trying to get the players out and saying, 'I was told to fuck off!'

'I knew then there was something wrong,' says Billy, which, as things turned out, was something of an understatement.

Kevin Moran was so pissed off with everything and with his injury, that he was seriously considering giving the entire thing up. 'I was thinking I wasn't going playing hurling again and that was the truth. No way was I going to put myself through this,' he says.

Sean Power was then sent in to get the players out. They still didn't want to leave and but say they would, only because Sean was asking them. Four of the players travelled home with Sean Power in his car, where the conversation included phrases such as 'something has to be done' and 'he's lost the plot'.

Sean advised them, 'Please, lads, if you're having a meeting, please go to the county chair-man and do it in full knowledge of them because they're your bosses and you'll have to take advice from them.'

The players agreed that was the best thing to do. Those players who got on the bus did so in complete silence but the anger on the faces and the anger in their eyes spoke volumes.

On the way home, many of the players said it was time for Justin to go. They discussed what to do next and some decided they wanted Flynner's advice. Paul Flynn was driving home when his phone started to hop. Dan, Eoin Murphy and half a dozen more of the players rang him to talk about what they were going to do. Flynners was clear enough about what he thought should happen, 'but not in my wildest dreams did I ever think that it would'.

There had been no organised plan before the game to oust Justin if Waterford lost.

That evening, some players were more irate than others, and called round to each other's houses saying Justin had to go.

The main picture on the sports pages of the papers on Monday morning was the photograph that had captured the moment when Dan had turned his body away from Justin. 'To this day, I'd love to kill the person that got that because of the regard that I have for Justin. The one mistake I ever made under Justin,' Dan says.

Throughout the day everybody was talking about the picture even though Dan told them he meant nothing by it. Players were texting and ringing each other, wondering what was going to happen next. There were no definite plans but something had to give.

Later that Monday, Justin rang Eoin Kelly and told him he'd definitely be starting the next game.

Wayne Hutchinson remembers players would sometimes not have credit on their phones but that day texts were flying everywhere, some later slagging the main movers, saying if they hadn't credit on their phones, Justin would probably have survived!

On the Tuesday morning, after thinking about everything that had happened and thinking about the photo, Dan woke up and said to himself, 'I'm after disrespecting that man.'

The same morning, a number of the players decided to go for a run with Gerry Fitzpatrick on Tramore strand at 6.30 p.m. the following evening. Others heard about the run and decided they'd go too.

In the meantime, half a dozen of the lads in west Waterford were also due to go for a run on Clonea strand. They decided to head to Tramore instead to join the others. The entire panel knew about the run.

As the phone calls and texts were going around, the idea of a players' meeting after the run was mooted. Texts were sent that there was a run on the beach and a meeting afterwards, and said ominously that everyone was to be there.

Paul Flynn says that, also on the Tuesday morning, Justin rang him to say he was guaranteed his place on the team for the rest of the year. And this was after Flynners not even being good enough to make the bus, let alone the panel the previous week!

On Wednesday morning, Eoin was phoned again by Justin, again promising he'd be on the starting fifteen for the next match. Eoin thanked him and said, 'No worries.'

13

TRAMORE

There has been a hotel on the site of the current Majestic Hotel in Tramore for longer than people can remember. Most of the five-kilometre stretch of beach can be seen from the hotel, as can the amusement park below.

On the Wednesday morning, the hotel manager Mark Whelan got a call from one of the players asking if there was a room available for a meeting that night. Pat Flynn, the county chairman, had spoken with a few of the players, advising that any meeting should happen quietly and promptly.

The Lakeside room beside the bar was available and Mark was told there was going to be a players' meeting of the Waterford hurlers after a run on the beach and that they needed the room from after half past seven.

Sandwiches, cocktail sausages, teas and coffees for between twenty-five and thirty people were arranged and the room was to be set up 'theatre style', with a top table facing out into the rows of chairs. Mark was told the county board would be picking up the bill.

Meanwhile Paul Flynn had phoned an official with Tramore GAA and asked him if they could tog out at their clubhouse and shower there after a run on the beach. 'No problem,' came the reply.

Paul and Pat agreed that if he was required, Pat would be available to meet with the players after or during the meeting.

The players knew that even though Justin had been ratified for 2008 by the county board only six months earlier, the board members would not go against their wishes.

Stephen Molumphy spoke with Michael 'Brick' Walsh on his mobile, asking what the meeting was about, saying that he was scheduled to work that night. Brick told him not to worry about going to the meeting, that it was 'just some lads letting off steam'.

Selector Seamie Hannon says he didn't know about the meeting.

Pat Flynn says that, before the meeting, he had spoken with three or four players that he got on well with, asking them not to do anything rash but to keep him informed. 'I understood why it was happening because of the feelings we were getting in the lead up to it. The frustration out of Sunday and the players were afraid the year was going to be gone,' he says.

Pat didn't ring Justin before the meeting to tell him it was on, but believes he must have known it was happening because nearly everybody connected with Waterford hurling knew the meeting was on. 'I didn't ring him beforehand and I didn't feel I should have because I felt the players were meeting, they wanted to talk themselves and I thought it might have been a good thing, they might blow off a bit of steam and they might be after finding a way to bring it forward and save the year. I wasn't alarmed at that stage,' he says.

At 5 o'clock on the Wednesday evening, Roger Casey and the other back-room staff got a text message informing them of the meeting. He wasn't a bit surprised.

Gerry Fitzpatrick says he turned up that evening to go jogging with Ken McGrath because Ken was injured. 'Two other players had asked if could they come along. When I turned up there was more players there and I was going, "What the fuck!" There was nothing about that night that was planned in terms of me or the team or Ken or the captain or anything.'

Players started arriving in their cars for their run on the beach just before 7 p.m. It was to be a light session and was led by Gerry Fitzpatrick. While they were waiting for the rest to arrive, the others stood around talking about the meeting and what they were going to do.

Twenty-four out of the panel of thirty were present. The only reason the other six weren't there was that two were working and couldn't make it and Shane 'Shiner' Ahearne wouldn't let his boys go because the under-21s were playing the following night and he thought that it would be too negative.

Of the twenty-four, six were carrying niggling injuries or weren't in the mood for running, so eighteen went on the run. The other six stood on the beach and waited.

Word had somehow got out that the players were going for a run on Tramore strand. Gavin Downey, a photographer from the *Munster Express* newspaper, took some pictures, one was a very good one of Dan in the water, which would appear in the paper the following week.

'Tramore happened because too many players had been hurt,' says Tom Feeney. 'Justin had helped me and others become better players and I'd have huge regard for him but I just wish he did not have such an ego, he could have been a great man. Players that were not part of the six or seven lads considered the 'holy grails' had just had enough.'

The players went jogging across the strand towards the sand dunes – the same sand dunes which, a decade earlier, many of them had got to know so well while they were on the Neutron Diet.

They finished a two-mile jog and then a whole series of sprints, short and longer sprints and mixed them up with more jogging. They then jogged back the two miles 'as a warm down' and they were all back in the car park after a session lasting an hour or so.

After showering and changing at the Tramore clubhouse, they drove the short distance to the hotel where everyone had a sandwich and some had soup.

It was after half past eight before the meeting started. Gerry introduced Ritchie Bolger (a sports psychologist at WIT and independent facilitator for the meeting) to four or five of the main players and then left before the meeting started.

The twenty-four players agreed to talk about the current situation first – the problems, issues, feelings about Justin, what they could or should do. Some senior players did a lot of the talking at the start and then the others joined in, with nearly everybody speaking on the night. They agreed that other matters, such as who would replace Justin if he did go, would not be discussed.

The mood of the speakers fluctuated from sadness to anger and frustration. Most of the players wanted better. The players were told that some county board officers, including Pat Flynn, were aware the meeting and could come in to hear them at any stage.

Many players had made up their minds what they wanted before they went to the meeting. Kevin Moran was one who wanted a change because he felt they could either carry on and get nowhere or try a change and hopefully get somewhere. 'Justin did a lot of great things and didn't do anything bad to me. It was nothing personal it was for the sake of winning and my own ambitions, either change now or go nowhere,' he says.

Wayne Hutchinson remembers talking about whether or not Justin should go on his own or with the selectors too.

Although some players wanted Justin to go, others, while agreeing that that had to happen, thought the timing was bad. One player said, 'We're never going to win an All-Ireland with Justin but can we do this to him after all we've been through.'

The speakers did not make nasty contributions, there was no vindictiveness.

Another player asked, 'Can we win an All-Ireland under Justin?' Heads shook and many said no. Nobody said yes publicly.

Other questions followed.

'Are things going to get much better?'

Again, a lot of shaking heads. 'Not really,' murmured a few lads.
'And do we deserve better?'

'Yes.' The reply was resounding.

Another player said, 'It's a shame to say, but this definitely has to
be done. We want to win an All-Ireland and if that is to happen,
Justin has to go.'

Brian Phelan says he wouldn't be one for blaming managers
all the time because players have to sometimes blame themselves
and that when he went to the meeting, he hadn't made up his
mind about what should happen because Justin had been good to
him over the years.

Jack Kennedy's mind wasn't made up before the meeting either
as he felt some blame must fall at the feet of the players themselves.
'I had felt Justin was harsh sometimes with me but it definitely felt
bad, I felt sorry for him, but there was no other option.'

Other players spoke about the lack of proper structures and a
lack of professionalism in the Waterford setup.

The meeting broke for a few minutes and players went outside
and chatted in small groups. Some went to the bar and ordered
orange or Coke. A few people in the bar having pints saw Big Dan
and asked him what was happening. He told them the players were
just having a chat about a few things.

Pat Flynn was phoned just after 11 p.m. and he drove from his
home in Waterford city to the hotel. Paul had told him he was
going to be needed.

Before setting off, Pat rang John O'Leary, the county secretary,
and told him the players were meeting in Tramore and that he was
going out to meet with them. He drove to Tramore and waited
for another phone call that would tell him he could go into the
meeting.

Meanwhile, the players went back into the room and talked
some more. Some players said they thought Justin should be given
another chance.

Another senior player said that what they were contemplating –

getting rid of a manager mid-season – was a massive thing. He wanted to make sure all the players were aware of the ramifications.

Another said they would have to get rid of Justin because if they didn't, and then won their back-door matches and got through to another All-Ireland quarter- or semi-final, then Justin would probably be kept on for a further year, as he would be seen to have had another successful year as manager.

The back-door system, which helped Waterford probably more than any other hurling team in the country, was now one of the reasons being given for Justin having to go.

A flip chart of issues and grievances was written up.

Just before midnight, they decided there had been enough talking, and that they should take a vote. The motion that Justin should resign was to be put to the floor and everyone agreed it would need to be a majority decision. Cards and pens were given out to each player and they voted in secret.

The question was: Do you want Justin to stay? The players wrote their answer – yes or no – and folded over their cards before they were collected and put on the top table. Ritchie Bolger separated out the votes.

'I remember the votes were going bang, bang, bang to one side and next minute you would have the odd one going over to the other side,' says one player. 'There were only four on one side.'

Ritchie counted the votes – twenty for Justin to go; four for him to stay.

Dan Shanahan, the villain in the papers with that famous picture, was one of the four who voted to keep Justin. He didn't think Justin had been there too long and didn't agree with 'deliberately getting rid of a manager, in mid-season especially'.

There were a lot of thoughts going through his head that evening, as there had been in the days leading up to the meeting. 'My name and my pict ure in the paper had been seen as one of the things that got rid of Justin and that is pure horse shit.' But the votes were cast, the decision was made.

The next move was to wait for Pat Flynn. When he arrived at the meeting a few minutes later, he was surprised at the turn out. 'Wow,' he said to himself, 'This is serious.'

He was told by the chairperson that a long discussion and vote had taken place and that the outcome was that the players wanted Justin to go. He was shown the chart listing the players' thoughts and grievances. He didn't try to dissuade the players; he just listened to what they had to say and asked them why they were calling for Justin to go now. He was told it was all on the chart for him to see.

Pat spoke with the players about the consequences, the dangers and how Justin would react. The players knew that, apart from Babs Keating with Offaly in the 1998, Justin would be the only manager to be sacked mid-season in the history of hurling. The players also reminded themselves that when Babs went, his replacement, Michael Bond, led Offaly to win the All-Ireland.

'I told them Justin could walk away or Justin could stay,' Pat says. 'I asked them what they were prepared to do and what they were going to do.'

It was now 12.30 a.m. and the players asked Pat to leave so they could discuss the points he had raised.

Pat went outside and looked out at Tramore Bay, and thought about the enormity of what was happening. Ten minutes later, he was called back in and the players told him why they believed they had to go the route they had voted for, they main reason was that they'd lost confidence in their manager. When Pat suggested they meet Justin to talk things through, he was told that things had gone beyond that point, that it was too late for talking. Pat asked them if there was anything that could be done 'for the sake of the team and county and the supporters'. Couldn't they all sit down and talk? But it was clear from the players' reactions that there was nothing that could be done.

'So I said that I'd ring Justin in the morning and convey their views. They didn't want to meet Justin and they didn't want Justin ringing them, because some of them felt, probably, that Justin would talk them round,' says Pat.

Before the meeting finished, they appointed a five-man team to represent their views, a committee of sorts, including Ken McGrath, Paul Flynn and Tom Feeney. The list of grievances was now outlined on an A1 sheet of white paper.

The players said the under-21s and the two missing from that evening's meeting needed to hear what had been decided. They agreed to have another meeting the following night after the under-21 match, with the venue probably being the Ramada Hotel as that would be where the under-21s would be having their post-match meal.

It was after half past one before meeting ended. Just before it did, the players agreed not to talk about what has been discussed, especially to the media.

Only Pat was to ring Justin to tell him what had happened and he would do that in the morning, because it was too late to ring him that evening.

The players drove home from Tramore, with some thinking the decision they'd made was the right one; that it took balls to do what they were doing. Most were buzzing when they got home, their minds all over the place. Some wouldn't sleep much that night. The wives, girlfriends and parents that were still up, all wanted to know what had been decided.

The next morning, Pat Flynn got up at 7 a.m. and thought about what he was going to say to Justin.

He knew the rules as set out, and was aware that he was in no position to sack the manager. Even the sixteen-person executive of the county board couldn't sack the manager – it could only be done by a full meeting of the county board. That was something that would take time to organise and could mean things would get very messy. If Justin didn't agree to resign, things would get very messy indeed.

Around the same time, Stephen Molumphy got a call from one

of his team-mates telling him what had happened at the meeting. He couldn't believe it and said he'd be at the meeting that night at the Ramada Hotel.

At 9 a.m., Pat Flynn rang Justin on his mobile and asked if could meet with him, even in Cork, to tell him some important news. But Justin told him he was heading away to west Cork. Pat then told him that the players had met, and that the bottom line was that they had lost confidence in him. 'Justin said he wanted to meet them and he'd talk them around,' recalls Pat, 'but then he said that if they'd lost confidence in him, there was no point in him going down.'

Pat told him the players didn't even want to talk to him.

'The conversation lasted about five minutes,' says Pat. 'He accepted that if he had lost the dressing room, that was it. He didn't sound angry, he sounded more or less like himself and just accepted it.'

So after seven roller-coaster years with one of the most exciting, dynamic and heart-breaking teams the country had ever seen, Justin McCarthy – the man who brought them three Munster titles after a thirty-nine-year wait and a National League title but who couldn't get them to an All-Ireland final – resigned.

In his seven years, he had missed only two trainings sessions. He had covered up for many of the players misdemeanours. When his players were working well, they were the Brazil of hurling and their individual flair was sometimes breathtaking, but, unlike the South Americans, something was lacking and they could never close out the really big games.

Most of their goals under his reign were created by strokes of genius (Flynn's rockets, Big Dan's catch and shots, Mullane's shuffle and strikes, Kelly's dynamism and anticipation of breaking balls) and very few by actual well-constructed passing movements. None of it mattered now. He was gone.

It was agreed that none of the players should ring him.

'We knew what we'd get if we rang him!' says Tom Feeney.

Pat Flynn rang three players and told them Justin had accepted their decision. This shocked them. They couldn't believe it would happen so quickly.

He then rang some members of the county board and called an emergency meeting of the sixteen-member executive for 9 p.m. that evening, immediately after the under-21 Waterford–Limerick match.

Meanwhile, Justin rang Seamie Hannon and told him that Pat Flynn had phoned.

'The players don't want me,' Seamie remembers him saying. 'They don't even want to talk to me. I've no option, there's only one way to go and that is to abandon ship. They don't even want to talk to me.'

Seamie couldn't believe it either. After all the years, this is what it's come to. 'Well if you're going, I'm going with you,' he told Justin.

Seamie says Justin had been told not to ring the players but, at this stage, says Justin wasn't bothered if he never went to see Waterford play again or even visit the county. For a man who had driven to Waterford countless nights, this was some change.

Justin rang Nicky Cashin, who told him he was going to resign as well. 'I was so disappointed at what happened and couldn't believe the ingratitude,' says Nicky of the players. 'Some people are very impatient. I think a lot of the younger players didn't want Justin to go.' Justin rang Michael Ryan and then phoned Pat Flynn to tell him the selectors had all resigned – a form of solidarity and support for the man. Pat told him about the executive meeting that night, and Justin gave him some words to read out.

'He may have been emotional, but he wasn't crying – he was still very strong,' remembers Pat.

The word spread amongst the players and back-room men.

On hearing the news, Dr Tom Higgins was surprised and felt sorry for Justin, thinking the players should have let him finish out his year and that the decision was harsh and hasty. 'But he never looked like squeezing an All-Ireland out of them,' he says.

Jim Dee 'got on super with Justin' when he was there and he was surprised and disappointed with everything. 'We were great, great friends and we'd go off to watch matches together. We went everywhere to matches when we weren't playing. Yet, when he left, he never spoke to me again. That hurt me, it did. I had nothing to do with it.'

A lot of the players and squad members from the senior panel were at the under-21 Waterford–Limerick match at Walsh Park, which, in itself, wasn't unusual. They would normally have been at this type of game, lending their support and seeing how the lads got on against a very good Limerick side. But this evening, it was different. There was intrigue in the air.

Many of the players had gathered on what was known as the far side of the pitch, opposite the main and only stand. There was no terracing, just a dry, decades-old mud bank.

After the game (which Waterford lost 2–17 to 1–7), the county board executive (minus one or two) gathered in the meeting room above the dressing rooms. Pat Flynn told them what had happened and explained that Justin had resigned and, after some heated words, the executive accepted it.

The executive knew they couldn't have removed Justin as manager, but they could accept his resignation. Pat told them that Justin had said he couldn't come down anymore, that he was resigning and that all the selectors were resigning as well.

It was now up to the main officers of the board, including Pat, to find a replacement – and quickly.

The meeting of the county board officers finished at 9.30 p.m. and Pat Flynn was tasked with writing a statement for the half a dozen or so reporters waiting outside. Just before 10 p.m., he came out with two other officers and read the statement. The sports bulletins after the news for the rest of the evening, carried the news that Justin had gone. Text messages and phone calls spread around Waterford hurling folk very quickly. Justin McCarthy's son, also called Justin (who's a reporter for Newstalk), had a statement ready on behalf of his father and he phoned the media with that.

Then Pat drove out to meet the players.

They'd been meeting as planned at the Ramada Hotel, the senior players joined by the under-21 players who were on the squad. One or two of them said they would have voted differently at the first meeting.

Pat Flynn arrived and told them about the events of the day, that Justin had stepped down as they had no confidence in him and that he couldn't come down to them anymore. He told them also they were going to have to step back and leave it to the county board to find a new manager.

Stephen Molumphy gave a five-minute speech, airing his views and saying he didn't agree with what was being done. Then, the meeting discussed possible replacements. They hadn't been asked formally to come up with a list, but it seemed a natural thing that they'd come up with some ideas. Names such as former Tipp hurler and manager Nicky English (first on the list); Liam Griffin, the former Wexford manager; Donal O'Grady and John Allen from Cork were also mentioned.

Liam Griffin says he wasn't contacted but friends in Waterford would have known he wouldn't have been available because of his work commitments with his hotel business, 'And I wouldn't have considered it if I was asked because even though I love Waterford hurling and have great respect for them, I would only have managed Wexford.'

In the middle of it all, someone mentioned Davy Fitzgerald, the former Clare goalkeeper. A senior player said, 'If that man comes in, I'm walking.'

The four main names were written on a sheet of paper and Pat Flynn was to contact them to see if any would be interested and available. Meanwhile, the players would have to train, so they agreed to meet at 8 o'clock on Saturday morning.

'I personally thought O'Grady and John Allen wouldn't do it,' says Paul Flynn. 'I thought Griffin might for three months. I thought it might have appealed to him to come in bang, bang, bang and get out. I think the position would have appealed to most fellas. I think Nicky might have gone for it only that Tipperary were still bobbing around for him.'

The following day, Justin's resignation was the source of many conversations in the county. The public reaction could best be described as mixed.

'I think people looking in obviously thought he had done so much, many people were disgusted,' says Paul Flynn. 'And the national media had a right go at us. Unless you were in there and got the brunt of it of what he was capable of, I don't think you would see how necessary it was but if you were friends of a player or related to a player you probably knew because you would have heard a player talking about things. We were probably seen as the bad guys I think.'

Paul Flynn didn't get any personal abuse. Dan Shanahan got more than a couple of text messages from people giving out about him and the other players. At one stage, there was an abusive, anonymous letter sent to the county board offices addressed to Dan. And the gardaí were called in to investigate threatening text messages to Dan's phone. No prosecutions followed but a number of people were spoken to. A member of the back-room team also got at least one nasty text message and thought about going to the guards with it, but decided against it in the end.

Meanwhile former county chairman, Paddy Joe Ryan (the man who brought in Gerald and Justin) thought of Davy Fitz and, through intermediaries, Pat Flynn got Davy's number and vice versa and contact would be made between the two.

John Allen and Donal O'Grady say they weren't asked about the job.

After being asked if he would be interested in the job, Nicky English texted back: 'Tell the lads wd love to do it but cdn't manage against Tipp.'

The players met at 8 a.m. on Saturday at Walsh Park for training under Gerry Fitzpatrick. It was the first time they'd met up with the back-room team.

Later that day, Pat Flynn rang Seamie Hannon. 'Would you consider staying on as a selector?' he asked.

'Not a fucking chance,' replied Seamie. 'Are you fucking codding me or what?'

Seamie still couldn't believe what had happened. He couldn't believe Justin had been given no option by Pat Flynn. That the county chairman had taken it upon himself to tell Justin he wasn't wanted and that he hadn't called an emergency meeting of the county board executive to discuss the matter. He says that until his dying day, he'd never forget what had happened. He was thinking the players had come out of it fairly well. None of the players had rung him and he still thought about the time when none of them came to his mother's funeral.

He believes the Tramore mutiny had been started by just a few senior players. 'I'm not saying we were the best management team in the world, we made mistakes, but what also killed me was that after the Limerick game in 2007 on the train back to Waterford, they all said, 'Sure Limerick got some goals, and we want to stick with you.'

Later that day, Davy Fitzgerald was at home in Clare. He'd heard from a friend in Waterford that his name had been mentioned. He knew of the other names that were in the pot, and he was fierce excited to be in the same bracket as them. Savage excited. He'd been managing Limerick IT and thought the reason he was being considered was because he'd done well with them. He was wondering if he'd get a call over the weekend when his mobile started to ring.

Pat Flynn asked him if he would be interested in managing Waterford, saying that he was on the shortlist.

Davy told him straight away he was interested, that he'd be totally committed and thanked him.

Pat was delighted with his enthusiasm. There was only one other strong candidate in mind but he felt Davy was the man for the job. Pat had told him that a decision hadn't been made and that he shouldn't talk to anyone about it.

When he hung up, Davy was beside himself. He'd love the job, he'd love being in the thick of it all, that's where he liked it. He says he didn't ring any of the players and didn't tout for the position at all. He was thinking that maybe they'd want him to come in for two or three months and try to steady the ship, but he was also thinking that if he got the job, he could do a lot more, he'd show them what he was made of as a manager.

He'd thought about what had happened to Justin too. He had written in a newspaper column a few years earlier that he thought Justin should have gone, and still believed that nobody could stay around as a manager if they were not winning 'two or three All-Irelands'.

'Justin had got as much as he could from the players,' he says. 'He could have walked away a massive hero and that would have been the right way to do it. It wasn't nice the way it ended up for the players because they came out of it terrible and it didn't do Justin any good either. Maybe it could have been avoided. Personally I think there should be mediation, and for the players to sit down and have a compromise.'

He couldn't judge Justin as he'd never had him as a manager but he didn't think they'd have got on. 'He had an unreal team. Could he have achieved more? I don't know. He's a good hurling man, he loves his hurling, whether I like him or not. But Waterford has as good a set of hurlers as anybody else – I think they were good enough to win an All-Ireland.'

But they hadn't.

Justin used to tell his players, even when they lost, to walk with their chests out and heads up. He had made Waterford the 'High Kings of Munster' three times, an amazing achievement for a team that had no minor or under-21 success. For some, he was 'unlucky' in that when he was managing Clare in the 1970s, he came up against a Cork team going for a three-in-a-row and, as Waterford manager, he faced another Cork team going for three-in-a-row and a resurgent Kilkenny team.

In Ballyduff Upper, Seamie Hannon talked with Justin on the phone again about how the meeting might have swung so massively in favour of a vote to oust him. They thought some of the lads might have been influenced by others who had an axe to grind, a kind of I'll-just-roll-along-with-it attitude.

Justin asked many questions. 'Can you tell me what happened, Seamie? Why was there such a revolt? Did you detect anything?'

Seamie couldn't answer.

Seamie's heart was broken for Justin. The next time he saw him, he told Justin he had the look of a man who had aged ten years. He thought Justin had treated all his players so well for seven years, that he had mended and banded their hurleys, that he had loved each one of the players as he would his own children.

Getting the cows ready for milking one morning, his mind was so much on the saga that he wasn't concentrating and got a kick from one of his cows that nearly broke his fingers. He was trying to think if there was some way it could have been staved off. He believed he didn't have an axe to grind with any of the players and kept thinking, that if the players had met with me or Justin and said, "We need somebody to take us to another level", they could have avoided a confrontation.

He rang Sean Power and a few of the other back-room team. Sean told him he saw it coming.

'Fuck it. I thought I was sharp but I didn't see it coming,' says Seamie.

The only player who drove up the hill to have a chat with Seamie was fellow clubman Stephen Molumphy, and Seamie appreciated it immensely. They leaned against the farm wall and talked, with Seamie telling him to keep on hurling as he had a long career ahead of him and a lot to contribute to Waterford. Seamie had always been good friends with Stephen and he remembered well the year Stephen lost his father in in a tragic accident when Stephen was only a young boy.

The following week, Seamie attended his niece's wedding and Justin went to the 'afters' where he again told Seamie, 'If only I could meet the players and talk to them and say it's this, this and this … it's terrible bad if you can't talk out a problem with anybody.'

Dan Shanahan was at home. He told people that he had the utmost respect for Justin and always would have. But he didn't ring Justin because he was afraid to contact him. 'I didn't know what way he'd react to me. I just didn't know. What would I say to him? I wouldn't have known what to say to him.'

Although very few people rang Justin, Peter Kirwan, the physio, is one who did – just to say thanks, and Justin was delighted to get the call.

The following Sunday morning, at around half past eleven, Paul Flynn was at his kitchen table when his mobile rang. It was Davy Fitzgerald phoning on his way to Dublin for *The Sunday Game* analysis. He spoke for about ten minutes and told Paul about what he had planned for Waterford, that he was a winner, that he was going to put Ken McGrath in at full-back, that he had 10,000 drills ready to go for training and that he had a good trainer to bring down with him.

'Look, Davy, I don't have any influence good, bad or indifferent on who's going to be appointed manager,' Flynners told him. 'But if there's one person you don't remove, it's Gerry Fitz.'

Pat Flynn was under fierce pressure as there was a county board meeting scheduled for the following night and he wanted to have a manager and selectors in place before then. He didn't want it to drag on.

He rang the other main officers and they agreed Davy was the man for the job. That evening, Pat tried to ring him but his phone was off. It was off because he was on the television and Pat Flynn sat down to watch *The Sunday Game*. When Pat Spillane asked Davy live on air if he was going to be the next Waterford manager, Davy pushed the question aside.

The next morning, Pat Flynn rang Davy and asked him if he'd like to do the job. And he said he would, he'd be delighted to. He was thrilled. He had only finished playing hurling in March and now he was to be the manager of one of the top four hurling teams in the country. 'A lot of lads from around my place just couldn't believe it,' he says.

He knew he'd have to give up his job with RTÉ and that the terms and conditions of his appointment with Waterford still had to be worked out, but he also knew that those things would all come good.

Later that morning, Paul Flynn was playing the eighth hole at Faithlegg golf course when his mobile rang. It was Davy again.

'He went on a bit,' says Paul. 'I can't remember what he was saying, because I put the phone down on the green, took my shot and when I lifted the phone back up he was still talking.'

Pat Flynn had to get selectors and as Ballygunner and Ballyduff Upper had been in the county final the previous year, they would be a good place to start. Pat had a meeting of the county board that evening in Dungarvan and he wanted everyone signed up before then. The June meetings were normally sparsely attended (fifty or so) but he knew there'd be twice that number turning up in Dungarvan.

As the news of Davy's appointment spread, a man in Cork thought about what had happened for many hours, days and weeks afterwards. He promised himself it would never happen to him in the same way again. Thinking about his years with Waterford, Justin McCarthy believed he had overachieved with them.

14

A CLARE MAN IN WATERFORD

Kay Casey's washing machine was worried.

As a top of the range Whirlpool, it'd been working hard over the years, washing all the jerseys but, now, Davy's appointment spelled trouble and it shuddered at the thought of what was to come.

Maurice Geary was also in shock. He had been asked to be a selector for the county he loved so much. From watching all those young lads growing up, he was now on the verge of being an intimate part of their lives again.

Pat Flynn had just phoned him to ask if he wanted to work with Davy.

Maurice was manager of Ballyduff Upper, the county champions, and was highly respected and liked. His initial reaction was not to get involved, his disappointment at what had happened to Justin clouded things for him. Added to that, all he knew of Davy was what he had seen on the television – and from what he had seen, he thought the man was half mad.

But he talked with his family and some friends in Ballyduff. He felt it'd be unfair to ring his club-mate Seamie Hannon, as he thought it might be backing him into a corner. Even in the small village, their paths didn't cross much nowadays, even though they'd played on the same full-back line in those hammerings by Cork in the early 1980s.

He knew he might never get another chance like this and rang Pat Flynn to tell him he'd do it. Pat told him Peter Queally from the east was going to be the other selector, to complement Maurice from the west.

The next day, Davy came to Lawlor's Hotel and met Maurice and Peter, the back-room staff and some county board officers.

They were impressed with Davy's eagerness, enthusiasm, business-like approach and his talk of a plan. Pat Flynn was impressed and frankly amazed by Davy and the amount of preparation he had already put in, knowing there were only a few weeks to go before the game against Antrim and then Offaly. One of the biggest demands he made was that there were to be two sets of training gear, all personalised, and that each set had to be washed after each session they had been used for. Davy wanted his players to train in the same style tops, shorts and socks – he told Pat it was a new start, a new message that everyone was to be treated the same. And because there would be more training sessions, two sets would be needed. They'll be like soldiers preparing for battle.

'Anything else?'

'O, yeah, two towels for each player. And a psychologist. And 150 sliotars each night for training!'

Pat set to work.

Meanwhile, Stephen Molumphy was feeling bad about the way Justin has been treated and he rang him to see if he'd be at home later and would let him visit. He drove down to Justin's home in Passage West and they had a chat. Stephen could see how disappointed and sad Justin was about the whole situation. The young player thanked Justin for all the great work he'd done with him and the team over the past years, and thanked him for all the faith he'd shown in him in particular as a player. He told him what had happened was a pity. He then asked Justin what he was going to do next, and Justin said he didn't know.

'Well, whatever you do, thanks a million for everything,' Stephen said.

Justin liked Stephen, they'd always got on well, and he was delighted the young man had called down to see him. He was the only player who had contacted him so far, and would be the only player to call to see him. It was a terribly sad ending to a romance which had started so brightly on a Dungarvan nightclub dance floor.

The next chapter in the turbulent journey of these Waterford players was about to start in the home dressing room of Walsh Park.

It was a Wednesday evening and Davy had arrived early with his instructions on what he needed. On his drive down from Clare, he'd been thinking about what lay ahead. He knew his first night was going to be, in his own words, 'fair fucking intimidating'.

He was about to step into a bunch full of serious characters, men who, in the past, he had railed against and cursed with all his might. He remembered the days in the 1990s when he and the ruthless back line that were the foundation of the great Clare team of the era used to pick on Paul Flynn in particular.

As the danger man for Waterford, Flynn had been targeted by Clare. Everywhere he went, he'd get a slap or a comment. And it didn't matter who was on him. Davy remembered players in the Clare dressing room agreeing to go for Flynners because they felt that if they got him riled, got him talking, they'd get to him and throw him off his game. He remembered the day when in the Munster club championship against Ballygunner, he had saved two penalties from Flynn. But then there were the days when Flynn had beaten him with one of his marvellous shots.

With his hand on his heart, Davy knew he had no hatred for Waterford. He'd been on All Star trips with John Mullane and Tony Browne and found them brilliant fun. In particular, he remembered a trip to the States and a story they told about when they found themselves at a Baptist mass one Sunday morning after a night out and sang as loud as anybody else in the church.

But in the past few days, people had been telling him he was mad to take the Waterford job, with some talking about the team being gone, having lost the bottle. But Davy didn't think so.

He was taking the job because he was going to be their friend, their confidante, their manager, their saviour. Because if they didn't win a few matches, the Waterford fans were going to eat them without salt!

And Davy Fitz knew the way he wanted it to be.

The balls and cones and drills were ready on the field as the players started arriving. Dan and others said hello as they went inside. Davy told Pat Flynn he was as nervous as when he played in All-Ireland finals.

With everyone inside and togged out, Pat Flynn took Davy and selectors Maurice Geary and Peter Queally into the dressing room. 'Lads we have the most up-and-coming manager in Ireland at the moment – Davy Fitz!' The players clapped, some more than others.

He started nervously, and why wouldn't he? He'd been public enemy number one for years for many Waterford fans. Some players thought he was mad taking the job too, that he had some nerve to become their manager. Davy's stomach was turning. 'I never thought I'd be standing in this dressing room coaching some of you guys. I know a lot of us are after having our battles down the years but I'm here with ye now.' He added that he wanted to give it everything. He talked briefly about how he knew most of them from playing against them and he said he believed they could go far this year. He let them know he was delighted to be there, that training sessions would be more frequent and more intense, and that he wanted everyone to wear the same training gear.

He looked around the room. Some of the players were glancing over at Paul Flynn, who was looking down at his boots.

Paul Flynn had been thinking back to three years earlier when Waterford had beaten Clare in Thurles by nineteen points. He knew how hard Davy had taken that humiliating defeat. Flynners also knew that the players had to shut up and get on with the

training and that many of them didn't really care who was
appointed.

The first thing Davy had to do was see how fit the players were
– from what he could see, they weren't fit enough, their hurling
was slow and they were stale. He decided they were going to have
to train a lot harder than he thought. He knew it might have tired
them out and left them vulnerable in the forthcoming games
against Antrim, Offaly and Wexford, but he had to take the
chance.

He knew as well that he was going to try Ken McGrath at full-
back. He had been thinking about it a lot and believed the position
was still one of the problems, as Waterford were conceding so
often.

The changes at training started straight away. Everybody was
to beat every session, even the walking wounded. And nobody was
going to come along with their clothes on to stand on the sidelines. Training bikes and weights were brought out and a player
carrying an injury was to do something, no matter how little.
Physio Peter Kirwan thought back to Justin's era, when an injury
would have meant a rest.

Davy had asked Maurice Geary to 'oversee training' and to liaise
with the players. Maurice liked to be involved, liked to have the
whistle in his mouth and to be in control. But he found out very
quickly that Davy wasn't into this with him. Training was hell-for-
leather and Davy was taking command. He was trying to do
everything. Maurice knew he wanted to be more involved, but so
be it. At least he and Peter had full input into team selection,
which was good.

Davy tried to get to know all the players personally, each one
on the panel. The players liked this because some always felt Justin
had his favourites and thought he didn't even know all their
surnames, he was so focused on his starting fifteen.

To help him get the players' minds right, Davy told them he
was bringing in a psychologist, John Carey, to talk with them

both as a group and individually. The players were a bit cagey about the idea. After all his years, Dr Tom Higgins thought he'd seen it all.

John Carey (whose phrase was 'chalk it down') had always thought of Waterford [players] as being nice hurlers but ones who could fold on a big day. It was his job to help stop that happening. With his previous involvement with Cork, he thought he might have met some resistance in Waterford but he never did. He interviewed all the players one-to-one and then collectively. 'There was an awful lot of unhappiness in the camp about how things had evolved beforehand, even those outside the so-called 'Golden Circle' of players. But they were all very open to the newness of what I was trying. They were a different kind of player from those in Cork in 2004 or 2005 so I pitched it somewhat differently but all of the Waterford players responded very well to what was being discussed. Some players who weren't having a great year, such as Dan, spoke a lot,' he says.

Doc Higgins believes it wouldn't have mattered who came in to manage the team, the players would still have responded. They had to; they had to prove to the public that they hadn't been the problem – that Justin had.

The doc had worked under many Waterford managers and while he thought Davy didn't know the meaning of management style, he liked him. He'd seen the famous clip on YouTube of Davy giving a team talk.

'That's what he's like,' says the doc. 'If you think that's normal, well and good, but it's not for me.' The doc left at the end of the season, citing the fact that his pace was gone and he couldn't get across the field quick enough to an injured player!

Sean Power liked Davy. 'He has wonderful attributes, he's very sensitive, kind and approachable. I really like his involvement in the Share a Dream Foundation for helping sick children.'

Roger broke the bad news to his wife Kay about Davy's kit requirements and so came the moment of truth – would the

Whirlpool agree to the new terms and conditions? Only one way to find out.

'Mother of God that was some dose,' says Kay. 'There were forty tops, forty togs and stockings but they were all initialled so when they were washed and dried, you had to get his jersey and you'd be looking for his togs and socks and put them into a small plastic bag – at least twice a week! Twice a week! It was crazy.' That was only the half of it too. When the team was playing a challenge match, the first fifteen jerseys go in on a cold wash for forty minutes and then they go in on a synthetic wash at sixty for an hour and thirty-five minutes to have them proper; a synthetic wash again; the other fifteen would go in on a cold wash and then Vanish powder – so four washes for one set of thirty jerseys!

'You have to because of the white in the jerseys,' says Kay. 'I think Laois and Kildare are the only other teams that have as much white in it. And then there's the drying! You can only leave them so long in the dryer because if you leave them in too long they will get wrinkled. We put them in for eighty minutes and take them out after thirty so they won't wrinkle. And then it's maybe put them on the clothes horse in the hall if I haven't my clothes on it and they can dry away with the night air.'

Kay's rural house became like a launderette most evenings after Davy landed, with washing going on five nights out seven.

'It's just that they are white and to get them perfect … In fairness they were giving about €30 a wash but by the time you would have washing powder done and time but we do it for the love of it. I just love it.'

And lucky for Kay, the goalie's jerseys have never run!

She's been doing it for seventeen years (the intermediates before the seniors); at times she got annoyed with it but kept it up. 'Sometimes it comes in and you'd feel like nearly crying. There were times when I was sick but I still love it – to have them come out proper that was very important because they're white and they're going out for the county on the field where people can see them.'

And then there were the forty bath towels; each one the length of a door; they decided not to torture Mr Whirlpool any more and bring them in the van to the launderette in Dungarvan the following morning – €90 a wash, four washes a week.

As for the 150 sliotars used every night, a few were lost each session, but not many. Sometimes, when he got home and the washing was on, Roger had to wipe them clean and put them in the shed, with the door left open to dry them.

'I dried them in the tumble dryer one night when Kay was gone to town,' he says, adding the dryer was never the same afterwards!

The players were now kitted out in their personalised training gear and Davy drove them hard, with clean sliotars flying in all directions. But he knew one important player was missing and, two weeks into his job, he rang Stephen Molumphy.

'How ya getting on?' asked the Ballyduff Upper player.

'Good. How's it going yourself?' asked the new manager. 'There's training on tomorrow night if you can make it. I know that thing with Justin and it shouldn't have happened like that. I've a lot of time for Justin but you only get a couple of years playing county and to be honest, you should make the most of it while you can.'

Davy had big plans for Stephen.

When they hung up, the army captain thought about it. He thought about what going back would mean, professional living in all but name. Giving up the odd pint, training every second day, not being able to go away with his girlfriend Niamh. He thought about Ken McGrath not having a summer holiday for years and other players only being able to have their weddings in the winter. The commitment was unbelievable.

But then he thought about the crowds coming on the field when they won, the pride in his family and club, and the joy he could help bring to a county starved of success. Sure wouldn't many a man have craved to be given the chance? He thought about what had happened to Justin. Having thought about it for a few days and talked with some of the people he respected most, he decided to go back – and the following week he started training again.

Stephen walked into the dressing room and the other lads said hello to him. Clinton Hennessy's nickname for him is 'John Rambo' and made a joke about Lieutenant John being back. The lads laughed and whatever tension there might have been because he hadn't trained since Justin left, went.

Out on the field, Stephen couldn't believe the change from before, with around 200 sliotars in the field and so many cones and training gear.

Around twenty minutes into the session, a player made a comment about Justin. Davy heard it. 'Everyone stop,' he shouted and called them all into a circle. 'Look I don't want to hear one other thing about Justin ever again. I've great time for him as a manager, the way it happened shouldn't have happened, but I don't want to hear his name again here, or anything disrespectful about him.'

If Davy said those comments to galvanise the squad, it worked. What also worked was the philosophy Gerry Fitzpatrick had been preaching for so long – that the players needed to spend as much time together, to do more than others, if they were to improve.

They spent practically the entire summer together for a crazy ten-to–twelve-week period, training four or even five nights a week, going on at least two weekends away where they trained at least twice a day, and involved themselves in some team-building events.

While not having anything against Stephen, a few of the players were privately annoyed that he had gone away for the best part of a month and was now straight back on the team as joint captain. 'It happens in every sport but it is wrong – but best of luck to him,' says one player.

A few players found it hard to get used to Davy's style – 'I didn't like somebody barking at us like he did,' says a player – it was so different to Justin's style. But the training was different and what's different is normally good.

Waterford played Antrim in the first round of the qualifier back-door system and beat them comfortably.

Dave Bennett started against Antrim but knew he hadn't played very well. He talked with Davy, who criticised him for hanging back around the half-back line which hadn't been his instructions. Dave told him, 'I was asked by our full-back and centre-back on the day, Ken and Tony, to do that because they had pulled out so far. I was doing it for the team, not myself. If I was doing it for myself, I'd have gone up to the forward line and tried to get myself ten fucking points.'

The Thursday night before the next game, which was against Offaly, Davy told Dave Bennett he was being dropped.

Waterford played well against Offaly, with Eoin Kelly in particular having a great game, and they got through to play Wexford, whom they also managed to beat. But they were struggling to score goals and put teams away. In the matches against Offaly and Wexford, they beat them by a combined total of seven points. Kilkenny had beaten the same teams by a combined total of thirty-seven points!

'If we're brutally honest, Eoin Kelly carried us through the Offaly and Wexford games,' says Dave Bennett. 'If he hadn't responded so well, we would have been out.'

Waterford had fallen over the line against Wexford (winning by a point, 2–19 to 3–15), knackered and running on fumes but had been just ahead when it mattered. And then in the last fifteen minutes against Offaly, Kelly had given an absolute exhibition. At one level, Waterford wasn't playing well as a team and yet they were in another All-Ireland semi-final.

But then they had had to get to the semi at least because if they hadn't, the fans would have been highly critical of them and what they had done to Justin. At least they had now done as much as they had ever done under Justin and, in some way, they had been redeemed. In the nine weeks since Davy had arrived, the players had done as much training as they had in the first four months of the year under Justin.

However, the match ahead was when they felt they were better without him – that they didn't need him! The master had taught them all he knew, but now the students had mastered the art of winning semi-finals.

Waterford beat Tipperary in the 2008 All-Ireland senior hurling semi-final. It was an amazing achievement considering how good Tipperary were all that year – National League and Munster champions and favourites to go to the final. But Waterford prevailed.

That night, they celebrated their great victory and went to bed in the early hours of Monday morning. They knew that an even bigger battle lay ahead in the form of a final against one of the greatest teams ever to grace a field in the 125 history of the GAA.

15
THE AGONY

On the Monday morning after Waterford had beaten Tipperary, some players had small hospitals in their heads. But nobody minded. Phone calls were made and a few lads from the west were on the way to the city. Davy had told them not to drink that day or they'd be gone. But as some of them congregated in Becketts on the Dunmore Road in the city, a Ballygunner pub, they know there was safety in numbers. 'Sure what's he going to do, drop us all?' Some didn't go to Becketts but, they might have been somewhere else. Some didn't drink at all, some only had a few pints, others a few more – it wasn't often you won an All-Ireland semi-final.

But word got back to Davy and, the following night, the training session was savage with lads sweating buckets of Heineken. He ran them to exhaustion. Parents had brought their children to witness a Waterford team training for an All-Ireland final for the first time but what they saw was a slaughter. He had them hitting tackle bags at ferocious speeds. He wanted more, harder, faster. It was *Rocky* stuff. Pure torture.

There is an old rule of coaching and even business management: 'Never threaten something unless you are prepared to carry it through.' He had specifically warned them in the dressing room after beating Tipperary that if anyone went drinking on Monday, they wouldn't be training on the Tuesday.

At the end of training, Davy got them in a circle and showed them his All-Ireland medal, going round to each in slow motion, showing it six inches from each of their noses, 'That's what it's all about, you haven't one of those in your back pockets yet! There are going to be thirty of these handed out,' he said, adding Clare had won against the odds and they could too. And then he said, 'Right, who's been drinking?'

A dozen lads sheepishly stepped forward. But they had stood the test of very hard training and knew that when other county teams have a big win, they too have a few drinks on the Sunday and maybe the Monday and leave it at that, which is what they were going to do now.

No action was taken.

Maurice Geary was disappointed that some of the lads had gone drinking but didn't see it as a big issue.

The squad was told they were going up to Carlingford Lough at the weekend – and anybody due to work on Monday would need to take the day off. Part of the idea behind going away was to take the players away from the hype.

On Saturday, they went up to Dublin, stayed in the Portmarnock Country Club Hotel and trained nearby. Then they went back to the hotel and down to Portmarnock strand for a dip and a bit of relaxation. Later, at a meal back in the hotel, John Carey, the psychologist, was trying to work on the lads' heads to get them thinking correctly.

Later, the players went into a meeting room. Davy told them that he had utmost respect for Gerry Fitzpatrick and that he didn't know what was coming on, but he'd never question it. A DVD was put on. The lads were expecting to watch some hurling, some swash-buckling players strutting their stuff on a hallowed pitch, but, instead, they saw Kenneth Branagh on the screen. The fifteen-minute clip they watched was of Branagh as *Henry V*, walking among his troops, readying them for battle. Shakespeare's sixteenth-century iambic pentameter dialogue was beautifully delivered, without a sliotar in sight.

Players were amused, baffled.

'What the fuck is this?' murmured a few.

Gerry was hoping the players would be inspired by the speech Henry V made to his men on the eve of their greatest battle. But not many of the players were Shakespeare fans, and some reckon only around eight of the thirty-five got the significance of it. Gerry also said that honour was being in a position to fight; but in sports psychology terms, was this not deviating from the goal of winning? Gerry says they gave out slips of paper to the players explaining the context of the speech – if you weren't in a position to fight, you wouldn't be in a position to win. All you can control is your per-formance, to focus on that and have no fear of losing.

Later that evening, while *Match of the Day* was on, Davy went to Dan Shanahan's room and had a long chat with him. Dan hadn't been having his best season and Davy was trying to inspire him to greater heights.

Training the next morning was early, then they got the coach to the Four Season's Hotel in Carlingford. The first item on the agenda was a three-hour session of team building near Carlingford Lough with canoeing, monkey ladders and problem solving. Over the course of the weekend, the Waterford hurlers spent as many hours doing water sports and such exercises as they did hurling.

'It was all emotion,' says one player. 'The three weeks was nothing but emotion and not enough thought and hard factual stuff. Like, what are we going to do about Henry Shefflin?'

Another player adds, 'We didn't play enough matches amongst ourselves. And a lot of it was Davy shouting. Some of us felt like schoolboys.'

That same weekend Kilkenny were in Seafield in Wexford, doing nothing but light gym work and hard hurling.

That evening, the Waterford boys went to Cooley Kickham's ground in Louth for a helter skelter challenge match between the Probables and the Possibles. An enormous crowd turned up and the players were applauded off the bus. Some players were sore from the various exercises earlier in the day. That evening, they all went for a walk down the pier and Davy gave a speech. In some of his speeches, Davy talked about his involvement in the Share a Dream Foundation and how lucky the players are. Some of the guys thought this referencing to illness and finding joy in the present was brilliant, others didn't think it worked. With the one-hour match in Cooley and a twenty-minute game later in the week at training back in Waterford, they'll have had only about 100 minutes of match-time before the All-Ireland final.

Kilkenny will have ten sixty-minute matches in their four-week preparation … 600 minutes as opposed to 100. How much would it matter?

Davy knew the fans in Waterford were excited about the build-up to the final and decided to have two 'public sessions' of training where fans could watch and meet their heroes. The first one was planned for Walsh Park, the second for Fraher Field in Dungarvan.

More than 5,000 turned up on the first night, and players did interviews, trained a bit and signed jerseys and hurleys. Before the session, Peter from Tony Roche Menswear measured thirty players, three of the management team and Jim Dee for dark-grey suits for the final. But most of the back-room team weren't measured as they weren't going to be getting suits and it was noticed by some (but everybody would be getting casual shirts and pants to be worn the day after the final). Costs had to be kept down and even getting suits for thirty players when only twenty-four would be on the programme was a major achievement.

But for some players, suddenly there was a hierarchy. For them, the recipe of solidarity which up to now had got them this far was cracking; the bubble bursting. Davy had 'packaged everybody' in that they all wore the same training gear, they all went on the field together, players and subs stood together for the national anthem – why? Because solidarity was needed as many fans were against them after what had happened to Justin.

Later, some players spoke about chipping in to buy new suits for the back-room staff. Davy told the players said the 'suits issue' didn't matter; he told the players and the back-room staff to forget about it.

'It was never an issue,' says county board chairman Pat Flynn, 'and nobody ever came to me about it.'

But the GAA tradition of getting a suit for a final is deep rooted. Waterford 'suits of 93' and now the suits of 2008 sowed some doubts. 'A small thing became a big thing,' says one, while another says it wasn't right as it became a stumbling block.

Brian Lohan of Clare says something similar happened in the week before their All-Ireland final match against Kilkenny in 2002 when Vodafone, their sponsor, had mobiles delivered but four players missed out on phones because at least one player took more than he should have. It was a moment when 'solidarity' became only a word. 'We had a meeting about [the phones] and a few other things afterwards,' says Brian, 'because you share every moment with players at that level and we felt betrayed and let down.'

Training continued and an even bigger crowd turned up in Fraher Field the following Friday night. Before they were allowed in, the Possibles played the Probables, twenty minutes each half. Stephen Molumphy was on the Probables, and the others were told not to mark him, to give him free reign from his centre-forward role. It worked for the Probables but, at half-time, the Possibles decided to put Richie Foley on him. The Possibles went out and destroyed the Probables, scoring 2–7 without reply. The game was blown up before it was due to finish – it didn't look good. The fans were allowed in but so many had turned up that there were fears that some of the younger ones would get crushed.

Sports psychologist John Carey spent the best part of an hour being a bodyguard for Dan. 'They were pulling parts of his jersey off him. Afterwards Dan said that being in a final might never happen in his career again. I was worried that the occasion was going to take over from the match itself and it was impossible to hide from. If you play the occasion and not the match then you don't play. It's like telling a two-year-old in a toy shop to concentrate on learning their ABCs.'

Over the week, some players felt there wasn't enough 'distraction control', not enough was being done to minimise the hype on the players. 'Those nights all the fans were crazy and I do feel it got to the players,' says Jack Kennedy. 'Then there were people ringing the house; and you'd go to the shop and see cakes with your name on it. We got no advice out of the ordinary about how to handle it, we were going to do the same as we did against Tipp. We didn't really talk about it, when maybe we should have.'

As was noted by a former Kilkenny player, the hype was understandable, but stupid because the team hadn't won anything. 'Waterford is a garrison town, a soccer town. They would celebrate without winning anything, celebrate like soccer players … but then they weren't in enough finals to get used to it.'

The Waterford players were trying their best to embrace the build-up and not let it faze them. But it was hard to get the balance.

Davy Fitz didn't mind the emotion. He was into working with it, but there was a difference between emotion and hype. He wouldn't realise until after the game just how many of the players read the local papers and were affected by what had been written. 'If I had my chance all over again, I'd try to block all that out. If a player gets caught up on the hype, he is not tuned in to what is important in the game,' he says.

Up to now, what had been routine to Waterford was getting to All-Ireland semi-finals – 1998, 2002, 2004, 2006 and 2007 – and losing, but now they were in the final and nobody was quite sure what the best thing to do was.

Another senior player says, 'There isn't a time when they all sit

down and say, "Right, we're in the final – this is the plan."
Kilkenny can win an All-Ireland with three one-and-a-half hour
training sessions a week because on a bad Kilkenny team there's
probably thirty or forty All-Ireland medals in their pockets. Here,
you don't have that time.'

When the players returned to Waterford on the Monday, they
tried not to listen to WLR which kept playing the song, 'Don't
Stop Believing' – it was played 142 times in the four-week build
up to the final. The station also visited Ardmore and Mount Sion,
as each club had three players on the team. Local papers went mad
with special supplements and the national press and television
wanted a slice the action too.

Supporters went to extraordinary lengths to proclaim their
undying loyalty to Waterford: Michael Foley, a Portlaw farmer,
filled 300 manure bags to spell out 'Cats Beware'; lifelong fans
Michael Ó Faoláin (Dungarvan), Peter Flanagan (Tramore), the
Kearns family (Kilmeaden) and Gerry Walsh (in the city) all
painted their houses white and blue, as did many others, including
Alice Mullaly who painted the names of every member of the
thirty-man squad on the gable end of her house in Lismore Lawn.
Dozens of cars were painted white and blue across the county. And
schools had special jersey days.

On the Tuesday night before the match, the team still hadn't
been named but players were given envelopes containing match
tickets for their relatives. Those who were playing got more than
the others, so inadvertently players knew who was going to be
togging out for the final.

Thursday night, the last training session before the All-Ireland.
Walsh Park had pools of water on it in places after the heavy rain
all week. Some players were wondering how they were going to
do high speed ball work on such a bog? In Nowlan Park, County
Kilkenny, there were fumes coming off the balls they were hitting
the sod at such speed.

Davy had a few Kilkenny jerseys brought into Walsh Park and

got them put on the tackle bags, the type of motivation used by other county managers at times, in particular Tyrone's Mickey Harte. The players have to punch the bags with the jerseys and then drive into them as hard as possible. He told the players that this was a war that had to be won, that nothing was impossible, that they were not to stop believing – that they were going to create history.

At the end of the session, Davy got the players in a circle on the field and, holding two balled-up Kilkenny jerseys in his fist, told the players that those who wore those jerseys didn't think anything of them. 'They think they're better than us. They think they invented hurling. They think nothing of you.' And he threw the jerseys on the ground.

Some of the players didn't know how to react; they thought it was like a scene out of *D'Unbelievables*.

When the players had made their way to the dressing room, Davy, hurley in hand, told them that he didn't think some of the Kilkenny forwards were as tough as people made out, in particular Tommy Walsh and Eddie Brennan. He also told them that nice guys don't win anything. Seamus Prendergast was to be marking Walsh and the Kilkenny back was to be 'softened up' on Sunday. Eoin Murphy would be marking Eddie Brennan. A third player was also included in this instruction but when he got on the pitch, he didn't do anything, saying it didn't feel right.

For anybody who knows the honesty and brutality of the Kilkenny Club Championship, this would be nourishment for them because Kilkenny players love a good physical game.

For some players, this 'softening up' was no big deal and was part of the process that teams did in hurling and Gaelic football all over the country. But for others it wasn't what Waterford was about; they knew the Kilkenny players well and didn't believe it would have any effect – at worst, it would backfire and inspire Kilkenny, the best team in the country, to mix it up when necessary. Players such as Eoin Murphy were not like Colin Lynch or Ollie Baker of Clare in the past – even though Murphy was a great hurler and not afraid to get involved when necessary, he was generally regarded as one of the nicest and quietest players on the panel.

'Some lads straight away didn't like what he said,' says a player. 'Eoin Murphy was one of the quieter chaps and the Penders were the same way; it wouldn't be in them; they wouldn't be that type of hurlers; and I'd say it definitely played on their minds.'

One of the back-room staff says it didn't cause undue tension in the squad, 'But Seamus Pender will tell you they'd never done that and they didn't know what they were doing. The Penders in particular are too quiet. They are lovely lads.'

Some of the players didn't see the wisdom of mixing it up with another player in front of 82,000 They had no problem hitting a chap a good shoulder in a fifty–fifty ball when the game was on and thought it may have been better to mix it up when the ball was thrown in, when nobody would really notice. It was unnecessary distraction, something that would play on some players' minds as they tried to sleep over the coming nights.

Others thought it was a very naive thing to have said. And doubted very much if the selectors had approved the policy decision beforehand. One of the three players admitted to friends he hadn't slept well in the days leading up to the game because of the orders. And the matter would later be brought up at a county board meeting by Jay Prendergast, uncle to Seamus and Declan, who asked under 'Any Other Business' that a guarantee be given that it wouldn't happen again. He would see Seamus and Tommy Walsh 'tearing into each other' before the ball was thrown in. 'I was amazed,' he said, 'as we knew some order had to have been given because the boys were not that type of players to do that sort of thing.'

Others remarked that Waterford traditionally didn't fear Kilkenny and the results they'd achieved over the years showed that – beating them in the National League final of 2007. So why was it necessary for Davy to adopt this attitude?

Former Kerry footballer Darragh Ó Sé commented in *The Irish Times* about the tradition of lads 'flaking into' other players, saying it can only be done by players who are used to doing it (such as the Meath footballers in the early 1990s) and who wouldn't let it ruin their concentration of the game.

Former Cork manager John Allen says in the run-up to a big game that, 'An awful lot of communication is non-verbal and fellas receive signals from all different things. One of the big things for us is never build up the opposition.'

Davy Fitzgerald says Seamus Prendergast was told to mix it up with Tommy Walsh at the start but 'I never said we were going to timber fellas'. He adds they discussed many different tactics that week in the run up to the game involving strategy on the field, movement, positioning of players, etc. and that one thing doesn't cause you to win or lose an All-Ireland. Davy knew he had the players under his control for only a few months and he was doing his utmost to prepare them as best as possible to face a super-fit, super-skilled and star-studded Kilkenny team.

The team went to the Ramada Hotel for food and, afterwards, watched a ten-minute compilation DVD of the training sessions put together by Michael Hearn and team-bonding exercises they had done over the previous three weeks.

It included a message of good luck from one of Waterford's greatest sportsmen, cyclist Sean Kelly, and backing tracks such as 'Search For The Hero Inside', 'Days Like This' and songs by Van Morrison and the Lighthouse Family. It showed clips of scores from the games over the summer since Davy had taken over, Davy's voice saying, 'I've been as proud in my life.' The time was nearly upon them.

The build-up to the match was now reaching fever pitch.

As would be expected, Waterford Local Radio gave the occasion massive coverage, increasing the hype. 'Don't Stop Believing' by the band Journey was being hummed on the streets (the same song which the Chicago White Sox had used and which is also played at many US hockey games). Contrary to myth, the song was never played in the Waterford dressing room, but it may as well have been so pervasive is its tune.

The Waterford contingent met at the Granville Hotel on the Saturday lunch-time and got shuttle buses over the bridge to the train station. On the bus over, the players were joking about the 'mixing it up' and a senior player jokingly took out a blank piece of paper, pretending it was an imaginary list of players who had jobs to do! Everybody broke into laughter. Davy wasn't on the coach.

The 3 p.m. train took them to Dublin, where a coach ferried them the Marriott in Ashbourne, County Meath. There was tension building in the train and they were late getting to the Marriott so the roster for the evening was put back by an hour. Sports psychologists say 'you have to cool down to rev up' and 'being on time but not having too much time is a fine balance'. It was imperative that this was adhered to but things were already running behind.

Players were allocated their rooms. They had been given a choice of sharing or having a room on their own. Eoin Kelly got a room by himself as he leaves the television on late. He'd normally share with Dan, who opted for a room on his own too. The plan was to keep the starting fifteen together. Dave Bennett was sharing with James Murray, both knew they weren't starting. James will later say he had thought it was their destiny to win.

The players were quietly confident that they were going to beat Kilkenny, but, that Saturday, a few whispers start that those who had been asked to mix it up with Kilkenny before the start were not entirely happy.

Dinner was boiled chicken or pasta without sauce. Butter wasn't allowed for the potatoes. Then it was upstairs for most to watch the end of *The Premiership*, with players chatting in each other's rooms; Dan, Dave Bennett and Paul Flynn all headed to Eoin Kelly's room to watch the soccer.

They all gathered downstairs in the Blackwater Room and didn't have a talk about tactics that night as Davy said they were not there to talk about All-Ireland final that night but to try to relax. This is known as a 'blocking out' technique and sometimes it works, sometimes it doesn't. It was a different routine from before the Tipp semi-final. He asked who wanted to go to mass the following morning and most who raised their hands were from the west. In some other counties, players are all made to go as it is seen as an essential part of quiet time in a group situation.

Maurice Geary always believed that no matter what game is being played, you go in with a chance. Nobody could foresee what was going to happen. Apart from a difficult game against Tipperary, the six Waterford backs hadn't really been tested during the year; the team hadn't had its back to the wall and the run-in had been relatively easy.

After eight o'clock, everybody went into the next room, the Boyne Suite, and the room of forty or so was broken up into teams and a quiz started with Peter Queally and David O'Brien as MCs. It was all general knowledge and, as usual, 'the auld lads' won (the back-room boys!).

The night before the biggest match of their lives, the players were in the same hotel in which they'd stayed before the Tipperary game. Staying there had worked for the Tipp game, why wouldn't it work now? Kilkenny were due to travel up in the morning, no overnights before finals.

If the things they did that night worked, then every other team in the country getting to a final may try to replicate them in the future. If not, it may be one more item to add to the list of things that contributed to the result.

Three of the senior back-room staff were then put as judges for an X-Factor competition. Cards were drawn out of a hat for each table or team of four with tasks for doing impressions, acting or singing a song. It was a great concept and a bit of fun. It was about half past nine, and there was no alcohol involved – nobody would have a drink tonight.

Each table nominated a person for their act and scores were given. The atmosphere was brilliant and rising. This was the Crazy

Gang having a great time without a drop of alcohol. This was one of the most fun-loving teams in the country doing something to take their minds off the match for a few hours. But they're competitors too and no table wanted to lose. At the same time, Kilkenny players were in their own homes doing what they normally do. Noel Hickey was delivering straw to his uncle in Piltown that evening and says, 'The night before a match we try not to do anything out of the ordinary.'

As the talent competition heated up, one of the players took to the stage to whoops of joy from the others and he started stripping. He thought he was in the film *The Full Monty*, as mobile phone cameras caught the moment and most in the room were convulsed with laughter. A few, though, didn't. The evening (one lad later calls it 'the greatest ever hooley without drink') ended before 11 p.m. and the lads retired to their rooms, some with their adrenaline so built up, they'd have to stay up talking about it for an hour at least.

Wayne Hutchinson turned on *Up for the Match* on RTÉ. His room-mate Shane O'Sullivan told him, 'If you don't turn that off, Hutchy, I'm going to throw you and the telly out the window.' Hutchy turned it off.

Some thought the X-Factor competition was too much as it took some players a long while to get to sleep after it, something they didn't think would help them the following day. The quiz was perfect, even if the competition was maybe a bit much. For others, the evening would have no bearing on their sleep patterns or what happened at the final, and that it wasn't a big deal at all. And if Waterford won, it'd be the talk of the town, a stroke of genius and one of the greatest ever pre-match routines.

At least one player slept in the Waterford shorts he'd be wearing for the match, something he always did before big matches; another had a freezing-cold shower in the morning, something he only did on championship days, a kind of 'today is special' reminder.

Eoin Kelly texted his wife Sharon at 3.15 a.m. to say he was still awake but then he slept well after that. They were called around 9 a.m. and headed down for breakfast, afterwards some went back to bed for another hour or two.

Roger Casey believes they had too much time on the Sunday. Some went to mass in Ashbourne. Some of the seats had blue and white flags on them and the priest wished them well from the altar. Back to the hotel and it was only 10.30 a.m., there was a long time to go before they left at 1 p.m.

Roger's wife, Kay, didn't write any notes for Justin during his time in Waterford and there were none in the gear bag. But, for this match, she gave Davy Fitz a mass bouquet and with the help of near neighbour Lucy Walsh, a seventy-five-year-old Waterford fanatic, the jerseys had also been blessed with Holy Water (at a wedding in Ratoath the day before the game).

Meanwhile players were busy trying to do nothing – especially not read the papers.

And in the papers: *Sunday Tribune* journalist Enda McEvoy was saying: 'Goliaths To Slay Davy'. Former Clare forward Jamesie O'Connor suggested physicality between the two teams could be okay, while former Wexford player Liam Dunne warned about Waterford's ability to handle the occasion. On *The Sunday Game Live*, James 'Cha' Fitzgerald of Kilkenny described Waterford as 'electric hurlers' while Davy Fitzgerald said, 'I have tremendous respect for Kilkenny and Brian Cody.' And in the panel discussion, Thomas Mulcahy of Cork said that coping with the hype and the 'Big Match Day' atmosphere would be the key for Waterford.

Then it was time to pack up and have another team meeting in one of the function rooms on the second floor. Davy and the two selectors went through the tactics for the day. There wasn't a whole lot of shouting because, at this stage, there was no point to it, but he did throw in a few 'fucks' at the end, as most managers do. Some players thought he gave an excellent prep-talk and they headed out to the coach.

One o'clock and it was time to leave.

Eoin Kelly took up his usual position on the back seat on the right-hand side; Flynners was in the middle and Dan was there too; Ken and Tony normally sat together. For Kelly, it felt like any other game and he didn't feel any extra stress. The other, older comrades appeared the same but nobody knew what's going on in their heads. Dan and Kelly chatted away and everything seemed grand.

Most of the older lads don't have iPods. A few men's magazines such as *Nuts* are passed around, but no sporting sections of the newspapers. On his iPod, Kevin Moran has a lot of Kings of Leon, speeches from films; and like many players, he particularly likes Al Pacino's speech from *Any Given Sunday*.

As was usual for big matches, players had been asked to pick their favourite song and the compilation CD was now playing as they came in from Ashbourne. The first song that came on was a piss-take of Davy Fitz, with an impersonator pretending to be the man himself! Davy had chosen the song to lighten the mood, everybody started to laugh and in response to the laughter he told the players, 'I bet ya Justin wouldn't be doing this.' The collection included The Killers, Bruce Springsteen and Garth Brooks! When Garth came on, the young lads laughed, saying it was disgraceful and tried to pick out the oldie who had chosen the song.

The number of fans thronging the footpaths increased as they neared Croke Park, and the players were cheered like matadors. Coincidentally, the last thing that came on the CD was part of the Al Pacino speech, but for some, the emphasis in the speech of 'hell' didn't strike the right chord as they were entering the stadium. There's no way surely Waterford could be going into hell?

Big Dan suffered terribly from sciatica and as anyone who knows how troublesome the back can be, he'd been through an awful lot of pain. He'd been taking tablets before and after games this year just to play and he hoped it wasn't going to trouble him today.

Shane O'Sullivan was completely focused. He had a pre-match plan learned from the course he studied at college. He listened to

'Lose Yourself' by Eminem and Jon Bon Jovi's 'It's My Life' on his iPod. He thought about seizing the moment, because nobody knew what was going to happen tomorrow. He got a tingle, a shiver as the crowds increased and he tried not to look out the window.

The Waterford team was travelling on a J.J. Kavanagh coach (a Kilkenny bus!) because there were no DVD facilities on the CIÉ buses based in Waterford.

Seamus Meade of the GAA had issued details to Bernard Smith and the Competition Control Committee that counties should use buses to get below the 3.6-metre height restriction if they wished to drive up to the Hogan dressing rooms.

They came through the back entrance of the stadium complex, but Billy Costine was stopped 100 yards or so from the dressing room entrance and was told about the overhead pipe. He got off the bus and told the officials he would lower the coach using the 'ferry lift' and they'd get in no problem, but the officials were having none of it and a verbal row developed.

'I told them they were being unreasonable but they told me if we hit it, they'd have to evacuate Croke Park!' says Billy. 'I knew full well we'd get under it but they wouldn't listen. The cops came along and everything.'

The players were wondering what was happening and the delay was getting to a few of them; the tension was increasing and this wasn't helping. Billy told Davy they weren't letting them through.

Davy stood up, turned to the players and, referencing Nicky Brennan, the GAA president and Kilkenny man, said it was an attempt to upset them but that this type of tactic wouldn't stop them winning today. 'This is their way of trying to stop us but we're not going to be stopped today,' he shouted, before telling the players they'd walk up to the dressing rooms.

For some players, the mood had now changed – there was now a greater power against them other than the twenty players in Kilkenny jerseys they might face.

Two weeks later, the same thing would happen to Mickey

Harte's Tyrone team, and he said, 'Lads, bit of a problem here. We might as well get off and walk. No big deal.'

They all got off and walked the short distance into the players' entrance (the gear bags had gone in beforehand with Roger Casey).

They were to sit where their jersey had been placed and the players found their places before heading out to watch the minor match.

Physios Peter Kirwan and Emmett Costelloe got their potions and strappings ready. Michael 'Brick' Walsh had ankle trouble and got a strapping.

Four or five of the younger guys came into the room for rubs. Peter could feel the sweat on their legs, which is a physical reaction to anxiety and increased levels of adrenaline. He'd been so close to these boys over the past few years that he knew when some were going to have a good day or not. There were more who were nervous today than normal, and understandably so. He tried to relax them, he talked to them, knowing what to say.

Nearly a dozen got rubs; some were on the couch for a lot longer than normal; some needed motivating, others needed calming down. The signs were not good and he felt at least five would not play well.

With fifty minutes to go before throw in, Gerry Fitzpatrick took them to the warm-up area near the dressing rooms and went through the normal agility exercises to get them moving.

Then it was back inside for the talk.

Firstly, Davy got them to try to 'zone in' − a visualisation technique now advocated a lot by sports psychologists. He made sure they were all sitting down, then they put their heads in their hands and closed their eyes. He told them to visualise scenarios: if you were beaten to the first ball, what were you going to do? You were going to get it back. They had to visualise getting it back and hitting it up the field or over the bar. He wanted them to visualise those who had written them off, he wanted them to visualise their faces. This is a long way from shadow boxing where the Cuban boxer would block out the opponent's face before a big fight. They do this because they believe visualising creates anger, and anger is fear-based.

In the Kilkenny dressing room, Brian Cody wasn't using visualisation techniques; he was just telling the players to focus on their own game.

The Waterford players got more drinks on board and Davy reminded them of the tactics and what they were there to do. The tension in the dressing room moved to nervous energy as players were told to stand up and get moving. Lads bounced against each other, some slapped hurleys on their thighs.

It was time.

But these players – these first-time players in an All-Ireland final, what they have been dreaming of – had no physical or mental conception of what they are about to experience. No sports psychologist could have prepared them for what was about to hit them. They were carrying on their lean shoulders the expectations of a county starved of success since 1959.

The entire back-room staff had been told to be positive no matter what, even if a player was injured, they were to tell him he was playing well. Tom Feeney was to lead the subs in clapping the players out and back in later.

The teams hit the field and the noise was unbelievable. Kilkenny were out a full five minutes before Waterford, getting as many touches on the ball as possible. It was boiling cauldron stuff.

Waterford had a set warm-up routine which involved a number of specific drills. But the noise was so great, the players couldn't hear the orders being shouted by the selectors and the drills didn't seem to work. But with 82,000 people looking on it was too late to change them; that would have confused the players even more. With hindsight, maybe a less complicated routine would have been better.

As Waterford's warm-up went askew, Kilkenny manager Brian Cody was ice cool on the line, arms folded watching his players puck the ball over and back to themselves as if it was a warm-up to a normal match. In lines of three, they do jab lifts and simple striking exercises, getting up to sixty touches of the ball before the start. The Waterford warm-up wasn't going well.

'Our warm-up went arseways,' says a senior player. 'Next thing you know Davy's in the middle of us in a big line doing a warm-up and you're thinking, What's happening? This isn't part of the plan. And Kilkenny are down below and they're pucking balls over and back and they are so focused, shouting at each other and Cody is standing there his with arms folded.'

Earlier the All Star team of 1983 had been introduced to the crowd and Tipperary legend Nicky English was astounded when he saw Davy going in to help with the warm-up. He remarked to his friends in the stand at how agitated Waterford seemed to be and in the match, how the great Ken McGrath couldn't hit the ball fifty yards. 'I was thinking of that photo of the Waterford build-up and all those fans around the players in the darkness in Fraher Field. I knew it must have got to them.'

Cody had his Kilkenny team primed like never before. Waterford wouldn't know what had hit them.

Both teams lined up to meet the president. Mary McAleese shook their hands, and thought they were a very nervous-looking team. Back in her seat, she said so to GAA president and Kilkenny man Nicky Brennan, who concurred, saying, 'They were woeful nervous; you could see it in their eyes; and their hands were sweaty. And then for the parade, they shouldn't be looking up at crowd, that's a no–no.'

The back-room staff could see the players' expressions had changed in the few minutes since they'd left the dressing room. It wasn't good. There was now a noticeable fear on some of their faces.

As the players paraded round Croke Park before the game (with Waterford closest to the fans), former manager Tony Mansfield was looking down and could see some players waving to people they know in the crowd. They shouldn't be doing that, he thought.

Concentrate, concentrate.

The players all came together for the national anthem and stood looking at the tricolour. Waterford players, subs and back-room staff were all together underneath the Hogan Stand; Kilkenny's starting fifteen were in the centre of the field, undaunted. The likes of Henry Shefflin, with seven All Star awards, didn't do nerves.

First there was a minute's silence for Larry Fanning (who played on the victorious 1948 Waterford team). Then Cara O'Sullivan led off the national anthem and Davy was seen on the television cameras, clutching the two crucifixes that hang around his neck.

The crowd roared as the anthem ended and the players took up their positions.

In the corner-back position, Eoin Murphy went over to his marker Eddie Brennan.

But Eddie says Kilkenny and Waterford lads always got on great and this wasn't Waterford's style. Looking back on it now, Eddie Brennan says, 'I was surprised to be honest, he tried to give me a dead leg or whatever and I said, "What are you doing, Eoin?" Around the field, we had been prepared for some roughening up but if you're not used to doing something like that, it's bound to distract you in the run-up. I'm always of the belief you should only do what you are comfortable with. I realised then that Eoin wouldn't be concentrating on the ball. Sure, we got on great with the Waterford lads – a lot of our lads went down to Waterford drinking with them after they won the 2007 National League.' Eddie Brennan would go on to score two goals and three points from play.

Kilkenny county secretary Pat Dunphy says, 'In the Kilkenny dressing room, nothing has changed over the years. Cody stands in the middle, goes up to them and out they go. But our lads would have responded by doing what they do best: hurling.'

'I'm convinced that if the lads had pinched the Kilkenny lad's arses, it would have had more effect,' says one of the panel members afterwards. 'The Kilkenny lads were going for their fifth or sixth medal; they play All-Ireland finals for training; the physical aspect wasn't going to trouble them.'

Another player summed up the tactics as wrong. 'Total and utter madness; stupid carry on. He was bringing the Clare tactics to it and Waterford never did that.'

One of the players who had been given an instruction was thinking would he do it but he says he found it embarrassing and decided against doing anything – something he was happy about afterwards.

The rest of the Kilkenny team saw what was happening. It was retribution time. Time for business.

The ball was thrown in and Kilkenny's fire was lit – they lashed into it. Cha Fitzpatrick won a free after 2.5 seconds and before it could be taken, referee Barry Kelly had to separate Seamus Prendergast and Tommy Walsh (Tommy's helmet had been taken off in the pushing and dragging).

The Waterford players realised that Kilkenny knew exactly how to stop them. This was big-boy stuff, hard, uncompromising and physical.

'The slapping of the hurl they'd give you when you'd have the ball in your hand,' says Kevin Moran. 'You'd be thinking a hand pass is the easiest thing in the world but you couldn't even hand pass they were so on top of you. They just got everything perfect on the day.'

Many players would have sore forearms and hands, making it one of the busiest ever games for Waterford physio Peter Kirwan.

Roger Casey had seen it for years. 'You'd have the ball on your hurley and they give it this little tap; they have it off to perfection; or a little pull back on the arm. Why can't we do it? They are getting away with it and we are admiring them for doing it – some lads are waiting for it to happen.'

Kilkenny's expertise in hooking, blocking and catching was paying off – Derek Lyng hooked Jamie Nagle for The Cats' fourth point; then J.J. Delaney caught a high ball over Dan Shanahan, passed it on to Aiden Fogarty and it was over the bar. Then Eddie Brennan fairly shouldered Eoin Murphy over the endline; the resultant sixty-five gives Kilkenny a 0–6 to 0–2 lead after only nine minutes.

Stephen Molumphy thought the first fifteen minutes had been going quite well, when he got a second to breathe, and they were only a few points down.

But, suddenly, Kilkenny banged one in; then bang, they got a second goal; and then Shefflin drifted out to the right half-back position and put over a glorious score; then another went over. All this time, Waterford couldn't put one over the bar. Then, suddenly, it was half-time and Waterford traipsed off, seventeen points down.

Five of the Waterford players had to be treated for niggly things and some got more rubs as their calves and hamstrings were tightening.

The old failing of not enough Waterford players being able to catch enough high balls had come back to haunt them. The stats would show that in that first half, Kilkenny had won thirty-nine possessions out of the fifty-fifty tussles with Waterford only winning twenty-two; in aerial battles, Kilkenny won eighteen to Waterford's four. Kilkenny had scored ten points from ten shots (before Martin Comerford hit their first wide). Waterford hadn't pulled off any noticeable hooks or blocks. And Kilkenny would score four points in injury time at the end of each half.

Davy Fitz and the selectors were looking at the bolt of hurling lightening that had hit them in the form of Kilkenny. It was unreal. For all the great teams that have played in Croke Park, the stadium had rarely seen as perfect a performance.

Waterford hadn't been able to respond. That much was obvious. It was also obvious that Waterford did not have the midfield or half-backs to pick off long-range points when they were required. Waterford didn't have the kind of midfield fire power that gave other teams their swagger and confidence. There was nothing more uplifting for a county to see than a half-back drive out and hit a ball over the bar from ninety yards.

Thoughts were swirling through Davy's head. Were there any changes he could make to ease the pain? No. What else?

'We got too caught up maybe in the occasion, taking on too many bits of sideshows. The stuff at the start had nothing to do with it, you could see we couldn't react to what they hit us with. We just hadn't tuned in enough to what was coming, they were relentless,' he says. 'Kilkenny were way fitter and we were beaten by a better team: simple as that,' he says.

After the two Kilkenny goals went in, selector Maurice Geary wanted to be in the stand, not on the sideline. It was a genuine nightmare experience. No matter what they did, he felt it wasn't going to matter; Kilkenny were swarming like killer bees, putting on their finest performance. The game was a senior team against a junior team. He was also thinking that even though the game was only half over, it was now damage limitation. 'If Our Lord had come down to make a speech to them, it wouldn't have made any difference,' he says.

Peter and Maurice each said something about pride but, inwardly, Maurice was thinking, Will we go away now? Where's the bus?

The sound of the players breathing; the sound of their brains trying to comprehend what had happened and what was going to happen. The sound of silence.

Then Stephen Molumphy, Ken McGrath and John Mullane each said a few sentences about everybody completely letting themselves down; and that Waterford had fallen asleep in the last ten minutes of the first half. But it was all a daze. Waterford were choking as a team. It could happen to the very best in any sport at any time and it was happening to Waterford. The combination of negative thoughts and emotions was leading them to lose confidence and motivation, to move slowly and with less certainty, and to doubt their ability to compete.

The pressure of the occasion was also part of the problem.

Keith Ross Miller is widely regarded as Australia's greatest every all-rounder in test cricket. He was also an RAF pilot during the Second World War. He died in 2004 but his wartime exploits gave him a greater sense of perspective in sport. When asked by Michael Parkinson about pressure in cricket, he responded with the famous quotation, 'Pressure is a Messerschmitt up your arse, playing cricket is not.' And when Kenny Perry could taste history with a two-shot lead with two holes to go at the 2009 Masters and still lost, he said, 'Great players make it happen; average players don't. And that's the way it is.' The dividing line between winning and disappointment isn't about technique or athleticism or talent, it's about performing under pressure, hitting the shots when they mattered most.

What was happening on the field was a case study in 'choking' as the part of the Waterford players' brains that monitored their behaviour started to interfere with the actions that were normally made without thinking. Players began to second guess skills they had honed through years of practice. And the worst part about choking was that it tended to spiral: the failures built up on each other, so a stressful situation was made more stressful.

The Waterford players were like onlookers at the scene of an accident – witnessing somebody else's accident!

While Davy was outside the room, John Carey's role was to try to settle the lads. 'Looking back now, we should have cleared the room and have had just the players. I think the players knew it was gone and it was about damage limitation. In psychological terms, when you have the scoreboard, the clock and the ref all screaming at you that you're screwed, all you want to do is finish it and crawl away home.'

With Davy still outside the room, 'Brick' Walsh said a few words about doing it for their families and their relations in the stand, but Paul Flynn stood up and said to everyone, 'Sit the fuck down and shut the fuck up! Forget the mothers and fathers in the stand, there's a hurling match going on. Stop trying to compete with these boys in the air, break the ball, break the ball!'

Players were listening to him as he was suggesting some game-specific instructions.

Davy then came in after maybe ten minutes of the fifteen-minute break, called them together and reiterated the instructions. They would make drastic changes (which unfortunately wouldn't work).

The subs tried to gee up the players as they headed back out, but it was like saying best of luck to a cow as she headed into the abattoir.

The gods were with Kilkenny, and the slaughter continued with Waterford getting poorer and Kilkenny getting better. Kilkenny would continue turning over possession winning thirty-six of the fifty-fifty balls to Waterford's twenty-seven.

Dave Bennett couldn't believe how awesome Kilkenny were in the second half. 'No doubt they are the greatest team that has ever played the game because they're the greatest unit and ninety-nine times out of a hundred the man in the better position gets the ball.

Fans tried to laugh with comments such as, 'Give Waterford a ball as Kilkenny won't give theirs back.'

Some Waterford players just wanted to get off the pitch. 'It was heartbreaking and embarrassing,' says Kevin Moran.

The harder the Waterford players tried, the worse it got. Every Kilkenny player was on fire. Nobody, not even most Kilkenny fans, had seen them play as well.

Stephen Molumphy was thinking, I'm just going to make this as hard as possible on my guy; keep running; make it has hard as possible for him to get his medal. He was marking the great Jackie Tyrell, who got taken off. His replacement played great too. Molumphy, and every other Waterford player, was feeling angry and sickened.

Gerald McCarthy was in the Hogan Stand watching the match with some friends. He wanted to be there to see Waterford win. He knew he was now watching something of a horror unfold for the lads, some of whom he knew so well. With seven minutes to go, he left.

Everywhere for those wanting Waterford to win, it was agony. For Kilkenny fans, it was a joy to witness. As Waterford fans started to leave early, three middle-aged Kilkenny men in the Hogan Stand rose up and shouted, 'Lock the doors, make them watch!'

And then the final whistle was blown: Kilkenny 3–30, Waterford 1–13. A twenty-three point defeat.

After the game, Kevin Moran just wanted to shout, 'Get Me Outta Here'; wanted to get away from the crowd coming on the field. He met his mother who said, 'Hard luck', and another relation who said, 'Tough going out there, was it?'

Kevin had to walk away. He was not religious but at his father's request, he had gone to early-morning mass the previous day in St Benildus church in Waterford. His father said it would do him good and now, when Kevin met his father, he told him he'd never go to mass before a match again. 'If you hadn't gone to mass, you would have been sent off,' his father responded, in reference to a moment when Kevin fouled and could have been red-carded. They both laughed. Kevin knew that when he went back teaching in De La Salle College in Waterford, the south Kilkenny students would go on for years about this defeat.

Usually teams who finish runners-up are never remembered in the pages of history but not in this case – the drubbing will be remembered for ever as one of Kilkenny's finest performances and one of Waterford's worst.

In the dressing room afterwards, it was hard to describe the feelings. Davy Fitz went into his little dressing room beside the players' and cried.

This was a mortuary; the deafening silence was interrupted by grown men crying.

'Tony, Ken, Mullane, they were all crying,' says Billy Costine.

Davy went into the Kilkenny dressing room and congratulated the victors. Most of the Waterford players changed quickly and were gone before Brian Cody came in to offer his commiserations.

Noelie Crowley met Ken McGrath afterwards and Ken told him, 'It was like there was somebody holding me to the ground', so strange had been the feeling during the match.

Back in the hotel afterwards, Maurice Geary met friends who have travelled from America to watch the match. The more people he met, the more his head dropped.

People said they were happy to see Waterford in a final, but it was embarrassing. He met his wife Kathleen and their children, he knew the drinks would soften the pain a little but, in the morning, it would still be a nightmare. But three stalwarts from his club, Gerry Hurley, Pat Flynn and Eugene Hickey, travelled in from the Bewley's at Newlands Cross when they could very easily have driven home, and he met him at the lift. It was moments such as this that would raise his spirits again.

Back on the train, everybody thought it was going to be awful, especially when there was no crowd at Plunkett Station. It reminded Maurice of his days playing for Ballyduff when they would parade through the town on the back of a truck, no matter if they won or lost. He thought this was going to be just as bad.

But then they came across the bridge on the open-top bus and the players started crying – they couldn't believe that about 10,000 fans had gathered at the Millennium Plaza on the quay. Davy told those who had convened that he and the players would be back, better and stronger.

In the aftermath, players tried to grapple with what had happened. Brian Phelan reckoned Kilkenny were so good because they probably worked harder than any other team at basics, such as tackling and hooking.

Ken McGrath believes Kilkenny are the benchmark for every team, 'Hurling is everything for them over there. They're all grand lads, they're not in your face and they enjoy their wins. They win the big games. I wouldn't change who I play for – they're only across the river and the have All-Irelands hanging out of their pockets like!'

A few weeks later, at a golf society function in Cork, Paul Flynn, Dave Bennett and Tom Feeney talked about retirement.

Three weeks later, they did all retire, quietly they hoped. The papers and television reports carried the news, with Flynn mentioned in particular. In a subsequent newspaper article, Davy Fitz spoke about Feeney and Bennett retiring, saying something to the effect that they hadn't made the team last year, so maybe they thought there was no point in coming back.

Bennett was incensed. 'Justin was a lot of things, but he would have said, "Best of luck to the lads, they gave forty-five years service to the team", or whatever.' He was going to retire anyway and Davy wasn't the reason he left.

There were times over the years when Bennett felt he had been treated badly but he had never fallen out with Gerald or Justin and had loved his time since he first put on a Waterford jersey in 1989. He gave an interview to Denis Walsh in *The Sunday Times* saying what had gone on in the build-up to the match was 'mind-blowing'. 'In eight or nine years did you ever see Eoin Murphy hitting someone before a ball was thrown in – or Declan or Seamus Prendergast?' adding that these players had felt it was unfair on them in that it wasn't their fault – an apparent reference to managerial instructions.

'I just had enough,' he says. 'The enjoyment's gone, it was time to go. And, anyway, there was always more to life than hurling.'

Of course there is.

16

2009 AND 2010 –

THE AFTERMATH AND THE FUTURE

The shock of such a heavy, ignominious defeat cut deep into the psyche of many in Waterford city and county. After all the hype, the result was a calamity. Of course, nobody died, but the soul of Waterford hurling was severely battered.

Some Kilkenny people who worked and shopped in Waterford city walked around for months afterwards with broad smiles – their natural order had been restored, vindicated and made even more impregnable.

Waterford fans also realised that a potentially 'golden era' of hurling for them could be gone for ever – or, at least, could be going. The skill and number of players retiring, such as Paul Flynn, Dave Bennett and Tom Feeney, was enormous and only served to deepen the fans' depression.

In the years up to the end of 2008, Paul Flynn had been the second most capped player for Waterford, Tom Feeney the fifth and Dave Bennett joint seventh. Flynners scored in every Munster senior hurling championship game in which he played – a record that is hard to believe. And, even better than that, he scored from play in twenty-four matches, including his last nineteen.

When he retired, he was Waterford's top championship scorer.

Pos	Total	Name	Score	Appearances	Average
1.	253	Paul Flynn	24–181	46	5.50
2.	141	Eoin Kelly	10–111	31	4.54
3.	117	Dan Shanahan	20–57	43	2.72
4.	116	John Mullane	11–83	33	3.51
5.	105	Philly Grimes	11–72	35	3.00

If further proof is needed about to his importance, his position in the list of the top scorers in the Munster senior hurling championship says it all. He is second only to Christy Ring (who played for twenty-two years) and Flynn's scoring average is higher, which is a remarkable achievement when it is remembered that for many of his playing years, he was only playing one championship game a year.

	Total	Hurler	Score	Games	Avg	Era
1.	235	Christy Ring (Cork)	28–151	49	4.79	1940–1962
2.	184	Paul Flynn (Waterford)	20–124	27	6.81	1993–2007
3.	173	Jimmy Doyle (Tipperary)	16–125	29	5.96	1957–1973
4.	162	Charlie McCarthy (Cork)	21–99	32	5.06	1965–1980
5.	158	Eoin Kelly (Tipperary)	7–137	19	8.31	2001–2008

Fans were aware of just how good the hurling had been over the previous six years. Each year, All Star awards are given to the best fifteen players in the country and from their introduction in 1971 until 2001, only four awards had been handed out to Waterford hurlers. Then, from 2002 to 2008, sixteen awards came to the county.

Roger Casey attended one of the All Star ceremonies in Dublin and got on great with players from other counties. He could see the reverence Brian Cody was held in by his players, 'I could see some of the Kilkenny players and they were nearly sitting up on Cody's lap!'

Davy Fitzgerald was ratified by the Waterford county board and was making preparations to take his panel for the first full-term, knowing that he would need younger players to supplement his ageing panel. Peter Queally and Maurice Geary had both decided to stay on.

As for the washing, Roger told Davy that they just couldn't carry on doing it, so players would be washing their own training gear at home from now on.

Waterford wanted 2009 to be the season of 'redemption' and, in November 2008, the players got height and weight tests and some did training sessions in the woods in Portlaw. One of the players Davy asked to come for a trial match was young Noel Connors from Passage East, whose father had also hurled for Waterford in the 1980s.

'The toughest thing was walking into a dressing room with Mullane and Prendergast and others there and thinking, What the hell am I doing here? I was kind of shocked! And then you'd have the questions whether you're good enough to be there but you just get into it and on with it. And then you'd be worried you might be taking somebody's place, either in the dressing room or on the field. I sat beside Molumphy. He started talking to me and there were a lot of young lads there as well, which was good,' says Noel.

On 6 January 2009, most of the team went to New York but the younger lads who were new to the panel had to stay behind and do stamina training in Kilmacthomas and other places, which was a hard thing to do with very few players there. 'Torture,' says Noel. 'The eleven of us would train for three days in a row, then have a day off, then train for another two days. Then we'd train a few times at weekends, being out in Tramore maybe at 8 a.m. to run on the beach.'

When the rest of the panel got back, full training resumed and the younger players were introduced to the horror that is Aglish – a beautiful village in west Waterford but the place of nightmares for Waterford hurlers down through the years.

'The worst place to go training is Aglish,' says Noel. 'It's always cold, dark and wet in January and there's lots of running. Every time you'd hear the word, it would put a shiver up your spine.'

As an example of how routines have changed so much from

previous years, Waterford played Laois away in the league on a Saturday in February and everybody was up early for a run on the beach in Tramore at 8 a.m.

One of Waterford's most important engagements in the spring of 2009 was playing Kilkenny in the National League in Walsh Park on 1 March. Maurice Geary decided he would have a strong input into the pre-match talk and told the players, 'People expect us to hide because of the hammering we got from these last September but we should be proud of where we are; we've hurled so well over the past few years; you have to do this today for the county; this is a very important game for us and we're going to go out there and establish our credentials again.'

Maurice had seen it happen in the 1980s and 1990s – Waterford teams rising one year and then ever so quickly and easily, slipping way down the hurling pecking order. This time, the Waterford players rose to the occasion and won the match.

The night before they were due to play Dublin in the league, Davy took the team to see his friend, Bernard Dunne, box for a world title at the O_2 Arena. After the bout, which Dunne won, the players had got to bed around 1.30 a.m. Some had been inspired by what they'd seen and it would have a positive effect on them for weeks after; others would just be tired and would not play well the next day.

Later in the year, Davy would get Bernard to give the players a talk about winning in sport. The management team also got other motivational speakers, such as former Armagh manager Joe Kernan, organised former Irish rugby coach Eddie O'Sullivan to take one full training session, introduced stringent dietary require-ments for match weekends and had more talks from dieticians, kept up the ongoing hydration and urine tests and held a 'Power Training Programme' through March and April, with a lot of work with medicine balls, box jumps and sledgehammers!

The rest of the league campaign didn't get Waterford to the final but the players were getting fitter and fitter – their conditioning was improving immensely under Davy's new regime. On Friday, 22 May, the team went west for a weekend training session. They played Clare in Ennis, before heading on to Lisdoonvarna arriving at half past ten. The players were all up the next morning running the beach at Fenor at 8 a.m., with the rain pelting into their faces. They would train twice more that day at midday and 4 p.m., with separate backs and forwards training in the evening. It was intense, nearly military stuff, with players showering maybe four or five times during the day. Dinner was at 8 p.m. with a 'Way and Shape We Play' meeting for an hour and a half in the evening. The training was repeated the following day, with two tough sessions before they headed back to Waterford for a well-earned rest.

Then it was the Munster championship against Limerick with Noel Connors at corner-back getting his first championship start. 'I told myself before the first game, "There's no pressure because it's your first year and if you do badly, there's plenty more years." My father has been great too – he's been training me since under-8s!'

In a bad game, the scores were low, Waterford got 0–11 while Limerick only managed 1–8. Writing in *The Examiner*, Tony Considine compared Waterford to rotavators. Being from an agricultural background, Maurice Geary was fuming, 'To write off a team with some of most skilful hurlers in the country as rotovators – which are awkward agricultural implements – wasn't on at all. And I said so in the dressing room, I used that article in the replay to motivate the players.'

Waterford's backs were really to the wall and players knew it. On the Tuesday night at training, they all went down to the end of the pitch in Walsh Park. Tony Browne spoke, 'Of all the times we've been in tough situations, this is a massive, massive game. If we lose, it'll set Waterford back years and years, we'll go backwards. If we win, we can drive on and win the Munster final.' John Mullane spoke too, words which would motivate and inspire the players.

In the first game, Shane O'Sullivan had been given a specific role by Davy Fitz to mark Limerick's playmaker Donal O'Grady very closely. The public didn't know this and Shane received negative vibes from the fans. O'Sullivan spoke with Davy, saying that there was more in him than that and that he needed to be expressing himself more. Davy agreed 100 per cent and the shackles were taken off; Shane still had to keep a close eye on O'Grady but he could attack more. And he went out and played outstanding hurling and Waterford won 0–25 to 0–17.

Beating Limerick had put Waterford through to the 2009 Munster final against Tipperary, while the Waterford minor team ended a seventeen-year wait by beating Tipperary and winning the title.

Davy Fitzgerald told the players that this was their chance to make amends for 2008. Joint-captain Stephen Molumphy was very confident thinking, We're going to take these guys.

Waterford's plan of opening up the full-forward line and creating pockets of space was working as the Tipp full-back line were roaring abuse at each other. John Mullane and Brick Walsh were consistently brilliant and, for the first twenty minutes, the match was a great contest, with Eoin Kelly getting a rocket of a goal from a twenty-two-metre free after only six minutes. But then Tipp came back before Mullane scored a goal. Then the slaughter – three goals in ten minutes for Tipp, with the Premier men going in nine points up at half-time. And then, six minutes into the second half, another Lar Corbett goal.

'There were lads running in and out and we had a few goal chances and should have got them, but then Tipp got two goals,' recalls Stephen Molumphy.

Jack Kennedy was not having a particularly good year for Waterford and wasn't really enjoying his hurling. As an electrician, he had to work many Saturday mornings in Clonmel. He admits himself that he wasn't playing well in the first half and he was the first to be substituted (with Dan Shanahan coming on). Waterford had a terrible start in the game, letting in soft goals and Tipp were well ahead.

'I felt again I was the scapegoat,' Kennedy says. 'There was no doubt I wasn't playing well but there were probably thirteen other lads not playing well either. That for me that was final straw. I went straight into the dressing room but when half-time came, I went back out and sat in the dugout. I said to the lads after match, and to my mum and dad, that I was packing it in; there wasn't a doubt; I was only fooling myself if I went back. I was pissed off with Davy. I rang Jim Dee and told him; I didn't like things ending like that as I'd put in as much as any fella.'

Waterford played better as the game went on, but couldn't close the gap and lost, 4–14 to 2–16. Waterford fought bravely and pulled it back and only lost by four, but Tipp had been a vastly superior force.

This meant they now had an All-Ireland knockout quarter-final match against Galway in Semple Stadium and would be facing the in-form sensation from Galway, Joe Canning. The night before the match, Eoin Kelly thought, Joe Canning is just starting off his inter-county career and has a lot to prove. I've been very impressed with him so far with what he's done at the club scene but he hasn't done it on the inter-county scene yet, and it's a big step up.

Eoin wasn't worried about the pressure he was under as a free taker compared to Canning, saying all the pressure was on the young Galway man and as usual Eoin wanted to come off the field having scored more than the opposition freetaker – and with a Waterford win.

It was the first year Paul Flynn was not on the panel – the person who had taught Eoin how to visualise the free. If he was practising on a windy day, he'd always hit more against the wind as it was harder to go against the breeze.

'Flynners used to tell me to pick something from behind the goal, something in the middle, between the posts and go for that every time. I've adopted his style where I now stand back more and visualise it. I look at the posts and I pick out what I'm aiming for; it could be the line on the netting at the back. I talk to myself a little, helping me relax and blocking out the eejits shouting. And whether it's Croker or Thurles, I put myself back up in the Passage field.'

Eoin's mother used to go to every match but had become very sick and so had to watch on television or listen on the radio, something Eoin find's difficult to accept. 'I try to use it in a positive way, to win the matches and play well for her; I'd be thinking, Why should anybody be worried if you are young and fit and healthy and you appreciate it? That comes with growing up. When I was starting to take frees if I missed a few, I might want the ground to swallow me up but then I think, Feck that, I'm out here; there might be 50,000 or 60,000 people watching the match, I'm able to do it. I then thought of my mother, watching it at home on telly and I don't worry about anything. Fuck the rest of them is all I think. If I miss one, I have it in my head, yeah, I'm always going to miss one a day anyway, so that one is out of the way.

'She can't walk and I'm getting upset about missing a stupid free instead of relaxing … it's a game, it's not life and death; you put it in perspective and use it in a positive way. I've seen managers over the years, even when you've won the game, they talk about the negative stuff. They never talk about the fucking positive stuff. Jesus, you missed one ball. You might have got 2–13 but you missed one ball! Players don't talk negatively, so why should managers?'

Eoin outscored Canning that day and with a marvellous point by John Mullane in the dying minutes (and a miss from Canning), Waterford get through to yet another All-Ireland semi-final.

And the opponents, yet again, were Kilkenny!

Davy and the selectors asked the players what they wanted to do – to travel up the night before or on the morning of the match. The general consensus from the players was they wanted to be in their own beds on the Saturday night and that they'd travel up by train on the Sunday morning. 'Everybody thought it'd be good for a change from 2008,' says Peter Queally.

After arriving in Dublin on Sunday morning, they got a coach out to the Portmarnock Hotel and Golf Club, had some food and a puck around before heading to Croke Park. Waterford were 6–1 outsiders. Compared to the previous years, there were none of the issues and far fewer mistakes in either the pre-match build-up or the game itself – players and management had learned a lot,

Sunday, 9 August was to be redemption day for the tens of thousands of fans who had felt destroyed by the previous year's result. The Waterford selectors thought long and hard about their team selection and ran Kilkenny very close. The team made good and scored three goals, but were beaten 2–23 to 3–15. They had reduced the deficit from twenty-three points to five, which gave a better indication of where Waterford were at. This was a massive performance by the players considering the hiding they had got in the 2008 final; none of the issues which had arisen before that game came up for the 2009 semi-final and the players and the management team did themselves proud.

Maurice believed they really could have won that semi-final but, after the match, admits, 'a certain feeling of relief because if we got two hammerings in a row, it would have been very damaging psychologically'.

In 2009, Waterford had 109 team sessions (matches and training). The statistics show that from 2003 to 2009, Waterford had accumulated massive scores in most of their games. They were a very attacking team and one which entertained, playing with abandon and finesse. The problem was that their defence also conceded many scores – too many – and the fire power of the forwards was negated by the collapses of the defence.

They show that Waterford actually amassed more scores than their opponents – but in the crucial big semi-finals in Croke Park, they weren't able to repeat what they'd being doing so well in Munster. And Croke Park is where it's at.

		Waterford			Other			Waterford		Other
Type	Date	Goals	Points	Total	Goals	Points	Total			
MHCFR	11/05/2003	2	26	32	1	12	15	11-May-03	32	15
MHCSF	01/06/2003	4	13	25	4	13	25	01-Jun-03	25	25
MHCSFR	07/06/2003	1	12	15	0	13	13	07-Jun-03	15	13
MHCF	29/06/2003	3	12	21	3	16	25	29-Jun-03	21	25
MHCFR	16/05/2004	3	21	30	1	8	11	******	0	0
MHCSF	06/06/2004	4	10	22	3	12	21	******	0	0
MHCF	27/06/2004	3	16	25	1	21	24	16-May-04	30	11
AIHCSF	08/08/2004	0	18	18	3	12	21	06-Jun-04	22	21
MHCSF	22/05/2005	2	15	21	2	17	23	27-Jun-04	25	24
AIHQGR21	18/06/2005	1	26	29	1	15	18	08-Aug-04	18	21
AIHQGR22	02/07/2005	4	17	29	1	3	6	09-Aug-04	0	0
AIHQGR23	10/07/2005	0	21	21	4	14	26	21-May-05	0	0
AIHCQF	24/07/2005	1	13	16	1	18	21	22-May-05	21	23
MHCSF	04/06/2006	1	12	15	3	14	23	18-Jun-05	29	18
AIHQGRA1	18/06/2006	3	22	31	1	14	17	02-Jul-05	29	6
AIHQGRA2	02/07/2006	1	25	28	2	20	26	10-Jul-05	21	26
AIHQGRA3	08/07/2006	2	17	23	1	13	16	24-Jul-05	16	21
AIHQQF	23/07/2006	1	22	25	3	13	22	******	0	0
AIHCSF	06/08/2006	1	15	18	1	16	19	******	0	0
MHCSF	17/06/2007	5	15	30	3	18	27	04-Jun-06	15	23
MHCF	08/07/2007	3	17	26	1	14	17	18-Jun-06	31	17
AIHCQF	29/07/2007	3	16	25	3	16	25	02-Jul-06	28	26
AIHCQFR	05/08/2007	2	17	23	0	20	20	08-Jul-06	23	16

Code	Date					
AIHCSF	12/08/2007	2	15	21	5	11	26
MHCQF	01/06/2008	0	23	23	2	26	32
AIHQR2	05/07/2008	6	18	36	0	15	15
AIHQR4	19/07/2008	2	18	24	0	18	18
AIHCQF	27/07/2008	2	19	25	3	15	24
AIHCSF	17/08/2008	1	20	23	1	18	21
AIHCF	07/09/2008	1	13	16	3	30	39
MHCSF	14/06/2009	0	11	11	1	8	11
MHCSFR	20/06/2009	0	25	25	0	17	17
MHCF	12/07/2009	2	16	22	4	14	26
AIHC	26/07/2009	1	16	19	0	18	18
AIHCSF	09/08/2009	3	15	24	2	23	29
(total)				817			737

Date		
23-Jul-06	25	22
06-Aug-06	18	19
******	0	0
******	0	0
17-Jun-07	30	27
08-Jul-07	26	17
29-Jul-07	25	25
05-Aug-07	23	20
12-Aug-07	21	26
******	0	0
******	0	0
01-Jun-08	23	32
05-Jul-08	36	15
19-Jul-08	24	18
27-Jul-08	25	24
17-Aug-08	23	21
07-Sep-08	16	39
******	0	0
******	0	0
14-Jun-09	11	11
20-Jun-09	25	17
12-Jul-09	22	26
26-Jul-09	19	18
09-Aug-09	24	29
Total	817	737

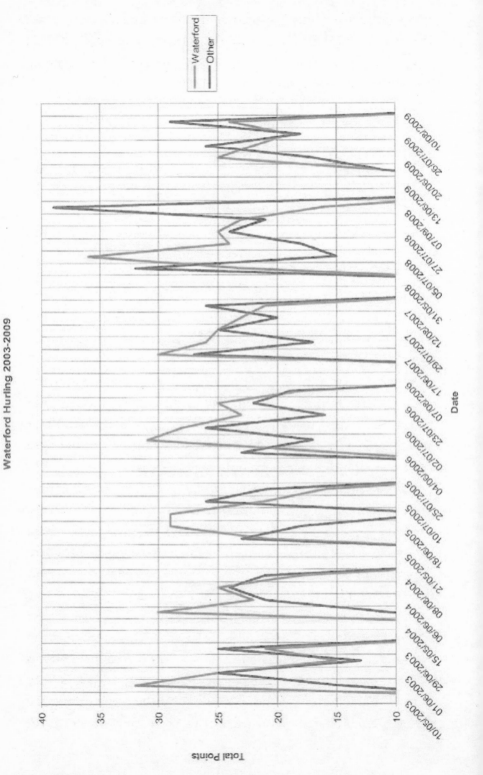

Davy made a passionate speech at the Waterford County Board convention about his plans for 2010 and with Maurice Geary and Peter Queally standing down as selectors, he got Padraig Fanning and Pat Bennett on board.

For the new season, hurling had a visual change too as every player was now obliged to wear helmets, which took a certain personality out of the game.

For 2010, Waterford were back out to 14–1 to win the All-Ireland, though expectations had changed somewhat. In an interview, with the *Irish Independent*, Tony Browne says: 'It doesn't break me up that we haven't won an All-Ireland. Not many teams have in our era because Kilkenny and Cork have been so strong.'

In February 2010, Waterford won the Waterford Crystal Trophy, beating UCC in the final, the first time they'd won the competition since 1998. But, the same week, the county board was told €100,000 had to be wiped off the training costs if the books were to balance for the 2010 season.

At the end of 2009, €327,681 had been spent on preparing the county senior hurling team alone, a figure down from €451,415 the previous year, when the team had to train for an extra four weeks and bore the costs incurred in reaching the All-Ireland. The bill for the footballers was up from €97,725 for 2008 to €132,343 for 2009, a lot lower than the bill for the hurlers, where sometimes just one training session could cost more than €2,000 when all the expenses for the management, back-room staff, players and meals, etc. were taken into account. The players (through the Deise Supporters' Club) raised badly needed money to help pay for their five-day training camp trip to La Cala in Malaga in April.

Davy had given many of the older players time off from winter training and they came back in late February looking refreshed and hungry for action. It also enabled Davy to try out younger players and gave them valuable match practice. A few players, such as Gary Hurney and Thomas Connors, would leave the scene during the season. Ken McGrath returned as did Tony Browne. In 1992,

Browne had been captain of the under-21 team and in the seventeen years in between had only put on two pounds in weight, such was his dedication to the cause. In those seventeen years, he had also played in fifty-two championship matches, an amazing feat – and he wasn't finished yet. He would play in the four big games in 2010, the first of which was a win against a young Clare team with seven players making their championship debuts. The highlight of the match was Declan Prendergast coming on at half-back and scoring three points.

Waterford were stunned when Clare's Darach Honan blasted home a thirty-three-minute goal and it looked like Waterford's decade-old problem of not having a towering full-back was going to haunt them again. But Liam Lawlor played well for the rest of the game and Waterford ran out four-point winners.

One of the many players now showing better toning and more strength was Eoin Kelly, who had been doing a lot of training with Waterford man Jimmy Payne. As an Irish boxing coach, Jimmy had learned a lot from trips to Eastern Europe and had brought a lot of the new methods into drills used by the Waterford hurlers in their training sessions. He also did many individual sessions with Eoin Kelly and others to get them super-fit, some of which involved running in the woods in Portlaw.

Boxing gloves at hurling training was something new, with the players pummelling each other in the stomach for sixty seconds at a time to build up their capacity to take hits. Players were getting used to Davy's shouting and roaring and the fact that, to a certain degree, tactics were being taught. And Davy was learning and changing too. They appreciated all the work trainer Michael Liddane from Clare and Joe O'Connor were doing – the swash-buckling days of Justin were well and truly gone.

Davy also got a team of statisticians on board, including lifelong Waterford fans Bernard Cullinane and his brother Kenneth. With one of the most modern systems in the country (specially commissioned by Bernard and taking three months and a considerable amount of money to develop), each match was analysed forensically. Eight people were positioned at league and championship matches with special hand-held devices and they sent up-to-the-second information, via wi-fi, to two laptops in the dugout run by Bernard and his colleague, computer genius Adrian Snow. There, the figures were compiled and printed out a minute before half-time and given to Davy and the selectors to see who had won ball, lost ball, made good passes, won possession, etc. Players performing well stay in the 'green zone' on the graph; those breaking even are in amber; but those playing badly fall into the red. After games, a report was completed with advice on how the stats could be interpreted to improve the team's performance for the next match, and each player was given an individual DVD containing the instances where they had been involved in play. Hundreds upon hundreds of man hours were put into this work.

'We have eleven people working on our stats team on any given match day,' says Bernard. 'To get everything set up, we have to get there six hours before a championship game and three hours before a league game. We had been at a Tipp–Clare challenge and knew, for example, that Cooney in the Clare backline might be vulnerable and where Clare targeted their high ball. We gave all the stats and our opinions as well to Davy – he loved the reports but not the opinion.'

Davy says the stats team did a great job for getting the facts. In mid-season, Bernard says there were difficulties behind the scenes in how the stats were being interpreted and whether 'opinion' should form part of reports.

After the win against Clare, it was time for the Munster final against Cork and another pulsating day in Thurles. A compilation DVD put together by Kenneth Cullinane of player pictures, training, 2004 highlights and lively music were played on the coach as the players travelled to the town.

Liam Lawlor was due to face the massive Aisake Ó hAilpín and the battle was expected to have a big bearing on the game.

'When we took up our positions,' says Liam, 'I put out my hand but he pushed it away and didn't shake it and I swore to myself he was going to be getting nothing off me.'

Kilkenny manager Brian Cody was in the stand and he noticed Lawlor's handshake had been declined.

Shane O'Sullivan got Waterford going with a great point and John Mullane was having a great match. Down at the other end, he hadn't planned it but Lawlor found himself resting his head on Aisake's shoulder a few times, a move that obviously infuriated the Cork man. There was a lot of pulling and dragging when the ball came their way but Lawlor was stopping his man from scoring goals, a crucial element if Waterford were to win.

The stats were coming in, showing the backs doing very well towards the end of the half and Waterford went in 0–7 to 0–6 up.

In the dressing room, Davy's great friend Bernard Dunne told the players to keep doing what they did naturally; to remain focused all the time; to go the twelve rounds and drive on till the final whistle.

Lawlor was booked on Ó hAilpín after the restart and, in case he got sent off, Davy decided to take him off and move Declan Prendergast to full-back. But events turned and Cork got two quick goals.

A few minutes later, with three subs about to come on for Waterford, Eoin Kelly caught a ball from Brick Walsh twenty-five metres out. He turned, pushed off the defender and unleashed an unstoppable shot past Donal Óg Cusack. (At a GAA testing day in Dublin the speed of Kelly's shots had been measured at approximately 151 kilometres per hour over a ten-metre distance, one of the fastest in the country.)

With Ken McGrath, and Dan and Maurice Shanahan now on the field, Waterford pressed, and got a free twenty-one metres out when Brian Murphy was blown up for playing the hurley off John Mullane. Kelly's low drive was saved but who was there to smash it home? Tony Browne! The Waterford fans, including Spud

Murphy and his wife June Fardey, whose grandfather Nicky had won eight county titles for Erin's Own, went wild.

From the puckout, Cork's Michael Cussen found himself clear and was lining up to make the winning point when Noel Connors caught and hooked him just enough for Cussen to miss. A brilliant interception to cap another brilliant performance. Final whistle, Waterford 2–15, Cork 2–15. A draw.

'We kept coming and coming,' said selector Pat Bennett on the field afterwards. 'The lads kept to the game-plan and kept going.' Tony Browne praised his team-mates for never giving up and Davy Fitz for working on that a lot.

Before the replay, Tony Browne realised he had another neck problem and, on the Saturday morning, went to see his old friend John Dineen, who treated him on his sitting-room floor. They joked about how John's treatments have brought him luck in the past – could it happen again tonight?

In torrid conditions, the rain lashed down on Thurles and the lights came on – the first time a Munster final was played under lights. Cork had some bad injuries, most importantly to Seán Óg Ó hAilpín and Jerry O'Connor. As the game started in front of only 22,763, Waterford dropped their half-forwards deep, flooding the puckout zones, and Cork didn't know where to go. Liam Lawlor's aim of knocking the ball away from Aisake all the time and getting it to the ground was working. Cork only scored one point from play in the first half but created three goal chances, with Patrick Horgan's nineteenth-minute effort miraculously cleared off the line by Noel Connors. Eoin Murphy made a marvellous hook with Niall McCarthy bearing down on goal and Clinton Hennessy saved from Michael Cussen.

Waterford came out for the second half 0–8 to 0–4 up; but Cork got a goal. John Mullane got three lovely points off Eoin Cadogan, his third being a thing of beauty, and Richie Foley put a lovely sideline cut over the bar. Eoin Kelly missed three chances to win it for Waterford after a Cork penalty had been saved by a combination of Clinton Hennessey and Shane O'Sullivan. The match went to extra-time.

In the dressing room before extra-time, Davy asked the players if they were tired – they said they weren't. He went round and looked each of them all in the eye, telling them they would win.

Big Dan was brought on and he latched on to a lovely quick pass from Eoin McGrath, found himself in space twenty-five yards out and sent a low skidding shot across Donal Óg into the bottom corner. It was only his second championship goal since the end of 2007 but would it be enough to Waterford their fourth Munster title of the decade?

For the final seven minutes, Cork piled on the pressure and when Cathal Naughton unleashed a bullet at the town-end goal, Tony Browne threw his body at it and it ricocheted off his helmet. 'He took it right on the head,' said Noel Connors, who was only two when Tony Browne made his debut for Waterford. 'That last five minutes were the longest of my life,' says Noel. 'When the final whistle went, it was amazing.'

Waterford had won 1–16 to 1–13. Fans poured onto the field and after he lifted the trophy, Stephen Molumphy (even though he hadn't planned a speech) thanked everybody passionately.

'The win that night was one of my top five ever moments in sport,' says Davy Fitz.

On the way home, Liam Lawlor told his good friend and team-mate Richie Foley that they wouldn't need any drink to celebrate, so great was the winning feeling.

Tipperary beat Galway which set up an All-Ireland semi-final with Waterford, a repeat of 2008. The build-up went perfectly for Waterford. All senior club games were cancelled and there were no injuries, and the training sessions were fast, intense and focused.

Two weekends before the big game, the team went for a weekend away to the luxury five-star Castlemartyr Hotel and Golf Resort. Driving their separately on the Sunday morning, they trained nearby and afterwards had Minestrone soup, potatoes and goats cheese, brown bread without butter and some ham and cheese. After some time to relax, they played a tough fifteen on fifteen at 5 p.m., during which Shane Walsh got a mild concussion. That evening it was over to the Garyvoe Hotel for a dinner of beef and veg followed by an early night. The next morning, everyone was up at 7.25 a.m. for a twenty-minute jog before a breakfast of porridge, scrambled egg and beans, followed by more training at 10.30 a.m. and lasagne at 1 p.m. Jimmy Payne and Bernard Dunne did all the training sessions with the lads.

Stat man Bernard Cullinane was surprised that Davy had not put together a comprehensive video analysis DVD on Tipperary, 'In the final ten days before the semi-final as far as I could see, no DVD tactical analysis or video work on Tipperary was carried out with the players bar one five-minute clip I put together myself for the players. I was worried we were going to be sitting ducks for Tipp and I privately conceded this to my back-room team the week of the game.' But some players such as Richie Foley said they did video and tactical analysis and the players were confident, 'I was full sure going into the Tipp game we were going to win.'

Meanwhile everyone celebrated Davy's birthday with a big chocolate cake and, afterwards, they all went to Kartworld in Watergrasshill. The twelve-lap race was some of the best fun they had in years, with Jerome Maher being presented with the Best Driver Award on the little podium. Then it was back to the hotel for a three-man scramble mini-competition on the golf course.

The feeling amongst the players was excellent.

On the Thursday night before the big match, the players were presented with their itinerary for the next few days, including a full diet plan. They went on the Saturday to the four-star Carton House Hotel in County Kildare, and saw the Manchester Utd reserve team (complete with Gary Neville) who were in Ireland for a tournament. (The Tipperary team had also been there the week before.) By now, tactics for the big match against Tipp were fine-tuned and the players felt relaxed.

That evening in Waterford, unknown to him, Ken McGrath's three-year-old daughter Ali was bitten in the face by a relative's dog, a Jack Russell who'd never harmed anybody before. She was be taken to Cork Regional Hospital for surgery on the Sunday morning and the family, although extremely upset, decided not to tell Ken as they didn't want him to be upset too.

After a mid-morning loosening out session on Sunday, the team went to Croke Park (there were no more problems with the coach). Ken got a text from a friend of Dawn, his wife, enquiring how Ali was. Ken rang Dawn who was at the hospital in Cork and she assured Ken everything would be okay, that the best surgeons were working on Ali and her right eye had not been damaged. Ken was very upset but spoke with this brother Eoin after which he decided he would play if he was called on. He would go to Cork straight after the match.

In the warm-up, as the 49,754 people took their seats, Ken strained a muscle and had to get an injection to ease the pain. Fans expected Waterford to do what they had done against Cork – hunt in packs, get men around the ball, hit hard and tackle relentlessly. But Tipp moved the ball quickly and with intelligence.

The Tipp defence had tightened up considerably since their quarter-final win over Galway.

Tipp had learned a lot from a challenge match they had played against Waterford in Semple Stadium a month earlier. 'Brick Walsh has a tendency to sit back as he did that match,' says one of the senior Tipp players, 'but only once in training for the semi-final against Waterford did we try out Noel McGrath at half-forward. It worked that day in training and Sheedy said he was going to go with it. We didn't watch any DVDs of how Waterford played against Cork but we just trusted our instincts and tactics. I was very surprised though at Waterford, particularly the backs, they weren't very vocal in Croker.'

Liam Sheedy says they didn't plan an overall strategy for dealing with Waterford's tactics. But Tipp hit some puckouts short and corner-backs Stapleton and Cahill were able to run fifteen yards and hit long over the Waterford half-back line, bypassing Brick Walsh. Davy had started with nineteen-year-old Brian O'Halloran as full-forward but the move wasn't working and he was replaced by Seamus Prendergast after twenty-one minutes.

A minute later, Lar Corbett caught a high ball above Liam Lawlor, turned and kicked a goal. Tipp's Noel McGrath had hit three from play in the first twelve minutes, and team-mate John O'Brien was lording it. At half-time, it was 1–11 to 0–08 with Mullane the only Waterford forward doing any damage. The half-time stats showed too many of the Waterford players in the amber rather than the green zone. 'Two or three of our players were not sticking to the game-plan,' says Davy, 'and when that happens, things go wrong. I think some of them thought we were playing too defensively and they wanted to change it themselves. Our tactics were right but some players didn't stick to it.'

Waterford got it back to three points in the forty-sixth minute but Tipp pulled away again.

On fifty minutes, Waterford's Eoin Kelly was taken off, angrily shouting at Davy and the selectors as he walked off that there were others that should have been taken off before him. He knew his namesake on the opposition wasn't having a great game either, even though both players are capable of doing something special. And, sure enough, in the last eighteen minutes of the game, Tipp's Eoin Kelly got two goals. Then Ken and Eoin McGrath and Dan Shanahan were brought on, with Waterford finishing with five of six of the starting forwards in the stands. Ken McGrath played excellently for the time he was on, a testament to his mental strength, physical courage and sheer determination.

Eoin McGrath tapped home a consolation goal for Waterford near the end but it finished 3–22 to 1–19, with Waterford shooting eight wides to Tipp's ten. At the final whistle, Tipp didn't over-celebrate, they exchanged jerseys with the Waterford lads but headed down the tunnel, focused on the final.

In the Waterford dressing room, everyone was shell shocked; some cried; but for some, it had happened so often, there were no tears left to shed. As for the tactics on the day?

'It's very hard to go between two Tipp players and trying to cover both of them, splitting them like,' says one of the players. 'Brendan Cummins is so good at the puckouts, he can put the ball in your mouth from forty yards; he drills them and it's very difficult to play against. So I don't think we were at fault. We all went out there to try out best.'

Richie Foley adds, 'In the Munster matches, Cork had played into our hands and changed their game to try to match our tactics; but Tipperary didn't do that; they held their positions and it just didn't work for us on the day.'

Davy Fitz said the better team won but Waterford hadn't done themselves justice and he blamed some players for not sticking with the tactics they had talked about, 'and for some reason we were a bit flat on the day'.

The next day, former Clare manager Ger Loughnane wrote in the *Star* newspaper that Waterford were not a Croke Park team and that Waterford were going for a poor imitation of Kilkenny's style but were going nowhere with it.

'It just didn't click for us on the day,' says Declan Prendergast. 'The build-up and everything was perfect. But on the day, it just didn't happen.'

'We just didn't get going,' says forward Shane Walsh, 'we used the same tactics we did against Cork and maybe we were a bit wrong we didn't change it a bit as Tipp had their homework done on us.'

Seven defeats in eight All-Ireland semi-finals since 1998 – a top-four team that just couldn't make the breakthrough.

Eoin Murphy agrees, 'We all tried our best. It's very nearly professional the amount of time and effort you have to put into it and people don't know how many sacrifices players make. It was very disappointing to lose another semi-final, but we'll be back.'

Outside, a disgraceful Waterford fan roared abuse at Sean Kelly, Eoin Kelly's four-year-old son, cursing his father. The child was very upset and when he found out about it, Eoin questioned whether it was worth continuing if that was the type of thing that a small minority of fans deemed acceptable.

Meanwhile, a car with a garda escort, organised by Waterford businessman Tom Murphy, was waiting to take Ken McGrath straight to hospital in Cork to see his daughter. When he got there, Ali was sitting up in the hospital bed delighted to see her daddy.

Everything was put in perspective.

17

CONCLUSIONS

So why haven't Waterford won an All-Ireland since 1959? Most accidents or events are a combination of factors and the same can be said of the journey that is Waterford hurling.

A sociological reason maybe?

There was so much money in Waterford in the 1970s, maybe some people didn't know what do to with it? Did this dampen the work ethic and therefore the thirst for success in other aspects of life? Was there a lack of the 'rural steel' which non–city players could bring to the setup? And to hide this problem, did the team develop a 'fun' attitude? The lads were always the best fun on All Star trips and on trips away.'

Maybe it's more specific?

Waterford legend Tom Cheasty, in an interview with Michael Hearn in *The Examiner* newspaper in 2002, saw the 'parish rule' as a massive hindrance to the county team developing. At present, players can play for other teams in the vicinity (as long as their transfer is agreed at county board level) which means, for example, you don't have to be living in the Ballygunner area to play for Ballygunner. This has led to a few powerful clubs getting more powerful because they could attract the best players and other clubs are then left floundering. So the game didn't develop in a healthy, more 'natural' way. But the parish rule has now been introduced for juveniles so that, at least, is a step forward.

And maybe history had a big part to play?

'If you have a history, things always come easier to you,' says Sean Power of the back-room team. 'Tradition in a big match gives you a head start. We were always edging to get over a line. We were good enough but when we needed a bit of luck, we never got it.

And then there were basic skills?

Ray 'Lay Lay' Barry believes too many Waterford players didn't have the basic skills. 'They make too many mistakes when they have the ball and it's too easy to get goals on a Waterford team. Justin didn't overachieve with Waterford, he was completely the wrong man; he'd be perfect to bring in a month before a championship match and get lads sharpened up for hurling but not for a nine-month period.'

Kilkenny legend Christy Heffernan, who lives and works in Waterford, says that over the decades there's been a lack of discipline through the club and county set up in Waterford, 'You see Kilkenny training sessions and there's severe hitting and no retaliation; that's what Waterford needs. There's a lack of respect for authority in Waterford, from the grass roots up. And that's down to each individual to change that.'

For Justin McCarthy, speaking in late August 2010, there were other reasons.

Talking about players on the periphery not getting proper chances, he believes he gave a lot of players chances and that he had an opinion about whether or not a player was going to make it.

'Nobody's perfect and I have my own style,' he says, 'and at the end of the day, we are only making a contribution to hurling, passing through. I could see when a player was good enough or not. People praised me for focusing on skills but I brought in a whole scope of things and had to deal with an awful lot behind the scenes as best I could. When you go training and you have thirty players and up to ten back-room staff, you have to be nice to them all. It's almost impossible but I tried always to be nice.'

As for tactics, he says you can have all the game-plans in the world to make the game easier but the philosophy of hurling is still the same, you can't make that easier. 'That's why Kilkenny are scoring and winning so well; they do the simple things well, get the basics right. When you go to the top level, your mindset has to change. Sometimes, fellas want the easy way out but they forget about the game. When I came to Waterford, I was basically trying to change a whole mindset of a team who'd been losing for forty years. In Cork, we never played a match where we thought we couldn't win. I was trying to bring that into Waterford; and when they won, they thought everything was great. I always want to win, I'm always competitive.

'It's a hard job, a hard game, and if you're not enjoying your hurling, you should give it up. I tried to look after players but you can only advise; you can't get too close to people because they'll lean on you and they won't grow up. They never realised how important we were to them and respectful we were of them. They were young; very few of them had families; you learn as you get older. You must look after yourself.'

Were the players ungrateful?

'I travelled to Waterford night after night and never had a lad say to me, "Jaysus, Justin, you must be tired after all the driving." I didn't make any money with Waterford and lost valuable money in wear and tear on the car over the years. But Waterford won't make or break me. I just love the game and I'm strong mentally and spiritually. We brought in some people to the setup but I didn't break the bank or put pressure on the county board finances with extra people.'

What do you feel about the Tramore coup?

'That comes down to a lack of respect. I would not have done that to them. I could have let them go at any time; people's minds' change and they get carried away with their own importance, get carried away with success, I never went down that road. Some of them thought they were bigger than the game but nobody is bigger than hurling, nobody owns the hurling of Waterford or Cork or any county. There's a different way of life in Waterford. What I was trying to do was give back a bit of respectability to a county that had underachieved.

'I like the underdog and I was only going there to help out. Players sometimes lean on the manager too much, fearing that if you leave the dressing room, their world will collapse; they have to grow up and realise they're men. I want to see respect for people in charge, I want to see discussion, but I can't do everything.

'I have all my notes from my time in Waterford and could write pages on each player. And some players didn't want to give me credit for what we achieved; then they held grudges and I was left to deal with a lot of egos and personalities – a lot of bluffers. We had leaders on the field but a lot of irrational players off the field. And sometimes they blamed everyone but themselves. I won manager of the month twice and I never heard a player say, "Well done." They wouldn't because it would give me too much credit.

'I was popular in Waterford because I respected people and I made the fans happy with the success. I never ignored a fella or the back-room staff. People got jealous and love to have you knocked. A friend of mine said he didn't know how I stuck it for six months never mind six years. I enjoyed my time in Waterford and I never doubted the players' enthusiasm but I don't think they enjoyed it as much as me.

'You will always get fellas who will chance their arm, but people have to learn to grow up and do things for themselves – you can't pamper people or they'll go soft; players had to grow up and learn for themselves and many didn't. When people get spoiled and soft, it's too easy to blame the teacher or the boss. It wasn't a fucking crèche we were running in Waterford.'

★★★

Waterford hurling is at a crossroads – but then hasn't it always been? Investing in the children seems an obvious place to start, and this is something many clubs are doing.

Some Waterford clubs are putting massive resources into underage facilities. For example, Ballygunner invested €1.8 million in a 100-metre indoor pitch with artificial grass. Training the young boys and girls, Billy O'Sullivan believes that if his team in the 1990s had been half as well prepared as Waterford is now, they would have made a breakthrough. In the future, he and many like him want the preparation of teams to be second-to-none.

Sean Cullinane says, 'It's in the genes in Kilkenny, in the breeding. If you see the under-12s in a small village such as Mooncoin, they have a Kilkenny style. They will have a core of five or six lads who have that little hand pass, the flick, the touch. We work so hard in Waterford to do it and still haven't mastered it. It all starts in the schools. If you drive through Kilkenny day or night, you'll always see lads with hurleys. I'd always encourage my lads to go out and belt the ball off the wall and tell them, "If you break a window, don't worry about it!" An hour training on a Tuesday or Thursday is not enough to get your touch. And as for Kilkenny seniors, they can mix it also when they want – they are the finished article in every way.'

The commitment that the players have to put in over the years cannot be questioned – they train and train and train. But what about the rural–urban divide?

Michael Foley, deputy sports editor with *The Sunday Times* says, 'It always struck me that Waterford were a very urban group of hurlers, which is rare in hurling, and gives them a different personality as a team to, say Kilkenny, who source almost all their players from rural areas.'

This is something that Justin alluded to time and time again in his six years at Waterford.

Waterford also had very few 'centres of excellence' at second-level schools – there's no St Kieran's College like there is in

Kilkenny to develop its many talents. De La Salle and Lismore are now trying to bridge that gap. As is the Waterford Institute of Technology at third level.

'Waterford didn't have many players that came through the college system,' adds Michael Foley. 'I always wondered whether that spot of extra honing through Fitzgibbon Cup and the extra layer of hurling intelligence that winning teams have was slightly lacking in Waterford and may have accounted sometimes for them losing big games in Croke Park.'

Coach Gerry Fitzpatrick believes Waterford should have won two All-Irelands in 2004 and 2007. 'It's very fickle,' he says. 'I think that the closer you get … you have to wonder how much the All-Ireland is perceived, the final is perceived differently from the semi-final in the minds of everyone involved in it.'

Kilkenny man and *Sunday Tribune* columnist Enda McEvoy, a well-known admirer of Waterford hurling, said that the current generation's only failing was '… to materialise at a time when Cork had their most successful team in three decades and Kilkenny their most successful team ever. The recent past was very nearly glorious for Waterford. The near future remains gloriously unwritten.'

Even though Kilkenny have been so good for the past five years and Cork were so good before that, Dave Bennett thinks of what might have been. 'On any given day, we could have beaten any of them but it just didn't happen and it's a shame because of the individuals that we had.'

Waterford was the least successful of the Munster hurling counties and this is one of the reasons why what happened between 1998 and 2008 was so special.

Patrick Power, who, in 1998, wrote *Off the Ball – Waterford's Re-emergence as a Hurling Force* contends that a defiant mentality is now ingrained into the mindset of younger players – emerging talents like Martin O'Neill, Jake Dillon, Maurice Shanahan and the Connors brothers. 'They believe, every time they hit the paddock for Waterford, they're going to win – this is a psychological commodity you cannot put a price on, and may make the next decade the greatest that this county has ever enjoyed in senior hurling.

Waterford forward Eoin Kelly says, 'There was never a year when you'd look back and say you were fully satisfied. Unless you win the All-Ireland, you can't say it was a brilliant year! Every year, we thought we could win the All-Ireland.'

Paul Flynn, says, 'Yes, Waterford were good enough to win the All-Ireland; when you name the lads and see the talent we had, I think few other panels had the man-to-man hurling ability, other things come into the mix I suppose regarding what wins a match but man for man, as a hurling squad, I'd say Waterford certainly had the best if not the second best.'

Gerald McCarthy believes Waterford deserve an All-Ireland, 'But that doesn't give you any right to it. They could have won – they were good enough.'

Maurice Geary believes Waterford did not have enough strength in depth. 'We missed people in key positions and it's very difficult to slot somebody in. There area always occasions when players' forms will dip; Kilkenny can lose some great players, or Kerry in football, but both have players to step in.'

A goalkeeper of the standard of Damien Fitzhenry from Wexford or a full-back the calibre of Kilkenny's Noel Hickey would have helped.

Seamie Hannon believes Waterford could have won an All-Ireland if all the players' heads had been right at the same time.

Roger Casey thinks that if Waterford doesn't win next year, it'll be a while before the chance arises again. 'I don't know if there's a God but if there is, the players deserve it. We now have two or three great goalies when, in the past, the lack of cover there cost us big time. The lack of a good full-back and a good full-forward cost us too. We have the goalie position solved now, but I don't think we have the other two sorted yet.'

Unfortunately, Walsh Park remains a black and white photograph of the attitude that has been Waterford hurling over the decades. A county as proud and with as rich a tradition in hurling as Waterford deserves one of the best county grounds in the country. Even Carlow, the only county never to have got an All Star in either football or hurling, has a great county ground. There are countless unpaid volunteers in Waterford GAA all over the county and they deserve all the praise and thanks they get for the countless hours they put in to promoting the games.

The €22 million development at Carriganore on the outskirts of Waterford city is to be welcomed and is a physical manifestation of all that is positive in Waterford. Here is where the future hurlers of Waterford will hone their skills, where athletes will emerge and hopefully prosper. Waterford is finally moving into an era where it can become good at various field sports at the same time. The relative success of the Waterford footballers is testament to that new-found confidence.

The Industrial Revolution which came to Waterford city in the 1960s and helped create soccer heroes such as Johnny Matthews, Shay Brennan and Peter Thomas is being transformed into a revolution in the professionalism of the county's amateur sports-men and women. Waterford senior hurlers have helped change the culture of the city and county, giving people hope and belief; and they can take a lot of credit for that. The Waterford hurling team was always one of the most working-class GAA teams in the country; they should be proud of that heritage and take the passionate best from it as they move forward. Inspirational performances on the field can inspire so many others in all aspects of their lives. The key now will be to harness that, nurture it, love it.

To do that, the people that must come first are the players – they are the unpaid labourers and artisans, the slaves of our imaginations. If they feel it best to stay at home the night before an All-Ireland final, then so be it. If they feel they should be given jobs by the county board, promoting hurling in the schools, then they should be so employed. Some of the Waterford hurlers spent so much time in their youth on hurling, that they have very few qualifications; not many have third-level degrees. They hurl because they love it, not because it will get them jobs but if they end up on the labour scrap heap in their late thirties, will all the years slogging in Aglish have been worth it?

The schools are where it's at, and that's where it must be concentrated. That's where the focus always begins in Kilkenny, so why not in Waterford? And then the clubs should begin to win more county championships because it's badly needed.

Peter Kirwan advocates multi-functional screening with an advanced 'return to the old days' where all training was done from the feet up, involving hips and pelvis with nothing done sat down. Static weights and some gym work can do more harm than good. He sees other counties already moving ahead of Waterford in terms of getting children as young as ten to run properly and fall properly. 'A fourteen-year-old with back problems needs to be put right because if he isn't, he'll be in trouble in his early twenties.'

The best type of county championship is one in which the title goes to five or six different clubs over a decade. That encourages more and more players to believe they can win, and they train harder and longer to achieve that goal. In Waterford from 1994 to 2006, the title was shared between Mount Sion (seven times) and Ballygunner (six times) before the stranglehold was broken when Ballyduff Upper won in 2007.

Clubs across Waterford are only now investing heavily in ball alleys – was it a coincidence that D.J. Carey and his fellow county men have some of the best handball exponents in the country? Justin McCarthy swore by the ball alley and the skills you can learn there; he's right in that respect. Some Waterford clubs are investing in facilities befitting professional soccer clubs in England.

And what, then, about an Academy of Hurling in Waterford – cutting-edge training techniques, top-class facilities and money rolling in as other counties send their players to learn from the stars?

And what of those stars which have shone so brightly?

For the past twelve years, Waterford has had a core of eight to ten players who have excelled, performed heroics, brought untold joy to thousands and done themselves and their families proud. Some are literally on their last legs, others will reach that stage sooner than they think, while those remaining hope others will emerge With Big Dan gone, another personality who brought so much joy has been removed from the national stage. The journey for some is over but will others ever get to go where they want? Will it be another ten or twenty years before such greatness is bestowed on the Waterford hurling world? The onus of responsibility on these players' shoulders was ultimately too great for them to carry on their own. Issues of all different kinds came to the fore, like a heavy fog obscuring their brightness.

With expectations heaped on so few people, Waterford have needed these players to behave like robots for the past decade. But they are only human. And it's easier to change your lifestyle when victories are coming. Lifestyle does catch up with some players in game-breaking moments. Making sacrifices equals confidence, and the players have to learn not to be that tight-rope walker who looks down and falls just before he reaches the other side.

Waterford unfortunately have to become boring off the field if they are to win an All-Ireland. Their manager and management team (whoever that will be over the coming years) need to command total and utter respect and have the ability, skill and intelligence to take the players hand in hand to the promised land. As the great former basketball coach Hubie Brown once said, 'The notoriety of the coach is dictated by the execution of his players under pressure.'

A famous hurler said recently that if he won one All-Ireland, he'd retire straight away, a happy man. He should be saying he wants to win three All-Irelands and then he might consider retiring.

When Roy Keane criticised other Manchester Utd players for not wanting more after they won the treble in 1999, he was accused of being mad, psychotic. That's the type of madness Waterford needs now.

Nobody deserves an All-Ireland – it has to be won. And with the sacrifices demanded of players in every county, it's going to get more difficult, not easier. Hopefully, it won't be possible to write a book like this again because, hopefully, there will never again be such mistakes made and chances spurned by one group of players in such a short period of time. They don't deserve tears, they deserve respect and adulation for gifts which are not normally of this world.

Waterford are the Samuel Becketts of GAA because when they show us pain, despair and suffering, they do it with unusual courage and even comedy. Anybody who reads the faces of those Waterford players cannot but come away with a true sense of human fragility, grit and endurance.

This may be the last great team of individuals you will see in hurling or even in the GAA inter-county scene. They had a need to be loved and not judged ('If You Don't Know Me, Don't Judge Me' is the tattoo on Dan Shanahan's arm).

History, in the end, weighed too heavily on them, these flawed geniuses, these human beings who cried and bled like normal people. They were normal, that was the beauty; they weren't super-human, they were like you or me with hopes and expectations but they were different because of their gifts.

On their broad shoulders, they tried and tried and tried to carry everybody, but weren't able to hold up the other players, the management failings, families' desires, fans' expectations, a county's hope and a country's longing to see Waterford make a break-through of classical proportions.

This is the real tragedy of this epic journey.

But – of course – there's always next year!

ACKNOWLEDGEMENTS

The research and interviews for this book were done from June 2009 to August 2010 and there are too many people to thank individually; you know who you are and thank you very much everyone who helped.

I'd especially like to thank all the current and former players and their families who gave me on and off the record interviews for this book; and the back-room staff, past and present, in particular Jim Dee and Roger Casey. Thank you also to Gerald McCarthy, Justin McCarthy and Davy Fitzgerald and to all the players and managers from other counties who recounted stories and tales.

Thanks also to Waterford fans for their contributions and continuing faith into the future. Like the players, I have great admiration for you for coming back year after year after year in the quest for glory.

To sports journalists Kieran Shannon, Vincent Hogan, Michael Foley, Enda McEvoy and Michael Moynihan; Michael Hearn; Melanie Kehoe; Peter Francis; Dermot Keyes, Jamie O'Keefe and Patrick Blewitt of the *Munster Express*; Kieran O'Connor and Michael Byrne at WLR; Paddy Joe Ryan, Pat Flynn, Tom Cunningham and Waterford County Board members past and present; and the members of Gaultier and Passage East GAA clubs. And apologies and sincere thanks to anybody I've forgotten to mention individually.

Thank you to all in Hachette Books Ireland, especially Ciara Doorley, Peter McNulty and Breda Purdue, your support, advice and skills are second-to-none. Thanks also to Claire Rourke.

And to my wife Louise and children Isobel and Sam, thanks for your support, understanding and patience.